OVERCOMING
SHOCK

ADVANCE PRAISE FOR
OVERCOMING SHOCK

In *Overcoming Shock*, Zimberoff and Hartman pool their decades of therapeutic experience to differentiate shock from trauma, trace the many ways shock reorganizes our psychic systems, survey the many kinds of experiences which generate shock, and provide a pragmatic approach to the relief of shock. The authors digest a wealth of physiological and psychological information in clear, easy-to-comprehend prose which serves therapist, victim, and family member well.

— James Hollis, PhD, Jungian analyst and author of
Hauntings: *Dispelling the Ghosts Who Run Our Lives*

OVERCOMING
SHOCK

Healing the Traumatized Mind and Heart

Diane Zimberoff, LMFT,
& David Hartman, LICSW

NEW HORIZON PRESS
Far Hills, New Jersey

Requests for permission should be addressed to:
New Horizon Press
P. O. Box 669
Far Hills, NJ 07931

Diane Zimberoff, LMFT, and David Hartman, LICSW
    Overcoming Shock: Healing the Traumatized Mind and Heart

Cover design: Charley Nasta
Interior design: Scribe Inc.

Library of Congress Control Number: 2014930467

ISBN-13 (paperback): 978-0-88282-480-2
ISBN-13 (eBook): 978-0-88282-481-9

New Horizon Press

Manufactured in the U.S.A.

18   17   16   15   14   1   2   3   4   5

AUTHORS' NOTE

This book is based on the authors' research, personal experiences, interviews and real life experiences. In order to protect privacy, names have been changed and identifying characteristics have been altered, except for contributing experts.

For purposes of simplifying usage, the pronouns his/her and s/he are sometimes used interchangeably. The information contained herein is not meant to be a substitute for professional evaluation and therapy with mental health professionals.

ACKNOWLEDGMENTS

We are indebted to Dr. William Emerson for first introducing us to the concept and dynamics of shock, and for his mentorship regarding the clinical recognition and treatment of shock. We are grateful to Dr. Stephen Porges for his contribution to our understanding of the intricacies of the dual functions of the vagus nerve system. We value the inspired elucidations of Carl Jung's work provided by two giants in the field: Dr. James Hillman and Dr. James Hollis. We acknowledge the foundations for our work provided by pioneers in the field of trauma treatment: Peter Levine, Bessel A. van der Kolk, Christine Courtois, Judith Lewis Herman, Babette Rothschild, Ellert Nijenhuis, Allan Schore, Robert C. Scaer, Donald Kalsched, Michael Eigen and so many others.

We are also grateful to all of our thousands of students who have taught us so much about the concepts presented in this book.

TABLE OF CONTENTS

INTRODUCTION

How many times do we hear people say, "My spouse (or friend, boss, child, etc.) is so disconnected. I keep trying to connect with him (or her) but I can't seem to do it and I don't know what else to do." This disconnection is a common form of shock. Shock attacks almost all of us and also affects those with whom we may be in relationship, at different times in our lives.

A common example may be evident when we are trying to speak with our children, spouses, bosses or friends. We are telling them something that seems really important to us and we discover that they haven't been listening to a word we have said. Books such as *Men Are from Mars, Women Are from Venus* may explain some of these experiences; however, they do not address the more pervasive issue of people who do not hear us, because they are just not present. They may be in shock.

Another familiar example occurs when people emerge from a car accident: they are dazed, confused, disoriented and numb to physical or emotional pain. Their sense of self is bewildered and their memory is fragmented. Usually we say the person is "in shock." The term "shock" is used very often in our language to mean, "I wasn't present for the experience! I was in shock!" Hospital workers and EMTs are very familiar with this term in regards to accident and trauma victims and commonly utilize "smelling salts" to encourage the accident victims to return to their bodies, to consciousness. But we are learning now that shock not only affects accident victims or people with obvious physical trauma; it also silently and profoundly affects humans (and animals) when the stressor is less obvious, such as psychological, emotional and even spiritual distress.

THE EXPERIENCE OF SHOCK

What is shock? It is a physiological response to any distress that seems intolerable and in which a person feels intensely helpless. It is the body saying, "I can't deal with this right now; I need a moment to collect myself." In the case of a car accident, the person usually "comes back" after a brief time. But an individual who is consistently in shock can't take that moment; they must find a way to keep going despite the disruption, to live their lives in shock. This could be a soldier in a combat zone, a family in the aftermath of a natural disaster or terrorist attack or a child in an abusive home. Here the assault is on the person's psyche itself and it abuses their spirit, damages their self-esteem and undermines their courage to "come back" from the protective numbness of shock. And so these individuals develop ways of living their lives and doing what needs to be done, in spite of the handicap of constantly being in a state of shock.

The younger people are, the more affected they are by traumatic events. This is the case because youngsters have fewer resources to draw on to "keep going despite the disruption." A child has only a child's ways of coping. So when the trauma begins early in life, at such a vulnerable time, the abuse to the spirit is devastating. Worse, when it is perpetrated by someone trusted as a caregiver, shock takes over and becomes necessary for survival. This type of shock, the residue of long-ago traumas, may not look as obviously debilitating as a car accident or a school shooting, but it can nonetheless cause the same amount of internal damage to our spirits and send us completely out of our bodies into a place of numbness and dissociation. The number one factor determining how severe a soldier's or tornado victim's long-term PTSD will be is whether they suffered trauma earlier in their lives.[1] If the body still needs to "collect itself" even after all these years, then the person is not as resilient when facing a new traumatic event.

In this book we will discuss the two different responses to physical as well as psychological trauma. They are called *sympathetic shock* and *parasympathetic shock*.

In order to remember the difference, we think of parasympathetic shock as being "paralyzed," which helps us to remember which part of the nervous system is being affected. So if you are speaking to your co-worker, friend, children, spouse or anyone else in your life and glance over only to realize that they have been gazing out the window, staring at their cell phones or have been otherwise preoccupied the whole time you have been speaking, the usual response is to react with anger. But if you understand the nature of shock, perhaps you can now respond differently to these dissociative behaviors, which are often symptoms of parasympathetic shock.

A person who is in parasympathetic shock is like a deer caught in the headlights, frozen in time, staring into space and mostly nonresponsive. We have termed this distant look "shock eyes," which indicates a very low blink rate and a familiar stare of disconnection. This disconnected stare is most obvious in people who have just been in a natural disaster or who have witnessed a horrendous crime. Or, surprisingly enough, have been the perpetrator of that crime. They are walking around aimlessly with shock eyes and are seemingly very calm. After a traumatic incident like this, one might expect these victims to be crying, screaming or otherwise extremely distraught. Curiously, this is often not the case and one must wonder why. This is the same parasympathetic shock state observed in the shooter and described by survivors after the movie theater shootings in Aurora, Colorado, in 2012. We know, too, that this same shock state can be observed in your children, your spouse or even in yourself during seemingly everyday events.

Now, while the person you are talking to seems to be disappearing right before your eyes (parasympathetic shock), you may actually be triggered into your own shock state, perhaps becoming aggressive and frantically trying to get their attention (sympathetic shock). For example, you may have encountered a person talking non-stop without taking a single breath in between sentences, or what we call "shock talk." Sympathetic shock can manifest in many ways in our lives. It is very common in high achievers, professionals with to-do lists a mile long and folks who have a perfectionist standard for themselves and others. Another common, more socially acceptable term for sympathetic shock is *multi-tasking*. Juggling many things at one time is socially rewarded but it is personally costly because of how much else has to be neglected.

It is very important to understand that nearly everyone is in shock at different times in their lives and most people go back and forth between sympathetic and parasympathetic shock states frequently. So this book is not just for people who have had *obvious trauma* in their lives, since those people are often clear that they need treatment and perhaps have sought help from therapists. This book also provides a wake-up call for people who think everything is "just fine" in their lives and one day wake up to discover that their spouses have been having affairs or that their kids have been using drugs or that they have a major disease such as cancer. Or any of the other countless shocking events that indicate perhaps something has been brewing beneath the surface while you have been either in parasympathetic shock, walking around comatose and disconnected, or in sympathetic shock, running around like a rat in a maze or a hamster on an exercise wheel.

Don't overlook this concept, because you don't think you are one of the ones with trauma in your life. There are varying degrees of trauma and it is the ability to go into shock or into a dissociative state that protects us and yet also prevents us from seeing what has actually happened in our lives. This is why shock protects us and at the same time disables us by undermining our ability to face the truth. We often call this "the good news and the bad news."

It is the physiological shock state that serves to protect us from pain, fear or shame, giving us the opportunity to take time to "collect ourselves." We can observe these shock states during television segments of just about anyone who is being interviewed after a natural disaster, a school shooting or an accident. When asked for details, they often say, "I think I must have gone into shock, because I can't remember what happened after the explosion (or the shooting or the train wreck)." Quite often the witness *and* the victim, and sometimes the perpetrator, will use the same words, "I went into shock and don't remember." It is how someone like Chris Brown could seriously beat up his girlfriend Rihanna, whom he purported to love immensely, and then apologize profusely, saying he didn't remember what happened. The concept of shock further explains how singer Rihanna can look into the mirror only to see her previously beautiful face bloodied to a pulp, one eye swollen shut and the rest of her face black and blue from the violence her "beloved" had inflicted upon her and then be ready to accept his promise that it would never happen again.

It is also how a mother can yell and scream at her children and then wonder why they never listen to her. In this book we'll give the answers to these baffling situations by nurturing your understanding that we can be in shock for much of our lives.

When we use the term trauma, most people think of horrible experiences like those described. But it is important to understand some more common traumatic experiences that happen to all of us. If you are acquainted with a young baby or small child, take a moment to observe how fragile and vulnerable they are. A disapproving look, a loud noise or people around them fighting with raised voices may constitute quite an assault on their little spirits. They may begin to cry, which is their way of letting us know they are disturbed. Now imagine that little child is you. You are the tiny one in distress after hearing disturbing sounds, receiving a disapproving look from the one who you depend on for safety and security or being left alone to address your own vulnerability.

This infant will find a way to cope, either with frantic thrashing and furious wailing (sympathetic shock), or becoming frozen and still (parasympathetic shock). And a lifelong pattern has begun.

After being fortunate enough to study with many of the Humanistic psychologists in the 1960s, co-author Diane Zimberoff felt that she was ready to help others. Very quickly she became somewhat disillusioned when she began, as a young therapist, to discover the profound suffering and wounds that exist in many human beings. She knew deep down that there must be a faster, more effective method for helping people other than talking to them at length and so she was drawn to India to study and learn Eastern meditation and spiritual healing. When she returned, she also discovered hypnosis, which seemed to go hand in hand with the spiritual and meditative techniques she learned in India.

A combination of Western Humanistic Psychology and Eastern spiritual practices came together for Diane in the psychological healing technique that emerged from this synthesis. She named it *Heart-Centered Hypnotherapy* (HCH). The results were astounding as she began using the HCH with trauma victims, domestic violence survivors and sexually abused family members. Many of her colleagues were aware of these healing results, became as excited as Diane was, and requested that she develop a training program.

When she first began this training over thirty years ago for other mental health professionals, she had no idea where it would lead. The one outstanding revelation for her was all the therapists who were and continue to be attracted to this deep work. Diane soon realized that one of the reasons for their attraction, besides wanting to help their clients as she did, was their drive to understand and heal their own pain and dysfunction.

Over the years she has become convinced that the fields and the specializations that mental health professionals choose are definitely correlated to the personal healing work they as human beings are seeking to achieve. In the beginning of establishing The Wellness Institute, Diane generally was the one to answer the request for training. Whenever someone would call to take the training, she would always ask what his or her "area of expertise" was. The answers were quite revealing.

An example is people who called and said they worked in "crisis management." Once they began the HCH, it very quickly became apparent to them how, as children, they had to manage one crisis after another in families where the adults were not only creating the crisis, but then were unavailable to clean up their messes.

Diane's own awareness is that she was drawn to get her degree in Marriage, Family and Child Therapy because, as a teenager, she was the only *adult* present when her parents were drinking alcohol and partying. She became the designated family marriage counselor once the arguing began.

However, another more astounding awareness that developed after forty years of doing this work is that therapists, counselors and the majority of people in the helping professions also make up the majority of *seekers* on this planet. They are seeking answers and healing for themselves as well as for their clients. They are seeking to understand and relieve their own emotional scars in an effort to be more clearly available to others.

As Diane worked with therapists, she was devastated to realize that their pain, their human angst, their physical and emotional dysfunction is as great or greater than any other group of people. Her husband, David Hartman's and her purpose statement clearly emerged as a dedication, first and foremost, to heal the people who have the lives of others in their hands.

This book is dedicated to all of the wounded healers. Just like the parent on the airplane who must put on her own oxygen mask first so that she can breathe and become clear-headed, we as therapists must heal our own shock first in order to perceive the shock in our clients.

Chapter 1

SEEKING REFUGE—A CREATIVE WAY TO HANDLE SHOCK

Trauma. In psychological settings, we use the term frequently and we treat clients to undo the damage caused by trauma. This has been done effectively for years for many clients...but not all of them. Because it turns out that trauma isn't such a "one size fits all" term. In fact, it's become something of a controversial word among mental health workers as we debate how to use the term and how to treat the problem.

We're convinced after so many years of working with trauma that it can't be used with just one meaning or treated with just one approach, because of the nature of human beings. In biology, there is a term known as "homeostasis," where the body tries to maintain a balance point for optimal health. Like a tightrope walker, the body doesn't have to keep strictly to the midpoint—an exact body temperature or pH level—but it does need to remain in a constant state of flux to keep very *near* to that midpoint. The tightrope walker who isn't making minute adjustments every second falls. The same is the case with the body.

For nearly a hundred years now, we've used the term "stress" to talk about any kind of environmental factors—from food to pollutants, from germs to physical accidents or abuse—that push the physical body out of

homeostasis. So, on the one hand, it's the cause. But on the other hand...
what do we call it when we're not in homeostasis? We're "stressed," or we
have stress. So the term is used as both cause and effect.

If we're pushed too far out of balance, stress is no longer stress. Then it
becomes disease, whether as an ulcer, heart attack or other serious condition.
In the end, this might just be semantics. We change the term, however, to
recognize that the stress has reached a new level and to describe—with the
name of some disease—the resulting symptoms.

Yet stress doesn't just impact us physically. It also impacts us psychologically. As with our physical bodies, our minds and emotions need to continually respond to the environment to maintain a healthy, balanced state.
When life and/or other people push our buttons, we are stressed mentally or
emotionally. Hopefully these are minor stresses and we can keep our balance
and our psychological health.

When we are stressed often enough or deeply enough...we no longer call
it stress. We call it trauma. Like stress, trauma is used to mean both the cause
(the traumatic event) and the effect (the trauma that needs to be treated).
This is where we've reached a state of psychological imbalance, something
we're not able to recover from without treatment.

In fact, it's more complicated than that, which is why choosing the right
professional is so important. Because stress becomes trauma and trauma
becomes *complex* trauma—what we're calling "shock" in this book—on a
gradual basis. There's no magical point at which stress becomes trauma or
trauma becomes shock, because it all boils down to an individual's ability
to handle the stress and to maintain balance before it reaches these deeper
conditions. Where we really see the difference is in therapy, where people
respond to treatment *according to the depth of trauma they've experienced.*
Without the right tools for more than one depth of trauma, a professional
really can't help all the clients passing through his or her door.

What we can say is that the younger someone is at the time of trauma,
the more likely it is to be a complex trauma or shock. The more intimate the
relationship with the abuser, the more likely it is for the trauma to become
shock. The less chance there is for safety, the more certain the danger, the
more likely it is to become shock. The more pervasive the trauma, the more it
is repeated and the longer the period of time over which it is repeated, the
more likely it is to turn to shock.

When we pass by stress and enter into levels of trauma, we begin to see a split taking place, a sort of division between someone's essence, or "soul," and the ego or personality. The greater this division, the less the soul or the "real person" is controlling the ego aspect, and the more this ego comes under the control of an "other," which we discuss next. When this happens, less of the person's soul is able to function and accomplish his or her true purpose in this world.

THE LEVELS OF TRAUMA

You can gain a sense of how trauma becomes more severe and pushes us into different psychological responses through illustration. In the classic movie *Home Alone*, a child is left at home by accident and discovers that some crooks are going to try robbing his family's house, believing it to be empty. So he takes it upon himself to outdo them and he rigs the home to defeat them. The movie was written as a comedy but, given that situation in real life, it would be a horror film for most children, especially the younger they were and the more they believed in the power of adults.

Think of a child in that situation, alone at home and seeing through the windows that the house is under attack. Two men dressed in black with masks over their faces have parked their car out front and are coming toward the door. The child feels powerless to do anything about it, so she may react in a number of ways depending on her previous experience. This could include tendencies she came into this life with, what some may call karmic or God-given tendencies.

One reaction would be to go outside the house before they reached the door and scream for help. Another might be like the boy in *Home Alone*. She might grab a baseball bat or some other form of defense and do what she could to protect herself. But most children find that option very difficult, because in most cases, the marauders coming at them are not only more powerful than them physically, but also psychically, since the magical thinking of a child gives adults a kind of "bigger than life" power. So, more than likely, that child is going to lock the door and hope they don't break in.

If the men try the door, find it locked and decide to leave, the threat is gone and—depending on the child—the stress of the event may not become traumatic. That is, it might not have created some kind of lasting psychological effect that needs to be treated. Granted, the child may be more aware of the world she lives in, but this isn't necessarily an ill effect. This is an analogy for those things we see as threats around us that put us on edge, that stress us psychologically and that may have us withdraw or hide temporarily from a situation—maybe not physically but psychologically. As the threat passes, though, we can easily return without having been traumatized.

Let's say, however, that the men don't give up so easily and they break through the door. So now the child has to run deeper into the house and hide, perhaps behind a couch or under a bed. This is much like the way too many children have to run and hide more deeply within themselves from threats—not so often from intruders (strangers), but more often from those in their lives inflicting emotional, physical or even sexual abuse. Here, especially with severity and frequency, abuses or other violent situations become traumatic and cause the kinds of divisions or splits we'll discuss later in this book.

The child hopes at this point that she has tricked the intruders by hiding and that this will carry her through the trauma. But suppose they find her under the bed. Now what is she supposed to do? They have physical control over her at this point and there is nowhere deeper into the house for her to retreat. So the one remaining option she has is to cut ties with the environment entirely, for her essence in this circumstance to fully break away from reality so that it's protected from what is happening to her body. We and some other therapists refer to this primal level of dissociation as "soul loss," requiring "soul retrieval" in therapy.

There are times when we protect ourselves psychologically in simple ways from those around us—in ways that may stress us, but that don't cause any lasting damage or split that requires therapy. The more we are threatened, however, the more we need to retreat into our own inner "house," our own psyche. The deeper we go, the deeper a split may become. With the deepest splits from shock, we find that part of the soul itself is disconnected from a person, and as part of the defense process, the ego may associate with the abuser who is causing the shock. We see this dramatized in George Orwell's metaphorical novel, *1984*, when Big Brother's brainwasher O'Brien says to Winston Smith, the victim of his abuse,

> We shall crush you down to the point from which there is no
> coming back. Things will happen to you from which you could
> not recover if you lived a thousand years. Never again will you

be capable of ordinary human feeling. Everything will be dead inside you. Never again will you be capable of love, or friendship, or joy of living, or laughter, or curiosity, or courage, or integrity. You will be hollow. We shall squeeze you empty and then we shall fill you with ourselves.[1]

SHADOWS

Let's briefly mention shadows here, because while they aren't the focus of our book, they represent the response to a milder form of trauma. As we've said, any kind of psychic split from trauma is effectively a loss of some aspect of the individual, which is then replaced with an "other" who fills the void where the loss occurred. In the following chapters, we'll illustrate the deeper splits of trauma and shock.

In the case of shadows, the trauma is real but more tolerable and the "other" remains closely connected to the original "me." The split is put out of sight or "in the shadows," so to speak. But it's not an unconscious replacement that the ego is unaware of. Instead, this shadow is an identity of convenience, functioning in alliance with the ego to pursue their mutual goal of ensuring safety and satisfying needs. The shadow uses means that the ego would not, either because it is deemed to be bad or because it's beyond the capability of the ego. In either case, the ego's plea is, "Oh, *I* couldn't do *that*." Whether it is manipulation, seduction or being devious or defiant, the shadow replies, "Oh, but *I can*."

As with other forms of trauma, the victim *introjects* (incorporates attitudes or ideas into one's personality unconsciously) the traumatizer's powerful qualities into the shadow. In other words, the tactics used by this shadow are determined by those of the source of the trauma, either mimicking them, standing in defiance of them or attempting to mollify them. If the source of trauma is a raging father, the child may develop a shadow that rages, one that stands in judgment of rage or a shadow that fearfully tries to anticipate the father's needs and meet them before rage can erupt.

Chapter 2

FROM HYPNOTHERAPY TO PSYCHODRAMA—THE TERMS OF OUR TRADE

The conscious mind, even though it is very important, is only about 10 percent of our mind. This part of the mind helps us to think, debate ideas, reason and process short-term memory experiences, all very important tasks.

Yet, the unconscious mind contains a full 90 percent of the mind![1] It holds long-term memory, to help us "learn from our own history." This demonstrates the saying that if we don't learn from our history, we are likely to repeat it, making the same mistakes over and over again. So even though our conscious mind may completely *understand* our dysfunctional relationships or self-sabotaging patterns, it is not capable of making the necessary changes.

What we have discovered by exploring the intricacies of the unconscious mind is that from very early in our development, we draw conclusions about ourselves which are programmed into the deepest core level of beliefs about ourselves. And then we make decisions about how to behave based on those conclusions. This behavior is so deeply buried in our operating systems that the limitations of the conscious mind do not allow us to find them or change them.

An example of this would be growing up in an alcoholic or dysfunctional family system. Having the experience of sitting at the dinner table with an explosive parent who pounds the table and emphatically yells, "You're not leaving this table until you eat everything on your plate!" or sitting at the dining room table night after night with parents who are fighting, drunk or screaming at the children might cause children growing up in this family to draw the conclusion, "I'm a bad person." Or "I'm not safe, even in my own family." Then those conclusions may be followed by an unconscious decision about how to behave in order to feel safe. That decision might be, "I'll just become invisible—if I become really small, perhaps no one will notice me and then I'll be safe."

Later on in life, such people may wonder why they cannot really be successful in reaching goals in their lives. They become aware, perhaps in cognitive therapy or counseling, that they keep on sabotaging themselves, hiding their own light, so to speak. Getting it all figured out in the conscious mind is certainly a good first step. But after lots of time and money spent trying to change this behavior of self-sabotage by talking about it, analyzing it and deciding to be different, most of us have learned the hard way that the self-sabotage continues!

Hypnotherapy has proven to be a most effective and efficient path to creating change within ourselves and our clients. Through hypnotherapy we learn that the way to change these old, stubborn patterns that have plagued most people for a majority of their lives is to have direct access to the unconscious mind, discover what conclusions and decisions are still operating and re-program them. This is just like the operating system of your computer. If you don't upgrade the old system, it will no longer be functional. The old programs are just not sufficient to serve you. Hypnotherapy is a powerful tool in re-programming what no longer serves your highest good.

THE DIFFERENCE BETWEEN HYPNOSIS
AND HYPNOTHERAPY: AGE REGRESSION

Hypnosis is the process of getting a person relaxed and giving them suggestions that may or may not help them get their desired results. They may stop smoking or lose weight or decrease their anxiety. However, these hypnotically-suggested changes are often temporary, because while hypnosis has provided access to the unconscious mind and its "operating system," it has not addressed the underlying motivation for continuing behaviors, no matter how self-limiting or self-injurious. The actual motivation, the primal conclusions and decisions, need to be found, resolved and released.

The most effective and efficient way to discover the unconscious conclusions and decisions still operating in one's life is to go back to the source, back to the formative experiences which dictated forming those beliefs and choosing behaviors to deal with them. Hypnotherapy provides an ideal vehicle for that journey back to the source, because it provides us direct access to the unconscious mind where these long-term memories and deeply held beliefs are stored. We call that journey *age regression* because it involves much more than remembering a past experience; it creates the opportunity to re-experience a past event as if it is happening now. In age regression, an individual feels the emotions deeply, the body sensations kinesthetically and the trauma or conflict acutely. The experience draws in all the original chaos, confusion, immaturity and helplessness. There is a huge difference between the original experience and the age-regressed experience: this time the individual is not alone. The therapist is available to suggest alternative responses and to encourage empowerment. An individual in an age-regressed trauma can revise the original scene, can yell at the abusive parent, "Stop it! You have no right to treat me this way!" or can kick and scream and repel the attack of a sexual abuser. Then, in this newly created state of personal power and self-respect, the person's old conclusions about being weak or stupid or worthless unravel. New beliefs of self-worth and belonging and personal power automatically emerge. These new beliefs, together with the immediacy of a successful rehearsal of new behaviors, establish a profound shift in the person's whole being.

After thousands of hypnotherapy sessions and an immense body of research, we have determined that most of our lifelong patterns do begin very early in our lives—in early childhood, at birth, during our time in the womb and even at the moment of conception! All this invaluable information is stored in the vaults of our unconscious minds. Hypnotherapy is the key to unlocking this valuable wealth of information and to changing these patterns where they began. That's how a new pattern can emerge.

For people who have never experienced hypnotherapy, it may seem unbelievable that you could return to your early childhood or birth, let alone your conception, and that it could have an effect on your life. Yet many people have had these life-changing age regressions in hypnotherapy.

An example is Abigail, an intelligent, well-educated woman who has a small private psychotherapy practice. She wants to expand her services and begin offering groups. But something has kept her from taking the steps to make this happen. She balks at speaking to church groups or service clubs in her community, feeling a gnawing sense of doom at even the thought of standing before a group of people and being the center of attention. Abigail began a hypnotherapy session with this self-sabotaging fear, and very soon found herself back in the first grade, feeling humiliated by the teacher and her fellow students as she stumbled in trying to tell about her summer vacation. The therapist tapped her forehead and took her back to an earlier time when she had the same experience of shame. Abigail was a tiny fetus, only a matter of weeks old, at the very moment that her mother discovered that she was pregnant out of wedlock. Abigail's mother's fear and shame was palpable for the fragile new life inside her, and Abigail felt responsible ("If only I wasn't here, my mother wouldn't feel so bad"). Her conclusion about herself in that crucial moment was, "I am shameful. My existence causes pain for others."

How did this little fetus try to defend herself from the pain of that felt rejection? She decided to become as small and invisible as possible, to fly under the radar. The source trauma for Abigail was her sense of rejection at the moment of discovery, and that prototype experience was replayed many times throughout her childhood, for example, in her experience in the first grade. She had never understood the sense of doom that plagued her at even the thought of public speaking, and was powerless to overcome it no matter how many motivational talks she attended or recited to herself. But now Abigail understood viscerally the deep, existential basis for that fear—deep in her unconscious, it really was a matter of life or death! With her newfound insight and reclaimed sense of worth, she was much more able to bring her ideas forward, enroll her classes and even do some public speaking. It was now okay for her to be seen.

HYPNOTHERAPY AND JUNGIAN PSYCHOLOGY

These self-sabotaging, self-limiting aspects of ourselves are long-held patterns of behavior motivated by deep and unconscious beliefs and defenses.

In Jungian psychology these are called *shadow parts*. These shadow parts are actually hidden parts of our personalities—hidden, that is, to us but certainly not to our friends, family and co-workers. Shadow parts are akin to the blind spot in a rear view mirror. Even though the car passing on our left side is nearly upon us, we cannot see it. Examples of personal blind spots or shadow parts may be having the self-concept that we are loving, kind mothers, wives and friends and then losing control and lashing out at those closest to us, then later on acting as if nothing has happened. It's like the car we don't see in the rear view mirror until it is suddenly in front of us and we continue on our journey as if we had seen it all the time.

Another example is believing that we are fair, kind and accepting and then listening to the voice of our inner judge who stands back and mentally criticizes or finds fault with others, nearly continuously. Perhaps outwardly we act normally, giving them compliments about how nice they look, how accomplished they are or what great friends they have come to be. The running, shadow dialogue in our heads is quite to the contrary: "What an ugly dress; he/she is an idiot and will never get anywhere. I don't trust them as far as I can throw them." These inner dialogues indicate that our shadow parts have actually formed an alliance within us called a *complex* by Carl Jung, without our conscious awareness or agreement.

How does *Heart-Centered Hypnotherapy* interface with and enhance these Jungian concepts to make them more therapeutically available to our clients? First, with hypnotherapy we can actually slow down long enough to drop into the unconscious mind, to be able to hear the unconscious dialogues that play in our heads like a radio left on. These internal dramas, akin to soap operas, take on a life of their own, uncensored and uninterrupted. When we, the client and the therapist, enter into the dialogue through hypnotherapy, we become aware that this radio program has been playing for a long time. Through the wisdom of the unconscious mind, we can regress to the origin of this dialogue and discover the age of the child part that is hiding in the shadows, i.e., the blind spot of our rear view mirror.

Second, with hypnotherapy we can resolve the infantile, unresolved conflicts that gave birth to the immature parts of us that felt unsafe and had to hide in the shadows and recesses of our consciousness. As children, if we grew up in families where we were criticized instead of encouraged and loved only if we performed to an impossible standard, we had to develop some defenses in order to survive and not become completely hopeless.

It was a strong survival instinct that created our internal shadow parts that knew they could not be seen or we could have been punished to the point, in some families, where the abuse would have been even more devastating.

Without the tools of hypnotherapy, we are limited to using only 10 percent of our minds, which is the conscious mind. Like the blind spot in our rear view mirror, the limited, conscious mind can think, analyze and talk about the concepts of our deeply hidden shadow parts.

With Heart-Centered Hypnotherapy, we have complete access to use the full 100 percent of the mind. Having increased access to the unconscious mind allows us to drop down into our memory banks in order to expand our full awareness of when and how these young shadow parts and complexes were created. These complexes can be untangled so that the intertwining issues that were suffocating our human development can be resolved.

Through hypnotherapy, the client as well as the therapist is gifted with the ability to hear these shadows, determine what they truly need for safety and encourage them to emerge from their hiding places to be seen, loved and transformed!

THE BODY IN BODY-MIND-SPIRIT HEALING

The body is an integral aspect of our work with clients. The body, through symptoms and specific sensations, provides valuable diagnostic information about what needs to be resolved and healed in psychotherapy. By tracking changes in these somatic experiences through the course of therapeutic intervention, we can assess our effectiveness.

In a Heart-Centered Hypnotherapy model, people often discover emotions that they never knew they had or that they did not have language to express. With hypnotherapy, we can teach clients to identify their emotions and then to put an appropriate label on these feelings. It is surprising how many adults have no language to describe or express their emotions. The most effective way for them to have a surefire way of knowing that an emotion is, in fact, present is to bring their awareness down into their body and notice what is happening. Many people try to "think about" what they are feeling, which brings them into their heads and their conscious minds. The problem with this is that the feelings are not located in the head, nor are they located in the conscious mind. Emotions are rooted in the unconscious part of the mind and physically in the body. This is why hypnotherapy is so effective for mind-body work. Every emotion that we experience has a corresponding reaction in the body.

So, for example, when you begin to feel sadness, your eyes may begin to tear up and you may have a slight pressure in the center of your chest which is called the heart center. The heart center is not your physical heart, it is your emotional heart. When you experience joy, you may feel like laughing or smiling (a physical reaction) and you may feel a warm feeling in your chest, your heart center. Some people experience anger in their chests with a pounding sensation, rapid breathing and tightness, perhaps in the stomach. Fear often expresses as tightness or burning in the stomach or chest. Shame or embarrassment usually causes the person to put a hand over his or her eyes or cover his or her face.

The body never lies and is the most consistent reporter of our current emotional status at any given time. In Heart-Centered Hypnotherapy, we always ask clients to bring their awareness into their bodies to find the place where the feeling or emotion is located. Then we use the Gestalt Therapy approach taught by Dr. Fritz Perls of "giving that part of the body a voice" and letting it express to us our deeper emotions of which we are usually consciously unaware. What are your clenched fists saying? What is the pain in your neck telling you? What is the message of your indigestion? Give it a voice and let it speak.

Many people hold their emotions inside their bodies, which is what many of us were taught to do as children. When this holding in of powerful emotions has become a lifelong pattern, it can certainly lead to disease and chronic pain or illness. With the Heart-Centered type of therapy, the stressed person can learn to identify and release these powerful emotions in a healthy way so that the internalized stress does not lead to a fatal illness such as cancer or a heart attack.

Other people have not learned how to express feelings in a constructive manner and may hold them in until they explode and become abusive to those they love. Some folks express feelings in another unhealthy manner, with snide remarks, sarcastic allegations and rude behavior. They frequently use the statement, "I don't get mad, I just get even." This is an example of expressing emotions in a non-direct, abusive manner, and is what psychologists call passive-aggressive.

When clients are in a hypnotherapy session, they have much more direct access to their emotions located in the unconscious mind. Clients in the trance state are much more aware of their bodies and can be easily directed to notice and express in a healthy way the feelings that have been stored within the body. This release of emotions is like opening or loosening the valve of a pressure cooker. The steam can then be released slowly without exploding. This, then, is how hypnotherapy heals the mind and the body through the information revealed, expressed and released from the client's energy field. This is also the reason why hypnotherapy can be so successfully used by psychologists, clinical social workers, licensed professional counselors and school counselors, as well as by doctors in the field of integrative medicine.

THE SPIRIT IN BODY-MIND-SPIRIT HEALING

How does spirit fit into mind-body-spirit healing? While the person is in the hypnotherapeutic trance state, perhaps toward the end of the session, he or she often experiences a warmth, a sense of forgiveness, of compassion, of a love that extends out to humanity itself. This phenomenon occurs with such frequency during the hypnotherapy experience that we have not been able to ignore it. It seems to be a natural result of someone making intimate contact with his or her heart center.

We have learned after more than forty years of experience that many people are longing for some type of spiritual connection—a real, felt, deeply personal *experience* of spirit. Many times we have heard ministers, rabbis and other actively religious people say, "Right now I feel closer to God than I have for many, many years." This connection allows clients to reclaim what may have been missing in their lives since they were children: the deepest and highest parts of themselves. We use the term "soul retrieval" for this miraculous spiritual healing.

Heart-Centered Hypnotherapy is a particular approach to the use of hypnosis in psychotherapy for mind-body-spirit healing which, taken together, we call *personal transformation*.

We transform first *physically*, changing the structure and functioning of our bodies. We begin to understand the subtle energy of which we are composed, and learn to manage it for optimal health and growth. We gain conscious influence over many of the processes once believed to be autonomic, such as our sleep cycles, recovery from injury and illness, the functioning of the immune system and ultimately the process of dying.

Second, we transform *emotionally*, healing the wounds of unresolved trauma and growing in self-actualization (Abraham Maslow's term) or individuation (Carl Jung's term). This healing necessarily involves incorporating the full expression of ourselves, embracing the repressed shadow, the imperfection, the unworthiness as well as the wisdom and the transcendence.

Third, we transform *spiritually*, surrendering the ego to that which is greater than itself ("Thy will, not mine, be done"), finding our highest purpose in life and beginning to express it in every action. This involves reclaiming all the fragments of the Soul that have been dissociated or lost through identification with a narrow, too-limited self-concept.

Finally, we transform our *social context*, creating healthy community to support our highest level of functioning. We transform within the crucible of relationships, creating an identity and strengthening the resulting ego by facing our deepest fears and greatest challenges. We create and use safety and trust, encouragement and support within the heart-centered unconditional love of a healthy community.

PTSD AND COMPLEX PTSD

It has become clear in recent years that there are degrees of wounding in traumatization, some being more pervasive and complicated than others. One attempt to distinguish between them is the distinction between *trauma* and *complex trauma*, or *PTSD* and *Complex PTSD*. Complex trauma refers to trauma experienced as overwhelmingly intolerable, that occurs repeatedly and cumulatively, usually over a period of time and within specific intimate relationships which violate the human bond and sever the vital human connection.[2] The victim of complex traumatization is entrapped and conditioned by the perpetrator, whom the victim relies on for safety and protection.

In families, it is exemplified by domestic violence and child abuse and in other situations by war, prisoner of war or refugee status and human trafficking. Complex trauma also refers to situations such as acute/chronic illness that requires intensive medical intervention or a single traumatic event that is calamitous.

Unresolved complex trauma results in *Complex Post-Traumatic Stress Disorder (Complex PTSD)*, which produces apparently contradictory symptoms.

When children and adults are traumatized beyond their breaking point, they retreat inwardly to call on unconscious resources. The child tried fight or flight and it didn't work (the abuse got worse), so he had to stop responding with that behavior. But his body's nervous system didn't stop reacting with sympathetic activation, and this energy just built up because it was unsafe to express it. So he had to find a way to override the body's natural fight/flight response to stress and to tolerate the growing accumulation of undischarged energy.

The mind dissociates from paying attention to what is intolerable; the body dissociates as well, through compensating activation which we call *shock*. This is the central distinction between trauma and complex trauma, between PTSD and complex PTSD. This is the clinical definition of Complex Post-Traumatic Stress Disorder: Exposure to sustained, repeated or multiple traumas, particularly in childhood, resulting in a complex symptom presentation. This includes not only post-traumatic stress symptoms, but also other symptoms reflecting disturbances predominantly in affective and interpersonal self-regulatory capacities such as difficulties with anxious arousal, anger management, dissociative symptoms and aggressive or socially avoidant behaviors.[3]

These other symptoms are really defenses which formed early on and were effective at surviving the ongoing trauma by allowing body and mind to dissociate. In a sense, the person is now accompanied by a powerful companion, a protective *bodyguard* for the traumatized and overwhelmed person to hide behind. Creating this bodyguard comes at a steep price, however: the person must turn over to the bodyguard the set of defensive behaviors, the moment-to-moment decision making about when and how to protect him or her. So the bodyguard might perceive an imminent threat, whether there is actually one or not, and throw himself in front of the one he is sworn to protect, suddenly, without warning or explanation or even rational purpose.

That happens when I begin to experience loneliness and my protector ushers me into the kitchen to eat three pieces of cake; or when I experience that my boss is angry at me and my protector forces me into the nearest hiding place; or when I experience my spouse getting cozy with someone I consider to be a rival for her affection and my protector explodes in a jealous rage.

The result is a split in the individual. The bodyguard develops into a powerful neurotic pathology in the form of addictions, thought disorders, anxieties, depression and other self-sabotaging behaviors.

These behaviors are the *psychological component* of the protection, i.e., the adaptation to the perceived threat. Shock is the *physiological component*, the same dissociative and defensive pattern embedded in the autonomic nervous system. The bodyguard (who shares the body's real estate with the conscious ego-self) has conscripted the body to its service and manages to step into control, to take the steering wheel away from the conscious ego-self through control of the nervous system. The over-eater literally "finds herself eating desserts" despite the conscious ego-self's best intentions not to do so. The bodyguard has taken control of the part of her that carries the willpower and ability to make healthy choices by putting it to sleep (parasympathetic shock) or by distracting it with busyness (sympathetic shock).

It is important to recognize that the bodyguard is just doing its job, what it was selected for so long ago and trained to do: protecting you. It is not malevolent, bad or mean-spirited, any more than the ocean is when it rises up in a tsunami. It is just doing instinctually what comes naturally. We showed great courage and wisdom as children in seeking out and finding a powerful ally to help us deal with the trauma. Surely now as adults we can find the courage and wisdom to confront those same powerful forces (bodyguards) to renegotiate the arrangement.

The way to retrain or recondition the bodyguard is to retake control of the body's nervous system. When the bodyguard cannot usurp the body through sleep or distractions, the conscious ego-self is returned to its rightful place at the steering wheel. And then I can choose to say to the bodyguard, "Thank you for trying to help me, but right now there is no threat. So take a break. I'll take it from here. And that means I won't eat cake right now; I'm going to deal with my loneliness in a different way. Maybe I'll call a friend."

Hypnotherapy is a preferred method of working with both the psychological component and the physiological component of C-PTSD.

PSYCHOTHERAPY, HEALING AND TRANSFORMATION

In **psychotherapy**, we basically follow the prescription discovered by Freud of retrieving traumatic memories, bringing unconscious material into consciousness, expressing the attached emotions and releasing the trauma. In the process, traumas are resolved and we return to the normality of social adaptation, free of symptoms. Our goal is a well-adapted life with a sense of personal power and healthy relationships. The ultimate goal is a happy life.

In **healing**, we expand the goal of our intervention from symptom relief to system optimization. It might be seen as the difference between reparative medicine and naturopathy. We also bring spiritual connection (the client's and the healer's) into the process, accessed through intuition and experienced as the grace of God. We use more powerful techniques to access deeper levels of the unconscious, bringing forgiveness and acceptance. Our goals are self-actualization, the expression of unconditional love in healthy community and service to others. The ultimate goal is a harmonious, balanced life.

In **transformation**, we begin by following the same therapeutic process. We might call this phase of transformation *regressive*, going to the source of lessened capacity and healing it. We don't stop there, however. We continue the healing into the psycho-spiritual realm, overcoming normality and achieving (returning to) wholeness. We might call this phase of transformation *progressive*, evolutionary growth into *self-actualization*. We transcend the limitations of generally accepted ordinary reality. We release the attachments to people and things that keep us captive and limited and work toward karmic liberation, clarity of psychic vision (listening to and following the quiet, infallible inner voice) and reaching the highest expression of love in the surrender of the ego to the will of God. The ultimate goal is a life of moments so balanced and conscious that one maintains equanimity, composure and spiritual focus even at the moment of death.

People usually seek therapy for quick solutions to immediate problems. Perhaps they have an addiction or anxiety or a relationship issue which they know they need to address. Unfortunately, therapeutic treatment is symptomatic and can often result in symptom replacement.

Healing, on the other hand, requires an in-depth look at what life is about, the purpose and meaning of existence and how to more fully express oneself in this lifetime. In healing work, we recognize the interconnectedness of the whole person. We go deeper, to the level of early trauma, and resolve what was left unresolved. We know that true healing clears up the problem, symptom and cause, leaving the person healthy and prepared to fight off future infections, be they physical or emotional.

In transformational work, we see the symptom as a *clue* to the deeper spiritual issue with which the person is involved. The symptom can actually lead through the deeper emotional work, clearing out ego issues that block spiritual connection. For example, a person who is continually upset with his/her relationship partner is so preoccupied with these projections that it prevents him or her from looking deeper at the real source of the hurt and anger.

A hindrance to transformation is the support we may receive to not change. The process of transformation often results in estrangement from those who have been our companions in ordinary life. As we develop new insights, new interests, new life scripts and life goals, those in our companionship circle who haven't changed in a like manner are no longer able to effectively support us. They may even try to sabotage our growth in a new direction, and support us to turn back to the old ways. This is especially common with relationships that have involved addictions or other behaviors designed to keep us numb and asleep.

However, we can create *healthy community*, a network of new companions, like-minded and supportive of our newly expanded perspectives. This is a community of seekers on the same path who value consciousness over unconsciousness. After spending time with people who share our souls on the deepest levels, it is difficult to go back to cocktail parties and idle chit-chat. It becomes boring to spend time with people who are not honest about their feelings and are still highly involved in feeding their hungry egos.

ACHIEVING OUR ULTIMATE POTENTIAL

Uncovering these unconscious conclusions and decisions is important not only to repair damage caused by traumas in early life, but also in resolving any obstacles to achieving our ultimate potential in life. One of the most important breakthroughs in Western psychology has been the discovery that psychological maturation can continue far beyond our arbitrary, culture-bound definitions of normality, and that techniques exist for realizing our expanded potential.[4]

Abraham Maslow said, "What we call normality in psychology is really a psychopathology of the average, so undramatic and so widely spread that we don't even notice it."[5] Normality is a form of arrested development, where the developmental process has stopped prematurely, incomplete.[6] The work of developing ourselves into our full potential is *personal transformation*.

We have all experienced moments of transcendence, induced by religious ritual, a peak experience, hallucinogenic drug, meditation, near-death experience or other means. This experience provides a "glimpse" of the vast possibilities beyond normal everyday consciousness.

Many people now see development beyond normality as the logical culmination of human development. In the first phase of life, from childhood to middle adulthood, we are becoming individuals, learning to meet the demands of family, work and society. In the second phase, which begins, according to Carl Jung, with the "midlife crisis," we begin to turn inward, to reconnect with the Self, the center of our beings. In the first phase we built and developed our egos and in the second phase we transcend them.[7]

DREAM WORK AND PSYCHODRAMA

In our practice we use *dream work* and *psychodrama*, two specialized techniques which are adaptations of hypnotherapy. Psychodrama provides an opportunity for the client, in a group therapy setting, to structure his/her internal psychic reality externally and to interact with the representation created. The person whose story is being enacted selects other group members to play the roles of characters in the psychodrama, perhaps his boss, his spouse or his parents. We might also represent his fear, his courage or the feeling of isolation by having a group member play that part. Subpersonalities or shadows can be enacted in psychodrama very effectively, providing clients with a fresh viewpoint of themselves. The identified client has entered a hypnotic trance state, similar to a dream state or to the state one is in while in hypnotherapy, which adds to the intensity of the lived experience.

Psychodrama is highly effective because it is experiential; it taps deeply into unconscious material, it is corrective and it is a group process. Psychodrama allows an internal experience to be externalized and experienced from a new perspective. For example, the impact on a client's life of overwhelming responsibilities is immeasurably more powerful *experienced* in a physical way than it is merely *discussed* verbally and *known* cognitively. We might place something heavy on the client's shoulders to let him really experience how burdensome the responsibilities have become. "Give that heavy burden a voice. What is it saying to you?" Then we have words to correlate with his experience of the heaviness on his shoulders. Also, we concretize experience visually, kinesthetically and viscerally. For example, a family sculpture (a technique popularized by Virginia Satir), with family members placed physically in relation to each other, could demonstrate visually how distant the antisocial brother is and how clinging the oversolicitous mother is.

Psychodrama helps to access the deep unconscious, engaging the body kinesthetically and activating *body memories*, which take us like sonar to early traumatic experiences or other deeply-held unconscious material. When an individual is in the actual physical posture or movement that accompanies a traumatic reaction, it becomes more palpably real. We might assist a client, whose tendency is to want to withdraw in the face of conflict, to express it by physically walking away from his scolding spouse. Then he is confronted in a visceral way with the isolation and loneliness that he also wants to avoid. We can help him to walk into his relationship with his wife and to withdraw from her as many times as it takes for him to realize that he needs to find a new solution, something he hasn't tried before.

Psychodrama is corrective because in it we can re-write history. We can react differently than we did originally, saying what we couldn't then, protecting what we couldn't then and setting much-needed boundaries. A client can see the abused child who was him/her sympathetically, contrary to the judgments and shame which have filled his/her self-experience ever since. This correction often takes the form of re-working missed developmental stages. The corrective experience encourages the client toward re-experiencing the old, unsettled conflict, but with a new ending.

Advantages of group work include the efficiency of benefit to multiple group members of one member's session. Often, the participants who play roles in a session or those in the non-participating audience find their issues getting triggered during someone else's session. Also, participants benefit from the modeled social learning provided by observing other members' coping strategies, resilience and triumphs.

Dream work is an ideal way to access the deep unconscious. In our dreams, the lowest parts of ourselves—the shadows, unacknowledged urges and unexpressed emotions—speak to us. So do the highest parts of ourselves—the denied aspirations, spiritual yearning and wise acceptance of life's conflicts. Often, however, we need a supportive forum and a skilled facilitator to make sense of the messages our dreams are offering. In hypnotherapy or hypnotic psychodrama, we can invite those symbolic dream images to speak for themselves, just like we do with a sensation or symptom in the body: "Give it a voice and let it speak." Then they take on a life of their own, no longer constricted to the exact script of the dream, but opened up to a dialogue with the individual whose unconscious presented him with the dream in the first place. Who better to elaborate the meaning and message of these dream figures than the one whose mind presented them? Not the therapist, and not a book on dream symbols. Probably not the everyday, conscious mind of the client either; the magic of working with dreams in this hypnotic trance state is the access it provides to the part of the mind which created and offered the dream in the first place, the client's unconscious.

Chapter 3

RUNNING AWAY TO THE CIRCUS

Sometimes a traumatic event is so intrusive and devastating that the ego experiences it as overwhelming. The threat is greater and the response is to create a more divisive split. As with the previous example of the child trapped alone in the house, this typically happens because options for physically getting to safety are not available, as can occur in war, natural disasters or the situation of adults abusing the children in their care, since children (as dependents) need to keep living with their caretakers. In this sort of instance, the "other" that is created cannot stay connected with the victim's ego, serving as an ally like the shadow did. It must retreat deeper within, to unconscious levels.

Let's return to the example of the abused child. As the soul begins to split away from control of some aspect of the ego or personality, that fragment of the personality is forced to align itself with something else to run the show...and it connects with someone "bigger than life" to try creating safety and to meet basic needs. We use the analogy of "running away to the circus" to describe this need. The aspect of the child created in this manner is called a *complex* and it has a core of the child's essence, but it also has a much more forceful identity borrowed from circus characters from the "collective unconscious," a term coined by Carl Jung. The personal unconscious is a gathering of experiences unique to each individual, while the collective unconscious collects and organizes those experiences that are common to all of us. The trauma state associated with this complex is much more autonomous from the ego than any shadow, so when it appears, it explodes into activation—suddenly, unexpectedly and with power. It "possesses" the individual and compels the ego to comply. The ego gives in immediately because the arrangement is intended to insure safety and survival. And for those who developed the complex as children, it's been in place for as long as they can remember, in most cases.

The archetypal characters at the circus are indeed larger than life and carry the intrigue that has captivated humanity. Importantly, we could say that they're eager to be "adopted" by a child because then they too can split, allowing part of these great figures to essentially run away *from* the circus and go home with the child.

At this point, the child has a working relationship with the circus character, but the archetype is more powerful than the child and has a life of its own. The more traumatized the child is—the deeper the split—the more overpowering the circus character, because its power is needed in response to the trauma. In fact, when the trauma reaches a state of shock and effectively severs the child's soul or essence from running the show, the circus character completely takes over to the point of physiological changes.

Addiction is an example of how the autonomous complex (the part of the psyche that split off) can take control so that we cannot say no to it. Not, at least, until another, healthier adult (an aspect of the individual's adult ego not severed from the essence or soul) is ready to replace the archetype as protector and companion to the "inner urchin." We'll talk more about addiction later in this book.

Ultimately, though, we need to separate the essential or "real" person from the introjects (qualities and beliefs from parents, priests, teachers, abusers, etc.) that one took on and eventually identified with; and in the same way, to separate the individual from the archetype, replacing it with the original essence that was always meant to guide the ego. To accomplish this, we need to return to the circus to find the characters someone identified with and to finally undo the original bargain. However, the circus that was so easy to find when we were children—when we were full of wonder, awe and imagination, and also desperate for protection—may not be so easy to find as an adult. So we use ritual ceremonies, symbols, fairy tales, dreams and intimacy with another human being to find it once more.

The circus characters with whom the trauma victim forms an alliance are really archetypes who can fulfill the victim's needs that have arisen from the trauma: perhaps a sense of protection to allay existential fear, nurturance to soothe feelings of abandonment or proactivity to calm helplessness. This is why the circus character who is selected depends on the person, the trauma and the circumstance. Here are some examples of characters with whom a child may create this alliance:

THE BARKER

He reaches out with a hearty "Step right up," calling passersby to come and "play the game." He makes false promises, feeding the fantasies and hopes of family members. He is generally manipulative and not to be trusted. He knows how to tell "sweet little lies." He's the player who only loves you when he's playing. People often buy what the barker is selling, only to leave the encounter disappointed, if not distraught. He knows that it is the sizzle that sells and, not having much steak to offer, may not pose an insurmountable obstacle to getting what he wants. Once you buy the ticket, he has turned his attention to the next opportunity.

THE FAT WOMAN

The Fat Woman eats and eats and eats some more, using all that fat to protect her from her emptiness within or from unwanted advances from men. She has found a perverse form of control in her life, a way to deny control to those who try to tell her what to do with her body. Perhaps her mother wants her to be thin and delicate like a ballet dancer or perhaps her father wants her to be tantalizing and sexy. She is creating a buffer from the truth, a shock absorber.

Frankie is a very overweight woman who is desperate to find answers for herself. She ran away to the circus and became the fat lady at a very young age. One reason for this is that she perceived her mother to be at the circus and it was the only place they could connect. So they hid toget[her] dinners, baking cookies and cakes and generally being t[ogether] loved to cook, eat and entertain others through food. [She presents her] self as joyful, laughing and joking with others, and is a ve[ry] general. However, underneath, as is usually the case for t[hese] we find a very depressed and self-deprecating woman with a lot of skills and talents that she herself does not recognize.

Frankie appears extremely uncomfortable in her own body and candidly will say that she would love to lose the weight but nothing has seemed to work for her.

When we rescued her from the circus so that she could begin to recognize her true feelings, she became aware of just how scared and empty she felt inside. There were so many messages from a very young age about how stupid she was, "Can't you do anything right?" and "You'll never amount to anything." She felt shame and then she went immediately into shock, feeling numb and disconnected. We regressed her back to the source of the shame and she went back to being an infant, left alone in her crib with the bottle having fallen out of her mouth. No one comes; no one cares. There was scene after scene of being alone and hungry, then crying herself into oblivion.

This is a different type of abuse than many people experience. This is the abuse and trauma of severe neglect: a young baby with nobody there to care for her or to address her very simple need to survive. We call this *need shock* and we will discuss it later on. When basic survival needs are not addressed, the baby will often stop crying and just exist in a state of shock. The baby is quiet and has run away to the circus at this very young age, because staying in the real world is unbearable. This shock defense at such a young age is probably what kept her alive, but later on became a pattern that nearly killed her. And that is the irony of the shock defense. She eats herself into oblivion just to feel alive, in an attempt to meet these basic survival needs for comfort and to quench the overwhelming pain of deep emptiness and hunger within that she's had since childhood. And now the obesity is killing her! What was a protector has become a saboteur.

THE TATTOOED MAN

He is covered in designs, which are distractions from seeing what is underneath; tattoos make him appear not to be naked. The tattoos are intricate designs, sometimes beautiful or sometimes scary, but always captivating. tattoos are not really part of this man, although they seem to be. The are an elaborate, superficial disguise that says, "Go ahead and get lost in the anecdotes and minutiae of what I present to you; you'll never know the real me, because I'm hiding behind a maze of mirrors." The tattooed man decorates himself to attract others, and yet at the same time to deflect their attention.

THE MUSCLE MAN

He can guarantee safety because nobody messes with him. He is proud of his power and demonstrates it at every opportunity. In fact, he may tend to belittle others or bully them because it is a way of showing off. He spends an inordinate amount of time training and developing his power as well as trying to impress others with it. He always feels like he is competing with others and wants to be "one up" on everyone, belying an unacknowledged insecurity deep beneath the macho façade.

THE CONTORTIONIST

She can make herself small enough to fit into a tiny space. She is double-jointed, and will bend over backwards to accommodate someone else's requests or demands. In fact, she bends in ways that most people won't or can't. Her strength is the agility to compromise like a chameleon.

THE SWORD SWALLOWER

He willingly takes into himself what is obviously self-injurious. He knows that he can withstand the assault as long as he stifles any natural reflex or reaction, disconnecting from his body in order to use it for performance.

THE MAGICIAN

He is a master of sleight of hand, able to mystify others with his razzle dazzle, diverting attention from his trickery that creates the illusions. He alludes to a connection with higher forces and access to supernatural gifts, but in fact employs cheap gimmicks and tawdry tricks. The magician sometimes falls into the trap of believing his own publicity, forgetting that he is merely mortal and entirely fallible.

THE RINGMASTER

She is in control of everything: all three rings at once. She is a master of multi-tasking and appears capable of managing the chaos all around her with ease. She feels most at home with high drama, dazzling spectacle and a dizzying array of activities. She has learned to manage everyone in her life by selectively calling attention to one or two at a time. She shines a spotlight on the loudest noise, the flashiest act or the most demanding character. And then she redirects the spotlight to the next drama. In this way, she can be the center of attention without actually revealing anything about herself.

THE CLOWN

Clowns are very powerful. Some use gallows humor in order to keep everyone laughing and to distract them from noticing the clown's deep pain of loneliness or despair. Other clowns are sad and dejected, downtrodden and bullied or sneaky and mischievous. But in each case, the clowning is distraction to cover up a fear of intimacy, which feels too risky without the buffer of clowning around.

THE TRAPEZE ARTIST

She thrives on the thrill of freefall between letting go of one stable and secure home base and attaching to the next. She relies on her excellent sense of timing to avoid the disgrace and danger of falling. And she also must rely on her fellow trapeze artists to catch her when the time comes, and to hang on tight. When she becomes truly accomplished at this feat, she may be tempted to perform without a net in order to add more suspense. She can often be found flying high above the mundane details of most ordinary lives, dazzling other people with her extraordinary adventures. For this reason, she is actually quite dependent on those others to catch her when she falters.

THE TIGHTROPE WALKER

He keeps everyone looking up (away from what is really going on down below), fearing catastrophe but bringing relief when he makes it. He has learned to "walk a tightrope" between disasters on either side, and his movement is intensely constricted. He feels right at home in situations and relationships that demand concentration to navigate, and that allow no deviation from the "straight and narrow." The balance is precarious, and even the slightest tilt one way or the other would be disastrous. The balancing wires are almost invisible, so everyone believes the fantasy of his death-defying feat.

An example of this character is Ashley, a woman who came to us from a very conservative religious community. Ashley is the mother of three children, two boys and a girl. She was in a very dysfunctional marriage that began early in her life to a man from the church to which her family belongs. Her parents were behind the marriage and as a young woman, she felt she was pushed into this almost "arranged marriage." As she began to develop in her personal and professional life, she realized that being married to Fred was like having a fourth child. He was emotionally immature, unable to bring home a decent salary, and he floundered around in his life about what he wanted to be when he "grows up."

Ashley has known for quite some time that she is gay. She had no interest in sex with her husband, or any man for that matter. She has had several encounters with women about which she carries a great deal of shame and guilt, especially living in such a conservative community. She is realizing that she has grown up in shock due to fearing a very violent father and seeing a terrified mother, who herself was in a great deal of shock. The main way that Ashley has come to know herself is through hypnotherapy and Jungian dream work. Her dreams over the years have clearly indicated that she has a deep, dark secret buried beneath the surface, which she does not want to face or even look at.

At an early age, she learned to walk the tightrope between having her deep needs for love and nurturing from a woman met in secret and keeping up the pretense of being devoutly religious in a conservative community. Her affairs with women were usually started by the other woman, so Ashley was able to justify to herself that she didn't instigate the relationship. She also walked the tightrope, carefully balancing between her desperate need for love and appearing to maintain her image as a married woman, a devoted mother and a consistent churchgoer.

As the years went on, Ashley had a successful psychology practice. Her training, based on self-examination and personal growth, led her to finally release her shame and admit, first to herself and then to others, that she was gay. Next she was able to reveal that her marriage was a sham and that her children had been raised believing in lies; the lies that, as they got older, became more and more clear to them. She could no longer participate in the rigidity and shaming atmosphere of her church and her community. She could no longer keep up the pretense of being a devoted wife to a man she didn't respect, love or admire. She was married to an immature man and she was tired of taking care of him both physically and emotionally.

Finally, Ashley felt she could no longer keep up the highwire routine. She did have below her, however, the huge safety net of a very supportive professional community, which assisted her in moving to a new environment with like-minded people and gently stepping down from her highwire act.

She gained the courage to speak openly and honestly with her now-teenage children, who actually had watched her development and were not surprised at all that she was gay. Nor were they nearly as judgmental about her life as she had been. Ashley realized, as she peeled away the layers of shock that kept her frozen in self-deceit, that it was the shock that had allowed her to live in a dream world for all those years. It was the shock that kept her frozen in fear, shame and turmoil, and perpetuated the lie that all was well. No longer having to balance on that high wire, Ashley discovered a new zest for life along with increased creativity and the ability to manifest many more of her gifts that had been buried deep below the shame and fear.

THE ESCAPE ARTIST

The Escape Artist can always find a way out of every predicament and flees every entanglement before you know it. He always seems to feel trapped and that he therefore needs to extricate himself. Relationships become threatening or suffocating when the other person wants true intimacy, so it's time to leave. He doesn't want to stay too long in any one place or job, because the longer he stays, the more tied down he feels. He is at his best when the challenge is great, so he seeks out people who demand more of him than he is willing to give. That way he gets to do what he enjoys the most and what he is the best at: abandoning others. Actually, he is running away from ever being in the position of being abandoned by someone else.

THE STUNTMAN

He loves being shot out of a cannon because it requires one to be fearless. He is seeking attention and thrills through danger. Live dangerously, seek the thrill of narrow escapes and feel alive by cheating death. Sometimes one can achieve this by getting involved in a sinister or creepy subculture. The more spine-chilling the feats of daring, the more recognition he claims. And underneath the bravado, he has a numbing disregard for his own value and worth.

THE MONKEY/ORGAN GRINDER

The organ grinder plays his organ while a cute monkey sits on top, holding out a cup to take money. The monkey has a leash around its neck and is dressed up in cute little outfits to attract the children. The monkey looks appealing but is actually a captive and is being used as a ruse by the Organ Grinder.

Frances has recently had a series of physical problems. These directly followed some deep work she did to begin to take her life back from her very dominating mother who uses the church and church rules to control her and the entire family. Just as the monkey is the captive of the organ grinder and the organ grinder is captive to the circus, Frances ran away to the circus at a very young age to become a captive of her mother and the church. At the age of forty, Frances still lives with her mother, has never been married and described herself as feeling strangled, unable to move or breathe. After bringing all these deeply buried feelings to the surface, Frances ended up in the hospital with pneumonia for quite some time.

After she recovered and was about to continue to unravel the deeply repressed relationship between herself, her mother and the church, Frances slipped and fell on some ice, breaking a few bones, and again found herself in the hospital, unable to move or take back her power. She knew on a deep level that this was her internal small child, still afraid of confronting her mother. But Frances was determined to salvage her life and take it back from her mother and the church. She had a powerful dream where she saw a small child, trapped in a freezer, and then she saw herself as a small child with a dog collar around her neck. She knew these were powerful symbols of her life. Through the power of psychodrama done in a trance state, she was able to uncover the full meaning of the dream symbols.

Using the dream symbol of being trapped in the freezer, Frances regressed to age four where she had polio and was in an iron lung. They told her she could not move and tied her down so that she couldn't even if she wanted to. She was clearly in a deep state of shock, exemplified by the symbol of being in a freezer in her dream. She was terrified as no one explained to her what was happening and no one was allowed to touch her. She felt abandoned, terrified and confused. Her mother was not there and the nurses were very mean. The conclusion she made about herself was, "Something is very wrong with me," and the decision was, "I'll have to figure it out myself."

Then she was regressed again and went back to the cold, judgmental womb of her mother. She sensed that her mother was unprepared for another baby and would have had an abortion if it weren't for the church rules. Her father was also very unhappy, feeling that they certainly could not afford another baby. She was very underdeveloped at birth, due to lack of proper nourishment from her mother, and was placed in an incubator. She began to get the symbolism of the freezer from her dream on an even deeper level. The empty womb of her mother and the incubator were both places she felt trapped and were both devoid of warmth, nurturing or any type of support that a baby needs. Her need shock was severe and so she became desperate to please her mother and the church, because these seemed to be her only chance at human contact.

Another image came to her as she became older and that was that she was a monkey with a collar around her neck, performing for her mother and the church. She realized that she had been in shock her whole life, at least since the incubator, and that her mother led her around by the "monkey collar" with rules and regulations and fear of God's punishment all her life. Just a few of the rules were "Go to church every day, don't think for yourself, don't speak unless spoken to, your ideas are stupid, I know what's best for you," etc. In her psychodrama, she was the monkey being pulled by the collar.

But Frances began to pull off the collar to take her agency back. She said, "Your rules are choking me and I'm going to think for myself. I am going to make my own decisions and I *can* make my own decisions!" She became stronger and more powerful as she took her power back from her mother and the church. She knew it was her experience with pneumonia that brought her to awareness of how she was feeling suffocated. She felt thankful for the experience of being trapped in the hospital, which brought back the memories of the iron lung and incubator which kept her in shock much of her life. She reclaimed her power, her voice and her ability to think and make decisions for herself. This was a powerful session where the client, through a series of adverse experiences, was able to see her life more clearly and heal the deep patterns of shock that had trapped her for so long.

THE LION TAMER

Her job is to domesticate the wild ones, even at great personal risk. This can be a legitimate strategy for dealing with abusive caregivers: do whatever it takes to calm them when they begin getting agitated, anticipate their needs and provide them before the demands become abusive. Or perhaps crack the whip and try to overpower the wild one. The methods vary, but the lion tamer is always vigilantly aware of her lion's mood, hunger level and readiness for violence. Taming the lion is a great challenge and is never completely accomplished, but rather must be re-established in every encounter. And any self-respecting lion tamer will show off her prowess by placing her head in the lion's mouth; she knows that her success and reputation depend on demonstrating just how dangerous the wild one that she is taming is. So she has a perverse vested interest in keeping her lion wild.

THE JUGGLER

He is able to amaze everyone by keeping multiple balls in the air or plates spinning, attending to each one only enough to avoid it crashing to the ground. He challenges himself right to the limit of what anyone thinks is possible to balance, and as soon as he masters that challenge he adds another ball or another plate. More is always better. It requires focused attention, keeping his conscious awareness narrowed down to the immediate task at hand. There is always another task just at the point of crashing, demanding attention. It is never-ending and soon becomes exhausting.

THE ROUSTABOUTS AND THE CARNIES

These are unsavory characters who do the grunt work. They are the only truly essential ones in the fantasy because they hold it all together. They build the fantasy, day in and day out, providing the structure for the illusion. They are hard workers...but only until payday. In other words, until they get their short-term desires met. Then it may be time to go out and "celebrate." They can't understand why anyone feels betrayed when they do, because that was the only motivation for doing the hard work in the first place. The irony is that everyone needs to depend on them for the existence of the structure and yet they are truly undependable.

THE BUSINESS MANAGER

The Business Manager is busy in his separate office, counting the money and disconnected from the goings-on all around him. His only connection with the others in the circus family is to pay them off. He has a vital role, but manages to accomplish it while remaining detached. The office is an effective place to hide from involvement with others and to receive social rewards for doing so. He can hold himself as superior to the Ringmaster, above the high drama and dazzling spectacle, while capable of just as much multitasking.

Chapter 4

THE WITNESS PROTECTION PROGRAM

As we have said, a minor split of the soul from the ego may create a *shadow* in which a powerful archetype may begin to influence the ego, allowing it to act in ways that the soul would not normally direct it to. At that level, however, the soul is still present, and the shadow is consciously recognized by the ego. With deeper trauma, the split is more divisive; the soul has fled further away, and the archetype takes substantial control of the ego in a mutual agreement for safety. In the case of shock, the soul has truly "left the building" or split from an aspect of the ego, and the archetype takes control to the point of altering physiology.

We emphasize the point that as part of the ego splits from the true self, it doesn't just disappear. In its arrangement with one or more archetypes from the collective unconscious, it forms a primitively organized alternative self that has its own identity. When this happens, the soul has effectively gone into hiding, and we use another analogy for this called the "witness protection program."

We use this term because, in a traditional witness protection program, one who is under some kind of threat finds protection by not only relocating, but also by assuming a new identity. Without a new identity, the new location doesn't help, because you might still be found. So in the case of trauma, you may relocate by leaving the body, in a sense, or dissociating. You separate the conscious connection with the body, with relationships, even with your own spiritual identity. And so you relocate and create that new identity.

In the witness protection program, you have to get rid of any similarities to your old life to make sure you cannot be found, and this includes the things you used to do. Your work, for example. Prior to trauma you may act in a certain way; but once traumatized, there is a need for protection and a need to act in different ways, to become something you weren't before.

Maybe, for instance, you had to become really, really good. By this we mean being extraordinarily obedient, doing everything you're told right away. In fact, you don't even have to be asked—you anticipate the needs of those you perceive to be a threat (whether this is true or not, it's your perception that counts). You become hyper-vigilant, tuned in to abusers or other threats in order to proactively minimize pain or danger.

You can see this in the example of a young child. When a child is three years old, undisturbed by trauma, they'll tell you who they are. They have a very good sense of this. They know who they are, what they like and don't like, who they like and don't like, their favorite colors and music and so on. They know themselves. But once they go into this witness protection program, they have to change all that, because they are now so vigilant about what is being demanded of them by a potential threat and they need to become whatever it is that will minimize the danger.

Maybe Mom rejects me and I feel unloved if she doesn't have all her needs met, so I become a caretaker to satisfy all her needs and to make sure I am loved. Or maybe I am told that I am bad and this is why I'm being abused, and I believe this, because I'm being told this by my caretakers, these adults who have tremendous power and credibility. I start to act according to this new identity that's been handed to me.

It's important to remember, as we continue through this book together, that there is no fine line separating trauma from shock, although there are several elements we can look at that distinguish them from one another. Ultimately, what's important in therapy is that the two need to be treated differently, for shock involves a greater separation between life essence or soul and the ego itself and for this, a different therapeutic approach is required.

DISTINCTIONS BETWEEN TRAUMA AND SHOCK

Remembering that the shift between what we're calling *trauma* and *shock* occurs on a continuum, rather than at one defined point, and that symptoms of shock may develop differently for different people as they enter deeper levels of trauma, here are some of the distinguishing factors that help us understand the progress from trauma to shock:

1) ALTERATIONS IN THE REGULATION OF AFFECTIVE IMPULSES

As we continue along the continuum of trauma to shock and then beyond, we reach additional conditions such as borderline personality disorder, dissociative identity disorder (DID, better known as *multiple personality disorder*), associative identity disorder and so on. Each is a little bit further into the witness protection program: relocation, dissociation and re-identification. "I'm somebody other than who I started out being." Regulation of affected impulses has to do with self-destructiveness, so the further we go into shock, the more this will manifest.

2) ALTERATIONS IN ATTENTION

This has to do with the degree of dissociation, which sometimes incorporates amnesia. This includes the part of me that registers memory, so now those memories are stored in my body, because my body was here during the trauma but the rest of me was not. This is why portions of therapy involve bodywork, and why people often recover lost memories through this kind of therapy.

3) ALTERATIONS IN SELF-PERCEPTION

The deeper we go into shock, the more likely we are to identify with guilt or shame surrounding the traumatic experience, even thinking we are the cause of it. Often we give a client a teddy bear or some symbol of his or her own inner child, and ask that the client tell the child (his or herself as a child) how much he or she is loved, how beautiful and innocent he or she is. In most cases this is a powerful healing experience. But sometimes we find that a client pushes the teddy bear away, saying, "I don't want to have anything to do with her. She is dirty, she is stupid and I hate her." That's an indication of how deeply embedded that individual's sense of responsibility is for what happened to her. She is blaming herself for what happened to her as a child. We can use this technique over time as a measure of recovery, as she is able to slowly embrace that little girl instead of judging and rejecting her.

4) ALTERATIONS IN PERCEPTION OF THE PERPETRATOR
In some cases of shock, the perception is that "I am the perpetrator." And the deeper the shock, the more this seems to be true. We call this identification with the perpetrator "trauma bonding." This is one of the new identity options for the person who's entered the witness protection program. And many, many times, this translates into actually becoming the perpetrator on someone else at a later time—many who have been abused in early childhood become abusers of their own children.

5) ALTERATIONS IN RELATIONSHIP TO OTHERS
The deeper the shock, the more we lose the ability to trust or be intimate with others.

6) SOMATIZATION OR MEDICAL PROBLEMS
The nature of shock, as opposed to trauma, is that it is deeply embedded in the body itself—in the physical systems of the body: the nervous system, the heart, the brain, the limbic and hormonal systems, etc. This is why, as we mentioned previously, it is through those systems of the body that we can access information about the damage done and provide corrective treatment. This is a fundamental aspect of what modern medical practice is now calling integrative medicine. As we begin to understand the nature of shock and how traumatic memories are literally stored in the traumatized parts of the body, the use of clinical hypnotherapy can bring a whole new level of healing from trauma through understanding how to retrieve these long-buried memories literally frozen in the body. Unretrieved, they are silently at work, causing unease and disease in the body.

For example, a woman named Carol, along with her younger sister, was sexually abused from the very young age of three by her drunken father.

After several years of this, he then brought in his alcoholic friends to sexually abuse them. This continued uninterrupted by her mother, who had to work to support the girls since her husband drank up all the money. This left the two young daughters in a nearly constant state of vulnerability, where they had to "run away to the circus," and each developed several circus characters in order to survive the horrendous situation.

Since the traumatic experiences and memories are stored in the body, it is very common in these situations for young women to develop "female problems." This can include painful menstrual cycles, severe endometriosis and even cancer. When the doctors try to treat the "symptoms," the next solution is removal. Many women who have early hysterectomies often don't know about the abuse that happened to them because they have been off to the "witness protection program." Carol developed multiple personalities which were a result of needing to leave her constantly re-abusing father and his friends. Since her mother was unable to protect her, she developed a creative way to protect herself: literally new identities via the witness protection program. Her sister used alcohol and drugs to accomplish a similar escape from an intolerable reality, to self-medicate her shock.

Learning how to do mind-body work through clinical hypnotherapy can be the road that leads people out of witness protection and gives them the ability to return home.

7) ALTERATIONS IN SYSTEMS OF MEANING

Chronically abused individuals often feel hopeless about finding anyone to understand them or their suffering. They believe that nobody could possibly understand, and they despair that they will never be able to recover from their mental anguish. They have been exiled, for that is the nature of witness protection. You are cut off from every relationship that you've had, and you're denied the possibility of creating new ones because that would only endanger your safety. The whole idea is to be invisible.

Chapter 5

A CLINICAL PERSPECTIVE

We have been using metaphors of running away to the circus and the witness protection program to describe children's responses to trauma. In more clinical terms, the child's ego splits when encountering an intolerable threat to safety. This splitting defense serves a twofold purpose: one, to fragment a painful experience, rendering it less unbearable by a process of dissociation and compartmentalization and two, to attempt repair, constructing a new and less distressing narrative which renders trauma less threatening to one's personal sense of worth and identity.

According to Donald Kalsched, an expert in Jungian psychology, trauma can be defined as what happens when a negative experience cannot be dealt with through normal psychic defenses.[1] Then a second line of defenses comes into play, defenses that are invincible and archetypal (in the sense that they are not personally elaborated and cannot be personally controlled). And the defense against the psychic presence of abuse must be at least as big, absolute, and divine as the forces behind the abuse itself.[2] The child's immature ego exists on the "magical level" (advanced by developmental psychologist Jean Piaget) or "mythological level" (developed by Erich Neumann, a psychologist and student of Carl Jung) of consciousness, and any parent of a small child is familiar with the unconscious fantasies that structure all of his or her experience.[3] Here live the great bigger-than-life beings of the archetypal psyche and they can personify as either angels or demons, protectors or persecutors.

Kalsched highlights the vital protective role that dissociative defenses play when a person is threatened with intolerable trauma, psychic pain or anxiety which is severe enough to bring about psychic disintegration, or "the destruction of the personal spirit." He suggests that trauma produces a fragmentation of consciousness in which one part of the personality regresses to an infantile state and another part progresses to a false and omnipotent adaptation to the outside world. A child's psyche has to pay a huge price for this kind of archetypal defense, in that once the trauma defense is organized, all relations with the outside world are screened by this shield. What was intended to be a defense against further trauma becomes a major resistance to all unguarded, spontaneous expressions of self in the world. The person survives but cannot live creatively, continues to live but lives falsely, terrified of a future breakdown *that has already been experienced* but cannot be remembered. This is very common in people who have been diagnosed by our mental health system as Borderline Personality Disorder and Dissociative Identity Disorder. We believe that these are not actually disorders but rather creative survival defenses against intolerable, ongoing, abusive family situations.

Defenses are not only avoidance mechanisms, but also active constructions in the form of narratives, created in imagination and fantasy to support a positive sense of identity and personal worth when these are threatened by cruelty, hostility or indifference (emotional neglect) from those whom we love and on whom we are most completely dependent. To feel that one is of no value, unlovable or the object of hatred is unbearable. Trauma of this kind results in the defensive construction of imaginative narratives, which render the child's experience of it more bearable and less threatening to the child's very identity. Kalsched recognizes that "the inner sanctuary to which the beleaguered ego repairs in time of crisis is also a world that opens onto transpersonal energies."[4]

Jodi's Story

Jodi is the head social worker in a major psychiatric treatment facility. When you meet her, you're immediately impressed with her professionalism, competence and extensive ability to manage her staff. She also is perfectly groomed and wears beautifully styled clothing from the very best boutiques.

When we first began doing hypnosis with her, it was mostly to help her manage the stress of a challenging profession and marriage. After many individual sessions, though, we felt that it would help her to be in a group in order to break through some of the defenses that kept her trapped behind her façade of perfectionism. Her first assignment was to come to group without make-up—without her mask. It was stressful for her to even imagine being seen in public like this.

As we continued to work with her, we grew to understand the profound extent of what that mask was covering up. In the end, it took years of deep clinical hypnotherapy before Jodi was able to open up to her own truth. Jodi grew up in a devoutly religious family from an authoritarian, Eastern European background. Her father was the head of the household and his mother—Jodi's grandmother—lived with them to help raise the children and to protect their strict family tradition. So it's no wonder that Jodi and her sisters grew up as high achievers, always looking perfect to the outside world in a compulsive attempt to bring accolades to this immigrant family, which was trying desperately to assimilate into the American way of life.

During her therapy, it was revealed that Jodi's past was filled with addictive behaviors, which we saw as a way to continue numbing the pain she carried underneath her fancy façade. Jodi had used food and alcohol as far back as she could remember to numb the hurt which, along with fear and anger, consisted of deep layers of shame. In group, Jodi would always speak highly of her father, discussing at great length his many outstanding attributes and how much she loved him. When her father died, Jodi was devastated and spent months grieving his loss. Soon after, however, it started becoming clear that her beloved father had been sexually molesting her all during her childhood. In fact, her father had a very destructive, angry, erratic side to his personality that the whole family feared. When this facet of explosiveness came out, the mother or grandmother would send little Jodi upstairs to "quiet him down."

As we worked together, Jodi slowly began to let herself know what her role was in this devastating family process. It became apparent that her role was as her father's little mistress. Through the Jungian hypnotherapeutic approach, we saw how Jodi "ran away to the circus" and adopted several different personalities in order to survive. She had to find circus characters more powerful than her in order to deal with her abusive father. She became the tightrope walker in a childhood attempt to continue this delicate balancing act that had been assigned to her. Jodi also used the personas of the clown, to keep everyone laughing, the lion tamer, to keep her rageful father from hurting other family members, and the fat lady, in an unconscious attempt to perhaps repulse her father into stopping the sexual abuse. As she grew older, Jodi became the powerful ringmaster, always making sure that in one ring the family secret was being kept while in the next ring she was managing her father's sexual appetite and keeping him from attacking others. In the third ring, Jodi was going to school and getting good grades while also managing the family image in the community and at church. In order to be less internally conflicted about all these different roles, Jodi artfully dissociated or split off from these parts of herself.

Dissociation is a natural process that occurs when children (or adults such as war veterans) are placed in untenable, painful situations for which there is no other solution. Like the millions of children who are abused, Jodi could not literally run away from home, so she ran away to the circus she had created in her mind.

Chapter 6

THE PHYSIOLOGY OF SHOCK

A young man hiked into the desert and was working his way through a narrow crevice when a boulder fell on his arm and trapped him. Not only did he have to face the physical pain of having his arm smashed, but as time passed, he had to face the almost unbearable reality that there was no way of getting the rock off his arm and there was almost certainly no way someone was going to find him. So his only choice for survival was to apply a tourniquet and then sever his arm in order to make his way to freedom.

Thankfully, few of us ever have to face such a physically frightening and brutal circumstance for survival, but we're often faced with having to sacrifice something we want in our lives for the sake of something more important. In the midst of a home fire, people will do anything to save their children and then their pets in preference to their possessions. More along the lines of the hiking example, every day people around the world choose to drink dirty water that has a good chance of making them sick, because, ironically, they need the water to survive. So they choose the lesser of two evils.

In fact, the entire body operates in this way. Any time it endures a lack of nutrients, for instance, it asks the same question we would ask with a limited budget: if I only have so much, what do I *have* to spend money on, and what can wait? Just like a human with a credit card, the body will borrow from its own resources—like the minerals in the bones—to make sure that day-to-day function goes on as well as possible, even though that may make its long-term foundation a little more shaky. Maybe the body needs calcium to keep muscles contracting, including the heart. Probably worth stealing a little calcium from the bones if it's not getting the calcium from its diet, right? But what happens if that occurs on a regular basis?

As we've discussed, the physical body isn't the only part of us that uses this principle of "the lesser of two evils." While we always prefer ideal options from which to make our choices—happy and pristine surroundings, perfect nutrition, wise teachers, kind friends—circumstances are often far from ideal, and we have to do the best we can in the situation. Adults sent into war, children sold into slavery and indeed the child at home being physically, sexually or emotionally abused—all these instances may call for choices of sacrifice: "If I want to function from day to day, I cannot live in a state of shock. So 'someone else' will handle getting abused while 'I' handle daily living."

In effect, the abused child basically sacrifices part of her connection to her true self, her soul, in order to preserve it. By separating her true self from the abuse, this aspect of her life is able to keep its attachment and its control over other parts of the child's life. It's wonderful that our true essence can be preserved in this way, and that this allows it to continue taking part in our lives. But there are consequences to this splitting.

After all, our souls are really the life force that makes us individuals rather than just a biological entity or part of a collective mind. This life force is what allows us to have what many people call "God-given talents," whether these are for learning, for creating or for having a good sense of humor. This essence also knows how to deeply love and respect itself and others—something that seems to be missing in so many people who have suffered from shock.

The potential for shock is around every corner, from the moment of conception to birth to the patterns we're exposed to by our parents, teachers and the media. No child completely escapes the impressions of stress and trauma, even if he or she is only affected to a small extent. But picture the child who has experienced minimal trauma, from a loving conception to an easy delivery, from harmony in his home and classroom life to encouragement in learning and doing. Perhaps most important of all is regular assurance from both word and deed that he is loved and respected. Picture that child and know how eager he is to learn; how happy he is to show affection; how readily he laughs. This is the structure of the generally uninhibited soul.

The soul is inhibited to some degree simply by being in a physical body. The body gives it limitations and frailties. And while most parents would love nothing better than to give their children this idyllic kind of environment, the challenges of everything from global and household economics to jobs, politics, relationships, health, housekeeping and other errands seem determined to keep them from doing so. But the younger the children without substantial abuses in their lives, the more we see those brilliant soul qualities shining through their eyes.

As we get older, though, trauma and shock play their role in teaching us, either directly or indirectly. Subtle traumas happen even in simple instances like heading into middle school for the first time and being laughed at for being different in some way and so, as a matter of protection, we start to learn how to fit in rather than being that unique self that had so much light in it. This is when trauma teaches us directly. Then we may teach our own children years later that they need to learn how to fit in and we encourage them to hide their true selves, because we fear for their safety. Now trauma is reaching the child indirectly through us as parents.

As we split away from the soul—either in subtle ways, as with shadows, or in substantial ways, as with shock—trauma and shock really are the only other elements available to control how we function. They are the default programming when the soul isn't making choices.

Aspects of the collective mind come to us in the form of archetypes and guide our thinking. In this book we're describing these as circus characters. This helps us to deal with ongoing trauma, because we're now accompanied by a powerful companion (identified as a part of 'me' that I don't quite control). This could be the Muscle Man, the Fat Lady, the Clown or others. But whatever form these archetypes take, its original intention is to act as a protective bodyguard for the traumatized person to hide behind.

Having this bodyguard comes at a steep price, however, because when there is any perceived threat having to do with the original trauma—the trauma that created this relationship—then the bodyguard takes control with or without current permission, because permission was given with the original agreement.

THE PHYSIOLOGY OF SHOCK

Perhaps the most important key to understanding shock is understanding our built-in system for handling stress. This system is designed to protect us and, as with the "lesser of two evils" we mentioned, the results of having this system work for us aren't always ideal, yet they are *more* ideal than the alternative, which is basically death by stress due to a loss of homeostasis. But when we're pushed too far, to the point of trauma and shock, you can see the lasting results of this protective system in our behavior.

This profound influence on human behavior is found within the deep evolutionary streams of human nature, flowing through the hormonal and nervous systems, regulated by the instinctual "reptilian brain" (limbic system). That part of the brain controls emotional thought, including rage, fear, aggression and arousal. The influence of these systems is especially direct as imminent threat increases. Importantly for us, the "new brain"—the prefrontal cortex and especially the hippocampus—can moderate that influence, putting the reality of a threat into context and making mindful, conscious choices of behavior.

So in animals having both parts of the brain to work from, nature combines the two to deal with danger. First there's an old brain (reptilian brain) assessment of a situation. This assessment asks, "Is there reason to turn up the stress response system?" The reptilian brain may determine that there *is* reason for a stress response, but the new brain may provide context to the situation and thereby eliminate the need for the stress response. However, in those who have suffered from shock, the new brain cannot provide that context so the reptilian brain's decision remains and can only provide two basic types of response: fight/flight and freeze. Let's take a look at a zebra in the wild as an example.

ORIENTING RESPONSE

Engaged in its daily activity, a prey animal like a zebra has an "early warning system" that senses a potential threat. Perhaps it is grazing when it suddenly hears something hidden in the nearby grass. It enters a state of "alert immobility," becoming almost entirely motionless, and focuses its attention on sensory cues regarding the threat (typically sight, sound and smell). If no danger is detected, the zebra resumes normal activity without wasting energy on a fight or flight response. If danger is imminent, then fight or flight is initiated.

THE FIGHT OR FLIGHT RESPONSE

The sympathetic response (fight/flight) is most easily understood as an upsurge in emotion. In people, these emotions are experienced as coming "up"—anger, fear, excitement, desire, hatred—and, if expressed, involve movement toward the problem (fight) or away from the problem (flight).

So perhaps our zebra spots a lion. Immediately, the instinctual fight or flight response is activated and stress hormones are pumped into the body by the *sympathetic* nervous system to put all available energy into survival. Norepinephrine immediately calls into action certain centers in the brain to respond, including the *amygdala* (the center for emotional memories) and the *hippocampus* (the nerve center that provides a conscious structure and context for "declarative memory"—a form of memory relating to facts and events in cooperation with the cerebral cortex). Adrenaline surges and glucose is mobilized from the liver to provide energy to activate the heart, lungs, arms and legs in order to optimize impending fight or flight. Endorphins are released in the brain to create stress-induced analgesia (to reduce any pain).

If the zebra in our example survives the threat on its life, it then discharges the stress hormones in its body and resumes its normal daily activities. The discharge is primordial, reflexive and totally somatic, ranging from twitching movements to violent shaking. And a record of the successful survival experience is etched in the hippocampus to make future threats more survivable.

As we've indicated, you can see the lingering effects of this stress response system in those who have reached this overwhelming point (trauma or shock). In these cases, the sympathetic stress isn't shaken off in the natural way, and the sympathetic "symptoms" can be seen in behavior years or even decades after the traumatic event. Over time, the non-discharged nervous system response becomes deeply embedded somatically and is what we call shock. People who experience sympathetic shock are often involved in frantic, constant movement, talking quickly with run-on sentences and no opening for anyone else to get a word in edgewise. This is often accompanied by compulsive working, spending and shopping. Other nervous or anxious habits can include tics, insomnia, smoking, frequent accidents or the need to control. There can also be physical symptoms such as ulcers, allergies, temporomandibular disorders (TMD), gastrointestinal distress and hypertension. These are all attempts by the body/psyche to "drain the swamp" of excess energy that has become dangerous to homeostasis as it builds up with nowhere to go.

Excessive sympathetic branch activity can lead to increased energy-consuming processes, manifested as increases in heart rate and respiration and as a pounding sensation in the head.[1] Other symptoms include muscle tensing, clenching or grinding of teeth, tachycardia (irregular heartbeat), excessive sweating, pallor, tremor, startle, hypervigilance, panic, rage and constipation. Over the long term, such hyperarousal may disrupt cognitive and affective processing as the individual becomes overwhelmed and disorganized by the accelerated pace and amplitude of thoughts and emotions, which can be accompanied by intrusive memories as well.

FREEZE RESPONSE

Opposite to fight/flight, the parasympathetic action (freeze) is described as coming "down." Human emotions include disappointment, grief, shame, guilt and despair; or in a positive sense, contentment, peacefulness and satisfaction. These feelings involve a decrease in tension, a drawing of energy inward with a tendency toward introspection. Laughter and tears are both usually a sign of parasympathetic activity, because both reduce tension. Other physical symptoms may include heart palpitations, nausea, dizziness, indigestion, abdominal cramps, diarrhea, incontinence, social isolation and withdrawal, substance abuse, constricted affect (a lack of apparent emotion), denial, cognitive impairment and dissociation.

In the case of the zebra we've described, if the fight or flight is not successful, at the point of recognizing defeat and impending death he goes into a state of helplessness and hopelessness. Physiologically, this is the *freeze response*. It appears as "feigning death" because of the sudden and extreme immobility, which is a last-ditch effort for survival because a lion will not eat an animal unless she kills it first. If the zebra convinces the lion that he has just dropped dead, the lion walks away and the zebra lives. The stress hormones are not discharged, as they would be after a successful fight or flight. Instead, they are counteracted by a new cocktail of hormones activated by the *parasympathetic* nervous system. The pulse and blood pressure, previously elevated by stress hormones, are now forced to drop precipitously. In fact, the overall vital signs drop so sharply that there is a danger that the animal will fail to recover even if allowed to do so. About one-third of animals who feign death like this die before they can recover. The endorphins released in response to a threat persist during freeze/immobility, rendering the zebra analgesic in the face of the injury from the attack. At this point the zebra is in a state of passive dissociation—not unconscious, but in an altered state of "suspended animation."

If it so happens that the zebra survives the encounter after entering a freeze state, it enters a discharge sequence similar to the discharge of the stress hormones. The experience of escape is stored in procedural (unconscious) memory, increasing confidence and resilience for future threatening experiences.

If hormone discharge is blocked without causing death, however, the zebra suffers chronic physical symptoms of immune deficiency and a shortened lifespan, and behaviorally suffers depression and neurosis. You can see in people that excessive parasympathetic branch activity leads to an increase of energy-conserving processes, such as decreases in heart rate and respiration and a sense of 'numbness' and 'shutting down' within the mind. Such *hypoarousal* can manifest as numbing, a dulling of inner body sensation, a slowing of muscular/skeletal response and diminished muscular tone, especially in the face. Cognitive and emotional processing are also disrupted.

One example of this is animals in cages whose freedom of movement is severely restricted. Their resignation to "inescapable" trauma is called the defeat response, or learned helplessness, and represents a state of adaptation to living indefinitely with life-threatening trauma without further attempts to escape (fight or flight). Learned helplessness is the persistence of the non-discharged parasympathetic freeze response. We know this because blocking the parasympathetic nervous system (with a drug) also blocks the development of learned helplessness.[2] Here, unable to discharge and complete the process of recovery from the freeze response, the experience of inescapable threat is consolidated in procedural memory, reinforcing the tendency to freeze in the future.

Such prolonged exposure to elevated levels of stress hormones within the context of the non-discharged freeze response creates damage to the brain's hippocampus. And indeed, you can then imagine the impact on people who suffer regular abuse. Smaller hippocampal volumes, for instance, are reported in female adult survivors of childhood sexual abuse. This kind of damage leads to a loss of neurons and synapses (up to 18 percent), and results in corruption of thought processes and learning, particularly deficits of encoding short-term into long-term memory, and of envisioning future events that are different from the past.[3]

The traumatic experiences, then, etched in procedural memory but not converted into long-term memory, interfere with current working memory. In this case, past threats are perceived to be present threats, suggested by intrusive thoughts, flashbacks and hypervigilance. Not only does this obscure the ability to distinguish between past and present, but the repertoire of survival skills remains confined to those skills that were acquired up to the time of the trauma and people in this circumstance lack the resilience to learn new strategies. You could say that an aspect of these individuals is frozen in the past, because they lost part of (or much of) the connection to their essence at the time of the traumatic, shock-inducing event. In circumstances related to that trauma, at least part of their true selves is only connected to them in the past, while part of the present ego-self is a replacement from the archetypal members of the circus.

The Polyvagal Theory of Stephen Porges proposes two branches to the vagus nerve: one associated more with the older, reptilian brain and one associated with the more recent mammalian brain. He suggests that this dual nerve system gives us the freeze response on one hand and a calming effect on the other. While the polyvagal system directly operates only with the parasympathetic side of things, this control also operates indirectly as a "brake" on the sympathetic system, thus controlling both through its veto power, so to speak. Porges's work documents how the body, through the vagal nerve system, determines whether parasympathetic activation triggers disappointment and shame on the one hand or contentment on the other.[4]

The good news is that, in cases where either the fight/flight or freeze response hasn't been discharged correctly, the discharge can be facilitated therapeutically and damage to the brain and memory can be repaired. The hippocampus is part of the limbic system and is especially susceptible to hypoxic and ischemic damage (obstruction of the blood supply). Yet it is the only known region of the human brain that can replicate new neurons. Long-term potentiation (LTP) is defined as an increase in strength of synaptic transmission with repetitive use that lasts for more than a few minutes. In the hippocampus, LTP can be triggered by less than 1 second of intense synaptic activity and lasts for hours or more. This may account for the memory re-acquisition and re-contextualization that is possible when healing trauma. Through techniques such as catharsis, titration of threat cues, unwinding of bound undischarged energy and reprogramming of the perpetual fight/flight or freeze response, effective facilitation can indeed reverse the damage done and return the individual to a state of resilience and homeostasis.

Nature has given us this necessary and useful ability to enter fight/flight or freeze for self-preservation. It also gives us a way to shake off these states when they are no longer useful for us. In our zebra example, that survival after stress, which includes successful discharge of the excess stress hormones, results in increased confidence and resilience for future stressful experiences. Unfortunately, we don't always do this effectively, even when facing a one-time trauma, much less when facing ongoing traumas from experiences like war or abuse. We become stuck on either end of the spectrum of sympathetic or parasympathetic—often moving between the two, though most people will tend toward one or the other, as we see in consistent personality traits.

SYMPATHETIC AND PARASYMPATHETIC: SEEKING BALANCE

As we've discussed, the psyche will send the true self into hiding in the face of trauma and bring in an expert from the circus to handle the stress. Giving up this power over one's life has its own cost, but it's a better option than giving up life altogether due to sympathetic or parasympathetic overwhelm.

However, these systems will also try to retain homeostasis on their own. For instance, when the sympathetic system is activated, the body attempts to counterbalance this by activating the parasympathetic system, and vice versa. So if someone's revved up with anger (sympathetic), he might want to smoke a cigarette or eat a comfort food (parasympathetic) as a natural response for homeostasis. Robert Scaer describes this process in *The Trauma Spectrum*:

The autonomic nervous system of the trauma victim…is characterized by a state of instability, sensitivity, and a cyclical abnormality of its normal state of regulation. Homeostasis may be disrupted by excessive and disproportionate stimulation by one limb of the autonomic nervous system, a state that is characteristic of the trauma victim. Assaulted by internal cues of threat, the victim experiences

repetitive episodes of **sympathetic arousal that in turn reflex-
ively trigger deep parasympathetic dissociation.** The trauma
victim lives in a state of involuntary and disruptive autonomic instability and cycling.[5]

SYMPATHETIC AND PARASYMPATHETIC: AN EXAMPLE

The Runaway Bride was a widely publicized story that gave us a perfect example of sympathetic and parasympathetic responses in action. It was the story
of a beautiful young woman engaged to a wonderful man who was in love
with her and wanted to marry her. Just before the wedding, she suddenly disappeared, to the amazement of everyone in her life as well as millions of TV
viewers. The runaway bride, Jennifer Carol Wilbanks, ran away from home
in Duluth, Georgia on April 26, 2005, in order to avoid her wedding with
John Mason, her fiancé, on April 30. Her disappearance sparked a nationwide
search and intensive media coverage.

She finally turned herself in after three days with the whole world
searching for her. What was the problem that caused her to run away the
day before a wedding that she had dreamed of her whole life?

If you look at her eyes in the photos, she clearly looks terrified and yet she
could only smile and say she didn't know why she ran away or even where she
went. Sympathetic and parasympathetic shock is like being on either side of a
teeter-totter, going back and forth from one to the other. That is what happened
with her. She was riding buses, getting on and off of them for days. This is sympathetic shock: lots of movement, like constantly running away. While on the
buses, she moved into parasympathetic shock, which is like being "paralyzed."
She spent hours and days riding and staring endlessly out the windows. She
reported that she didn't remember where she went or what she saw.[6]

After she was finally discovered in a bus station, it was revealed that
she had anorexia, a disturbing eating disorder in which a person eats very
little because she feels fat. She had a great deal of shame about this condition and the constant stream of lies that accompanied it. As the wedding date
approached, she unconsciously realized that getting married would reveal her
long-held secrets, lies and shame to her new husband. That was more than she
could bare and, at that point, her shock was activated and other forces took
over so that she could escape without knowing consciously what she was doing.

CATATONIA: SYMPATHETIC AND PARASYMPATHETIC EXTREMES

These two propensities, the fight/flight sympathetic response and the freeze parasympathetic response, establish the basis for panic on the one hand and depression on the other. Stanley Keleman has worked on this formulation for many years, expressing that the first response to any stress or challenge is always arousal.[7] When that arousal is not containable—if it is so intense that it becomes "unboundaried"—the person becomes overwhelmed. There's too much excitation and not enough form, structure, context or containment. At the extreme, this becomes panic. To protect oneself from being overwhelmed or panicked, a person sometimes responds by holding it in, waiting, stiffening, squeezing and constricting: this is the freeze response, which heads in the direction of depression.

When there's too much excitation without form or containment, there is panic. When there's too much constriction and containment without a flow of activation, you have numbing, in which nothing can be aroused. This is depression.

The psychopathology labeled *catatonia* is an extreme example of the unresolved freeze response.[8] The *catatonic stupor* symptoms of immobility, rigid and waxen mask-like face, fixed and unfocused gaze or stare and lack of reaction to stimuli nevertheless accompany evidence of alertness: despite their apparent unresponsiveness, they often have a surprising level of mental functioning with awareness of events going on around them.[9] No longer considered solely a subtype of schizophrenia, these symptoms are present in about 10 percent of psychiatric inpatients, most often following situations in which the individual felt him or herself to be under profound threat (real or imagined) from internal or external perceived sources.[10] This is experienced as unbearable anxiety.

Depression is much more common than catatonia and psychologist A. K. Dixon linked the immobility response (which he termed *arrested flight*) with such depression symptoms as social withdrawal, reduced eye contact and psychomotor retardation.[11] So depression is conceptualized as a last-resort defense strategy, triggered by imminent, inescapable threat. Indeed, psychologists Paul Gilbert and Steven Allan suggest that such a blocked motivation for flight—the arrested flight—results specifically from feelings of *entrapment* and *defeat*.[12]

Andrew K. Moskowitz suggests that this pattern of anxious depression follows a specific cluster of experiences: "a perception of inescapable but at the same time amorphous danger, a sense of defeat and entrapment, and a sensation of imminent doom."[13] This is very much like the learned helplessness we see in animals.

A powerful and all-too-common example of this *learned helplessness* is the story of Stella. Stella is an overweight, master's level therapist who sat in our group session, completely in shock. She stared out the window, couldn't remember the practice we were supposed to be doing and couldn't connect with the other students. She walked around with a fake smile plastered on her face and the "shock-eyed stare" that is very familiar to us. Even though she is a very intelligent woman with a college degree, Stella couldn't perform even the simplest of practices. When it was her turn to "be the client," she described a deep depression which had plagued her for years. She had very little motivation to keep her private practice going even though clients were calling to try to schedule sessions with her.

Beginning her session, she was depressed about not being able to maintain any intimate relationship, with twenty-five years of sexual abstinence, fear of men and distrust of women. Stella had been having intrusive flashbacks of a naked man's rear end in her face. When we regressed her, she went back to a scene at age five, in bed with her father while her mother is standing in the doorway, glaring at her. She is wearing something very skimpy and is feeling, on one hand, that she likes the attention and being close to her daddy and on the other hand she is nauseated and filled with fear.

In the next scene, her father is kissing her with the smell of alcohol on his breath. Then he begins to force his penis into her mouth, as she is gagging, cannot breathe and fears she will die. As a way to get her out of the immobility of the parasympathetic shock, we instructed her to get into her body through movement. We told her to get up from the frozen shock posture she was in while reliving her abuse. We taught her some deep breathing and some bio-energetic motions to move the frozen energy into action. As she began to breathe and to move her arms, Stella realized that she had anger frozen throughout her body. Holding all this anger inside for so long actually had been the root of her depression, since it took a great deal of energy to repress these overpowering emotions.

At first she expressed her anger toward her father and the horrendous physical and emotional betrayal that she felt. Then her anger turned toward her mother, who often expressed relief that she didn't have to have sex with the alcoholic father. The mother, however, was also jealous of her daughter and the sexual attention she was receiving. Because of her inner conflict and unmet emotional needs, she hated little Stella and refused to protect her from the horrible abuse that happened right before her eyes. She was also in a parasympathetic shock state of complete detachment from what was happening and was frozen herself, unable to act.

The mother spoke about times when the father tried to kill her during many of his drunken rages. The father's sympathetic shock rages, sexual acting out with his five-year-old daughter and out-of-control drinking became unconscious triggers for the parasympathetic shock response of the mother and children who automatically became frozen in his presence.

Stella then regressed to a very early family scene, where her father was in a drunken, angry rampage, waving his shotgun around, threatening the family that he intended to kill them. He was screaming obscenities and shouting over the heads of Stella's little brothers and sisters. The whole family, including the mother, went into frozen, parasympathetic shock and could do nothing.

Stella was ultimately able to step out of the five-year-old shock state and become the loving, protective mother that she needed at that time. Once she moved out of shock, she was able to see the whole picture and realize that this was not her fault. Stella began to reclaim her adult power and give back the family shame to her parents, the grownups who were supposed to be loving and protecting their children.

Her recovery from these deeply entrenched shock states was not accomplished in one session. That was only the beginning of Stella's process of waking up to her life and reclaiming the skills that she had as a woman and a therapist. The hypnotherapy done in a therapeutic group is essential in uncovering the deep unconscious memories of what triggered the shock and sent the clients into deep states of depression and learned helplessness. By providing a consistent and healing group atmosphere, we are offering an emotional support system in which the clients feel safer and safer to explore where their shock began and to get loving feedback if they begin slipping back into these shock states. The group becomes the laboratory where the clients can try out their new behaviors as well as a community where they can laugh, have fun and learn to play, often for the first time in their lives.

An alternate form of catatonia, *hyperkinetic catatonia*, appears with *catatonic excitement* symptoms of apparently purposeless agitation not influenced by external stimuli.[14] This is an extreme example of the unresolved sympathetic fight/flight response, which typically precedes or follows the freeze response.[15] The important thing to notice here is that there is no clearly recognizable threat to attack or flee. The person with this condition is reacting to a perceived threat that doesn't actually exist in the present. Instead, it's a memory from his or her traumatic past. This inability to differentiate past from present leaves the person feeling threatened from all directions and from nowhere.

When the catatonic state becomes lethal it is called *malignant catatonia*. In such cases there is generally an extended period of frenetic activity (sympathetic response) followed by stupor (parasympathetic response) and then death. In most cases (80 percent) there is no medical cause of death.[16] Psychiatrist Ronald Gurrera argued that a hyperactive and unregulated sympathetic response, released from inhibition by the frontal cortex (via the hypothalamus), accounts for the death process, and suggested that "acute psychic distress" may be responsible for that disinhibition.[17] It is the same process as the zebra who dies following a death-feigning parasympathetic dive. What does that mean in layman's terms? The person has literally been "scared to death."

DISSOCIATION

While it often has a negative connotation because of its deeper, more complicated levels, dissociation is a valuable tool we all have available to us. It is really just a matter of moving our consciousness from our bodies and emotions, sometimes inward and sometimes to nowhere in particular of which we're aware. For instance, when we space out while driving or when we lose ourselves in front of the TV. In cases like these, it's a protective process that allows us to better handle the stresses of life. However, we can also see dissociation from body and emotions from efforts like meditation and prayer.

The more deeply we are stressed or traumatized, the deeper the shock state is embedded and the greater this dissociation becomes. In moderate dissociation, we may flow into neurological experiences such as freezing, losing the ability to think or feel, entering a trance or temporarily leaving the body.

As the split becomes more severe, a greater portion of us has gone into hiding by "running away to the circus," and we have a circus archetype offer its protection by coming in to run the show. We can see that we've given up control to "something else" when we give in to an addictive or compulsive urge, or when a patterned behavior (anger, jealousy, shame, loneliness) jumps in as the automatic response to some situation. Someone who is habitually in a hurry, busy-busy-busy, doesn't make spontaneous choices in every new situation but rather automatically feels urgency even when quiet calm and tranquility would be a rational and healthy choice. Perhaps his or her "Circus Business Manager" is running the show. When this level of control happens too frequently, it disallows the true person or soul from being involved in life, from getting to experience spiritual health, growth and transcendence.

To be clear, when splitting occurs, it is rarely a complete tear. The different parts of the psyche usually remain aware of one another, except in cases like Dissociative Identity Disorder (formerly known as Multiple Personality Disorder), where the part that has "run away" becomes lost to the remaining part, and each is unaware of the other. Where we do not have a complete split taking place, it is possible to have a variety of experiences.

For instance, a split may lead to a shadow. This means that the archetype is closely aligned with the rest of the personality. This shadow is able to get things done that the usual personality could not do, but *wants* to get done on some level. On the other hand, you may have a split where both portions are taken over by members of the circus and in these cases, the two elements may have various relationships with each other:

- **Competition** (My rational good ego tries to impose limits on my overeater by identifying as "The Critical Parent.")

- **Contentiousness** (My rational good ego feels self-hatred or deep guilt for what the other did "in a weak moment.")

- **Conspiracy** (My rational good ego makes excuses for and thus enables my overeater.)

- **Punishment** (My rational good ego responds to the overeater by saying, "Since you ate a candy bar, I'm just going to eat a dozen cookies. You're hopeless." Or, "Since you ate a candy bar, I'm going to deprive you of dinner tonight.")

- **Violence** (Microsuicidal behaviors like dangerous driving, unsafe sex, obesity and non-compliance with medical treatment.)

The relationship can be complementary as well; that is what we are working toward: a well-integrated, mutually supportive set of parts that cooperate synergistically.

The Theory of Structural Dissociation by Ellert Nijenhuis and associates proposes that each aspect of a split can be thought of as a cluster of mental/emotional states, and that we have both an "Emotional Part" (EP) and an "Apparently Normal Part" (ANP) created by this divide.[18] The emotional part takes on the trauma or shock, integrating it into this part of the personality and re-experiencing the trauma or shock when triggered by something that recalls it. The apparently normal part, however, splits off in order to continue running day-to-day operations. It fails to integrate the trauma, does not have a sense of it, and therefore is able to have such a disdainful relationship with the emotional part as in our examples above, where "my rational good ego" is really the apparently normal part. These autonomous parts of the individual share one brain, one heart and one nervous system. Yet they each have separate, identifiable patterns of reactions in the heart and brain.

The emotional part, or emotional personality, carries memories somatically, often pre-verbally, and experiences the memories of traumas as personal to itself. The emotional personality presents with the identity of a child, the arrested-development inner child stuck in time at the point of the original traumatizing event(s). The traumatized individual's apparently normal part of the personality does not experience memories of traumas as personal, or may have no access to them at all. The apparently normal personality, dissociated from her body and her emotions, presents as, for example, the precocious caregiver, willing to tolerate age-inappropriate responsibilities. She is condemned to live life "on the surface of consciousness."

When the emotional personality is activated, the individual tends to lose access to a range of memories that are readily available for the apparently normal personality, and vice versa. The lost memories typically involve episodic memories, i.e., personified memories of personal experiences. For example, when a woman who is "apparently normally" rational and cogent suddenly becomes consumed with jealousy, this alternate "emotional" personality cannot remember or accept that her husband is trustworthy and faithful, instead being preoccupied with memories of her womanizing father who abandoned her early in life. The two parts of her personality share one brain but do not share all aspects of it equally, such as memories or impulse control.

Imagine, then, that the emotional personality cannot function in the world like the apparently normal personality, because its part of the brain does not have access to the memories necessary to function in that way, and it's burdened with trauma memories that the apparently normal personality is not.

One research project on the physiology of dissociation found large differences in regional neural activity for these dissociative sub-personalities when they listened to trauma memory scripts. The apparently normal personalities, who did not regard the recounted memories as personal, had more activity in parietal and occipital regions which are related to lack of sense of self. The emotional personalities displayed decreases of heart rate variability and increases in heart rate frequency, systolic blood pressure and diastolic blood pressure. Studies link reduced heart rate variability with various outcomes indicative of emotional dysregulation, such as anxiety, depression and rigid attentional processing of threat. Increased heart rate and blood pressure are symptomatic of stress. Both dissociative parts of the personality responded differently to recounted traumatic memories, but did not have different physiological responses to neutral (non-traumatic) memories. Nijenhuis said, "Emotional personalities have strong emotional responses to traumatizing events that escape inhibition by prefrontal regions, whereas apparently normal personalities inhibit emotional reactions, while being depersonalized and not well in contact with bodily feelings."[19]

Translated into our terminology of the shock response, the apparently normal personality uses dissociation from somatic and emotional response as a defense. This part of the personality, protected by the alliance with its archetypal bodyguard, manages to avoid stressful feelings and thoughts that lead to anxiety or depression. The somatic defense is embedded in the autonomic nervous system as either sympathetic or parasympathetic shock. The emotional personality (regressed part) also uses dissociation as a defense but, without the aid of the bodyguard or complex, it's not nearly as good at it. The emotional personality has the memories, has the

physiological stress responses and is more vulnerable. The apparently normal personality has amnesia, has dissociation from the body and is the
more superficial "false self."

In our discussion of sympathetic and parasympathetic, we noted that if
a person's emotional personality tends toward the hyperarousal (fight/flight)
response not being effectively discharged, his/her apparently normal personality will tend to use *parasympathetic dissociation* as a defensive effort to
achieve a semblance of homeostasis in the body: "spacing out," being a "couch
potato" vacantly watching television or eating or drinking in excess or even
experiencing chronic exhaustion.

If a person's emotional personality tends toward hypoarousal (freeze)
response that is not effectively discharged, his/her apparently normal personality will tend to use *sympathetic dissociation* to achieve a semblance of
homeostasis: mindless busyness, incessant talking, chasing endless lists of
"must do's" and constant attentiveness to others' needs.

If a child exposed to trauma uses a predominately hyperarousal response
rather than a passive dissociative response, the child will be vulnerable to
developing persistent hyperarousal-related symptoms and similar disorders (e.g., Post-traumatic Stress Disorder, Attention Deficit Hyperactivity
Disorder and conduct disorder). These children are characterized by persistent physiological hyperarousal and hyperactivity, with increased muscle
tone, frequently a low-grade increase in temperature, an increased startle
response, profound sleep disturbances, affect regulation problems and generalized (or specific) anxiety.

In fact, those who suffer from PTSD are plagued with frightening physical symptoms which are characteristic of hyperarousal: accelerated heartbeat,
cold sweating, rapid breathing, heart palpitations, hypervigilance and hyper
startle response (jumpiness). These symptoms lead to sleep disturbances, loss
of appetite, sexual dysfunction and difficulties in concentrating, which are
further hallmarks of PTSD.

Conversely, dissociation in hypoarousal uses variations of the freeze
response, such as drifting consciousness, emotional constriction, social isolation, loss of contact with reality, derealization or depersonalization. This
kind of dissociation manifests as an inability to sense or feel even significant
events, a sense of estrangement, an inability to accurately evaluate dangerous situations or think clearly and a lack of motivation. The body, or a part

of the body, may become numb and the victim may experience a sense of "leaving" the body.

SOMATIC DISSOCIATION

Dissociation may be accompanied by split or altered perceptions not only of self and reality, but also of parts or regions of the *body*. As we defined earlier, when we reach the point of physiological response to trauma, we have reached the stage of shock. The body carries memories of shock in the form of sensations specific to the site of the invasive event(s)—for example, sensitivity in the temple area of the head caused by use of forceps at birth, or a tendency to gag or experience choking or suffocation caused by oral sexual abuse. In the same way as the psyche, the body or body parts can dissociate with a disconnection from feeling, numbness, withdrawal or hyperactivity. Whether dissociated or not, somatic memory, frozen in place, determines subsequent shock response: one's shadow behavior is embodied at the time of the overwhelming trauma.

Robert Scaer revealed:

> Dissociation, by this model, is a neurophysiological syndrome of central nervous system origin. It is initiated by a failed attempt at defensive/escape efforts at the moment of a life threat, and is perpetuated if spontaneous recovery from the resulting freeze response is blocked or truncated. Lack of recovery from this freeze response results in conditioned association of all sensorimotor information assimilated at the time of the traumatic event into procedural memory, to be resurrected at times of subsequent perceived threat as a primitive conditioned survival reflex.[20]

Based on the concept of somatic dissociation, the area of the body that is *not* feeling can be equally as important an indicator of stored trauma as body parts that *do* feel.

This comes about because the brain releases endorphins during trauma for analgesia, and the result is mental and somatic dissociation. Endorphins create relief from pain and also bring pleasure, even euphoria. Sometimes the traumatized individual has been conditioned to repeat either the trauma or experiences that provoke similar physiological responses, as a means of generating endorphins in the brain. Endorphins create a trance state, dissociated from one's actual circumstances in the environment. This means that there is a secondary gain of endorphin release (and the attendant pain relief and dissociation) when re-creating trauma or other self-injurious experiences.[21] Think of the thrill-seeker, the long-distance runner, or the sex addict who engages in dangerous behavior. In fact, "plane crash survivors have described getting a new-found 'rush' from subsequently putting themselves in risky situations such as skydiving or extreme sports."[22]

GENDER DIFFERENCES

As we cover this information on the physiology of shock, we should point out that there are marked gender differences in the response to traumatic violence.[23] Females are more likely to dissociate passively while males are more likely to dissociate through a classic "fight or flight" response. As a result, more males will develop the aggressive, impulsive, reactive and hyperactive symptoms (more externalizing), while females will tend to be more anxious, dissociative and dysphoric (more internalizing).

Studies by psychologist E. H. Carmen and domestic violence expert Peter Jaffe indicate that abused men and boys tend to identify with the aggressor and later victimize others, whereas abused women are prone to become attached to abusive men, allowing themselves and their offspring to be victimized further.[24] A girl tends to identify with the *projection* of the abuser, so she will adopt the self-image that he sees her as, whether that be a little doll or a prostitute. Identification with the abuser victimizes not only others but also oneself, just as collaborating with the abuser does. An aspect of one's self (integrity, esteem, compassion—the soul) must be sent into hiding and is cowering in fear not only from external threats but also from the aspect of self that sent it into hiding, the progressed or apparently normal personality. Confronted by the traumatized ego-self who demands to know, "Why are you hiding here?" the soul answers, "You would have killed me if I came out."[25]

Some of these gender differences are accounted for by oxytocin, a hormone that prompts labor as well as milk production in the mother. Oxytocin is also released during stressful events, prompting the uniquely female stress response of tend and befriend: tending to dependent children and seeking out social support.[26] Oxytocin's effects are enhanced by estrogen, but are antagonized by androgens, male hormones. Both male and female human subjects who inhale oxytocin in a nasal spray show increased trust in social interactions with unfamiliar individuals.[27]

THE HEART PLAYS A PART

In discussing the physiology of shock, we must discuss the important role played by the heart. While it's true that the heart is constantly responding to "orders" sent by the brain, the heart actually sends far more signals to the brain than the other way around. These heart signals have a significant effect on brain function, influencing emotional processing as well as higher cognitive faculties such as attention, perception, memory and problem-solving. In other words, not only does the heart respond to the brain, but the brain continuously responds to the heart.

There is substantial evidence that the heart plays a unique role in synchronizing the activity in multiple systems of the body, and in this way orchestrates the flow of information throughout the psychophysiological network. The heart is in continuous connection with the brain and other bodily organs and systems through multiple pathways: neurologically (through the transmission of neural impulses), biochemically (through hormones and neurotransmitters), biophysically (through pressure and sound waves) and energetically (through electromagnetic field interactions).

Sustained positive emotions such as appreciation, care, compassion and love generate a smooth pattern in the heart's rhythms. This reflects increased order in higher-level control systems in the brain and increased synchronization between the two branches of the autonomic nervous system. By contrast, research has shown that negative emotions such as frustration, anger, anxiety and worry lead to heart rhythm patterns that appear incoherent—highly variable and erratic. Overall, this means that there is less synchronization in the reciprocal action of the parasympathetic and sympathetic branches of the autonomic nervous system.

According to recent research, different patterns of heart rhythm (which accompany different emotional states) have distinct effects on cognitive and emotional function. During stress and negative emotions, when the heart rhythm pattern is erratic and disordered, the corresponding pattern of neural signals traveling from the heart to the brain *inhibits* higher cognitive functions. This limits our ability to think clearly, remember, learn, reason and make effective decisions.

In contrast, the more ordered and stable pattern of the heart's input to the brain during positive emotional states has the opposite effect. Ordered patterns *facilitate* cognitive function and reinforce positive feelings, emotional stability and perceptual clarity. This means that learning to generate increased heart rhythm coherence by sustaining positive emotions not only benefits the entire body, but also profoundly affects how we perceive, think, feel and perform.

Heart rate variability is considered a measure of neurocardiac function that reflects heart–brain interactions and the dynamics of the sympathetic and parasympathetic branches of the autonomic nervous system. There are six general categories or modes of psychophysiological function that can be detected by measuring heart rate variability:

1. MENTAL FOCUS

This is associated with impassive emotions experienced while attention is directed to performing familiar, cognitively engaging tasks or actions. This state is primarily one of mental attention to the task at hand and, as such, is characterized by little or no emotional arousal (either of a positive or negative nature) and low motor activity.

2. PSYCHOPHYSIOLOGICAL INCOHERENCE

This is associated with negative emotions such as anger, anxiety, etc., and is typified by an erratic and disordered heart rhythm pattern and intense activation of the sympathetic nervous system.

3. RELAXATION

This is associated with calm emotions experienced while resting from the effort and stress of everyday life. It is characterized by a virtually steady heart rate. There is a shift to increased parasympathetic activity (the relaxation response) and lower overall heart rate variability. This rhythm is also seen during periods of restful sleep. Many relaxation techniques are essentially dissociation techniques, whereas the psychological states associated with coherence are directly related to activated positive emotions, not dissociating from emotions.

4. PSYCHOPHYSIOLOGICAL COHERENCE

This state is associated with positive emotions such as appreciation, care, compassion, etc. It is signaled by a highly ordered, smooth heart rhythm pattern and typically with increased parasympathetic activity.

THE TWO HYPERSTATES

The remaining two modes occur under extraordinary or unusual circumstances. They are physiologically and experientially distinct. Physiologically they are both associated with very low heart rate variability; experientially, they are at opposite ends of the spectrum, with one mode being associated with an uncommon sense of inner peace and the other mode associated with extreme negative emotions such as fury and rage.

5. EMOTIONAL QUIESCENCE (STILLNESS)

The subjective experience of this mode is a state in which the intrusion of mental and emotional "chatter" is reduced to a point of internal quietness, to be replaced by a profound feeling of peace and serenity and a deep sense of being centered in the heart. First-person descriptions include a heightened awareness of the movement of energy both within one's body and between oneself and other people; the feeling of being "totally alive" and "fully present" in the moment; the experience of an all-embracing, nonjudgmental love (in the largest sense) and a sense of increased connectedness with one's higher self or spirit and with "the whole." This hyperstate involves a transcendent condition in which the individual's emotional experience involves the feeling of spiritual connectedness to something larger and more enduring beyond himself. Typically this state is associated with selfless actions and is also generative of bodily renewal.

6. EXTREME NEGATIVE EMOTION

This state involves violent, uncontrollable fury and rage or overwhelming fear and anxiety. Extreme anger or rage is subjectively experienced as an intense, highly focused state that is usually directed outward. Individuals describe their subjective experience of this state as one that is highly energized and seething with negative emotion, with a feeling of increased physical power and a corresponding reduction in sensitivity to physical pain. In this mode, the heart rate variability becomes very low due to excessive sympathetic outflow to the heart, which both drives the heart up to very high rates and inhibits parasympathetic outflow. This hyperstate tends to be an all-consuming state of self-absorption and self-focus. This state is usually associated with highly destructive behavior—directed at the self and/or projected out onto others—and has detrimental, even devastating consequences. Negative hyperstates lead to a depletion of the body's energy and resources which, in the long term, results in the degeneration of bodily function.

The two states associated with anger and anxiety exhibit very different physiological signs. *Incoherence* is generally typified by an erratic and disordered heart rhythm pattern, while the more extreme version of the same emotional content, *extreme negative emotion*, exhibits very low heart rate variability and a well-ordered heart rhythm pattern, which we would normally associate with the positive emotions. *Extreme negative emotion* reflects the inhibited affect of the *apparently normal personality* in the grip of parasympathetic dissociation shock, while *incoherence* reflects the volatility and emotionality of the *emotional personality*, which, if it is in shock, is probably in sympathetic dissociation shock.

Also notice something with the two states associated with positive emotions—*relaxation* and *psychophysiological coherence*. While both shift to increased parasympathetic activity and lower overall heart rate variability, the two have a significant difference. Relaxation is essentially a dissociated state (parasympathetic dissociation), while psychophysiological coherence is an actively engaged state (not dissociated or in shock at all). Again, we want to understand what determines whether one enters dissociated *relaxation* or non-dissociated *psychophysiological coherence*; also whether a person experiences emotional *incoherence* or the controlled rage of *extreme negative emotion*. In Jungian terms, what we're asking is whether the archetypal complex (the circus character) manifests as protector or as persecutor in a given momentary experience. The answer is related to—perhaps determined by—which of the two vagal nerve pathways is engaged to transport parasympathetic activation from the heart to the brain. This takes us back to the Polyvagal Theory proposed by Stephen Porges, where the two branches of the vagus nerve serve different adaptive behavioral strategies. The dorsal vagal complex is a slow-responding nerve that supports immobilization in response to threat (e.g., the freezing response, or death-feigning)—what we call parasympathetic dissociation shock. On the other hand, the ventral vagal complex is a fast-acting nerve that functions (as we mentioned earlier) as an active brake, or counterbalance, on the fight/flight sympathetic system. It can rapidly mobilize or calm an individual via its fast-acting inhibitory influence on the activity of the heart without mobilizing the slower-acting sympathetic nervous system. This branch of the vagus nerve is said to be involved in the modulation of respiratory-related heart rate variability, is non-dissociative and results in feelings of appreciation, compassion, general well-being and trust in intimacy (psychophysiological coherence).

For all the ways that shock can occur, for all the ways we can exhibit symptoms and struggle in our lives because of it, the bulk of our discussion on cause and physiology revolves around the sympathetic (fight/flight) and parasympathetic (freeze) stress responses. Keep this point in mind, so you'll see the pattern play itself out in cases cited throughout this book. This helps you to understand that beneath the complexity, there's a consistent way to look at it all.

SHOCK: SYMPATHETIC AND PARASYMPATHETIC EXPRESSION

HYPERAROUSAL (FIGHT OR FLIGHT)

1. Rapid breathing and heart rate, heart palpitations
2. Cold and pale skin, pallor
3. Dilated pupils
4. Raised blood pressure
5. Endorphins released to reduce pain
6. Hypervigilance, panic, rage, constipation, tremors, muscle spasms, hyperventilation, cold sweats, profound sleep disturbances, loss of appetite, sexual dysfunction
7. Accelerated pace and amplitude of thoughts and emotions, intrusive memories, difficulties in concentrating

8. Active dissociation: persisting physiological hyperarousal and hyperactivity, busyness, increased muscle tone, increased body temperature, hyper startle response (jumpiness), affect regulation problems and generalized (or specific) anxiety

HYPOAROUSAL (FREEZE)

1. Decreased heart rate and respiration
2. Warm and flushed skin
3. Lowered blood pressure
4. Endorphins released in the brain to create stress-induced analgesia
5. Helplessness and hopelessness
6. Sudden and extreme immobility (appears as "feigning death" or "suspended animation")
7. Palpitations, nausea, dizziness, bowel cramps, indigestion, diarrhea, incontinence, generalized weakness
8. Numbness, "shutting down" within the mind, dulling of inner body sensation, slowing of muscular/skeletal response, especially in the face
9. Social isolation and withdrawal, substance abuse, constricted affect, denial
10. Passive dissociation: drifting consciousness, emotional constriction, social isolation, loss of contact with reality, lack of motivation, body numbness, a sense of "leaving" the body, withdrawal, somatic complaints, anxiety, dependence

THE DISSOCIATION PROCESS

In the case of dissociation, a child first separates from conscious awareness of affect (numbing), then from knowledge (amnesia) and then from foundational beliefs. Jennifer J. Freyd provides a vivid analogy of the dissociative process, and how one might resort to numbing and further to amnesia:

Consider a circus performer who breaks a leg while performing stunts on stilts. Experiencing tremendous pain, she will not want to move at all, and certainly not stand up and walk. Instead she will wait until her co-performer gets help. On the other hand, if she has a similar accident in her spare time, alone, she will block perception of the leg pain and get up and hobble to get the help she needs. While the woman in both cases wants to avoid feeling pain, only in the second case does she block the experience of pain.[28]

Applying this to traumatic child abuse, numbing becomes functional when there is no help readily available, i.e., when the primary caregiver upon whom the child is dependent is the source of the abuse. Thus betrayed, the child must rely on herself to survive, using dissociation and memory repression to ignore the pain of hobbling on her psychically broken leg.

The more advanced defense, blocking information about the abuse—i.e., amnesia—is more likely to occur when:

- Alternative realities are available (abuse in the middle of the night and 'normal' family interactions in daytime, allowing the child to select one construction of reality);
- There is isolation during abuse (lack of social validation for the experience, allowing for cognitively consistent internal denial);
- Abuse begins at a young age (reality is defined by adults);
- There are alternative reality-defining statements by caregivers ("This didn't happen" or "He was only showing you how much he loves you"); and/or
- There is an absence of any socially shared explicit discussion of the abusive events, causing a failure of information entry into the child's explicit autobiographical memory.

With persistent incidents of trauma or more flagrant betrayal, next to be exiled is the child's world view (foundational beliefs). When enough information is blocked or denied, and when reality has been falsified, the child begins to delegate unbearable experiences to someone else: "Not-me." The "Not-me," a primitively organized alternative self, experiences things that we could not, endures assaults that our psyches could not, and must find a source of strength that we are not. And so the "Not-me" goes in search of help to find solace and protection or to avoid loneliness. Split off and isolated, she wanders through the realm of a child's imagination, looking for protection, companionship and nurturing. What resource will she find in the great Land of Imagination? Perhaps one of the circus archetypes or an imaginary friend in the guise of her favorite doll. A part of her personality has now loaned its psychic energy to this *other*, who takes up residence in the same body but who has uniquely different emotional and somatic settings, and who is experienced as "Not-me."

These maneuvers require disconnection of aspects of the child's ego, i.e., memory, affect, self-image. This disconnection splits off part of the child's identity, the part that is unacceptable to her conscious self-image and sends it "into internal exile." But more invasive abuse with even deeper levels of betrayal requires a more drastic defense and that is to split off part of one's essence.

Shelly, as a young child, lived in poverty with her single mother and three younger siblings. Often in families, we discover children being responsible for and raising other children, even from very young ages. Shelly was age seven and had in her care a set of four-year-old twin girls and a two-year-old brother. Shelly quickly learned to judge her own needs as childish and put them behind her and pretend to be an adult. She saw from an early age that her mother was struggling with being overburdened in her responsibilities of caring for and financially supporting four young children. Being very bright, Shelly realized that her mother was struggling with an alcohol addiction and dysfunctional relationships with men and perhaps was emotionally immature. Her mother left very early every day to work as a maid while Shelly was left with the children.

Each day her mother came home exhausted, often drunk and abusive. She ranted and raved about how the house was dirty or the children were unkempt and she blamed all of it on Shelly, the seven-year-old. Shelly grew up always feeling blamed for whatever was wrong and took on this blame even though she may not have had any control over the situation. When it all became too much for her, Shelly ran away to the circus and became the girl on the flying trapeze. She would grab onto one bar to keep herself from falling and all the while be frantically searching for the next one to grab onto. She never felt a safety net below her which caused her, as a seven-year-old, persistent anxiety. Life felt to this young girl as if she just kept flying from one bar to the next, praying she wouldn't fall and tumble to her death—always praying that she could just hang on for one more day.

One day Shelly was scrambling to clean up the house before her mother returned. She heard a commotion in the bathroom only to discover one of the three-year-old twins writhing around on the floor, foaming from the mouth. Shelly panicked (this was before 911 calls existed) and she was frantic trying to figure out what to do. She went into sympathetic shock and ran out of her house screaming down the street for help. Finally she got the attention of an adult neighbor who followed Shelly back to her home and the neighbor determined that Shelly's younger sister had ingested some rat poison. The child was finally driven to the hospital, but it was too late.

Shelly's mother was distraught and blamed Shelly for killing her little sister. Upon returning home, the whole family was in shock and no one could speak. Her mother went back and forth between sympathetic shock, screaming at Shelly and the others, racing around the house frantically trying to put things in order, and parasympathetic shock, staring out the window and drinking herself into oblivion.

Eventually, Shelly's mother left the house one day and did not return. In her deep grief and despair, she began drinking herself to death. The children were not only left with the shock of their small sister's horrible death, but they were left with the huge guilt of feeling that it was their fault and they were forever being punished by their mother's abandonment.

Shelly, being the wise little soul that she was, somehow continued to function, attend school and go through all the motions necessary to survive. She returned to her previously successful circus role of the trapeze artist, appearing to fly though life with a smile on her face while all the time grasping for the next flying bar to grab onto. "The show must go on" was her motto and so it did for Shelly. She learned to survive without any net to catch her.

MARSHA'S SHOCK IN A DOCTOR'S OFFICE

Marsha came to the group session we were conducting in a deep state of shock with what seemed to be severe psychological wounding. She could barely speak from crying so hard. She said that her pap smear had come back with some questions and her doctor had requested she come in. The doctor told her they would have to do a biopsy. She then proceeded to tell this horrendous story of a physician's assistant performing the medical procedure with no anesthetic or painkiller. She was bleeding profusely and felt that the assistant was not attending to her pain. Marsha experienced the procedure as physically as well as emotionally abusive, being performed by a completely uncaring assistant. Afterwards, the nurse came in and told her they would have the results of the biopsy in a few days, but that she should make another appointment for an additional procedure pending the results. Since Marsha had perceived the procedure as outright abuse, she now felt that the nurse was merely acting as if what they had done to her was perfectly normal. Given Marsha's perception of their insensitivity, she had the presence of mind and assertive wherewithal to say no to the follow-up appointment.

As Marsha was going into shock while telling her story, we offered her a warm pack to put on her stomach and gave her some water to drink. We asked her to slow down by taking some deep breaths, as we could see that she was in extreme sympathetic shock. She did this; however, we then noticed that several other people in the group were now also in shock. We saw some people looking very sleepy, eyes closing and slumping down in their chairs. That is the *parasympathetic shock* that affects people by making them withdraw. Others were shuffling papers, shifting in their seats or otherwise being somewhat agitated. This is *sympathetic shock*. Because shock is contagious in a group, we then took a few minutes to address the shock in the others by giving them hot or cold packs, drinks of water and some essential oils to smell (like old-fashioned smelling salts). We asked people to notice what was happening in their bodies. These reactions are subtle and usually not noticed in traditional group work. It is up to the astute therapist to be aware of the shock responses of all group members.

In her psychodrama, Marsha began with the experience in the doctor's office. She immediately regressed to childhood abuse that she always knew was there but had never been able to fully access before. She found herself at a very young age where her father was taking her to see the horses in the barn. As a young girl, she loved the horses and was very excited to go. But when her father got her into the barn, he proceeded to rape her there, where no one else could see or hear. There was intense pain and blood which her father quickly wiped up and told her never to tell anyone, especially her mother.

This felt similar to the doctor's office experience, since her father took her out of the barn after raping her and then acted as if nothing had happened, just as the nurse acted as if nothing had happened and expected her to make another appointment for additional procedures, even before the biopsy results came back!

Through her psychodrama experience, Marsha released a lot of her shock, which enabled her to fully express the grief, anger and shame that she had carried for so many years. She realized that she had been living much of her life in a state of parasympathetic shock due to ongoing rapes by her father. She survived in the only way that she could—in a state of dissociation. She had made the unconscious decision to be very good, very quiet and basically invisible in order to stay safe. Since she and her mother and siblings were all dependent on her father to support the family, she believed that she had no other choice.

After Marsha completed her painful story, we invited the whole group to stand up and just shake off the energy, the way that an animal shakes when they are recovering from the "fight/flight" or "freeze" stress responses. The physiology of shock is essentially the same as these fight/flight or freeze stress responses of the sympathetic and parasympathetic nervous systems in all mammals.

In our psychodrama work, we always have people change the unconscious conclusions about themselves and the behavioral decisions that were made by very young parts of themselves in order to survive. This is important in order to enact substantial, long-lasting change. It's like hiring a computer programmer to fix your computer by installing new software or changing some underlying code. Only in this case, it's your mind and body that are recoded.

In Marsha's case, the underlying conclusion she had made during the childhood sexual abuse by her father was, "I am a piece of crap. I am worthless. I deserve to be hurt." It is these underlying conclusions about herself that enabled Marsha to continue attracting abusive relationships into her life. We attract whatever is deeply programmed like an emotional/psychological magnet within us.

There are also behavioral decisions that young children make unconsciously during intolerable experiences in childhood. The decisions address how to behave and how to react to similar experiences during our lives. As mentioned above, Marsha decided to be very quiet, very good and invisible in order to stay safe. Another clear decision was, "When (Dad) is hurting me, I have to be quiet, not move and just take it."

The conclusions Marsha had made about herself, her "internal computer programming," were what led to the experience in the doctor's office. The unconscious decisions Marsha had made about how to survive caused her to let the abusive experience continue for over an hour without speaking up or getting off the table and saying, "No!"

At the completion of her psychodrama, Marsha made new conclusions about herself such as, "I deserve to be treated with respect." A new decision she made about how to behave was, "I speak up and express my needs!" After she returned home, Marsha called her doctor's office, expressed her anger about the procedure she had had and told them that she would never return to their office.

This is the healing of shock. It allows someone to stop responding to situations from programming and to respond, instead, from their own decisions. Today, Marsha has reclaimed her body from the shock response of dissociation. She has reported feeling much more alive and fully present in her life. She feels that she has reclaimed her full consciousness and her power to make clear decisions.

Sympathetic/Parasympathetic Shock Questionnaire

Perhaps you are wondering if shock is affecting you.
Take this questionnaire to discover the effect of shock in your life.

SYMPATHETIC SHOCK

On a scale from 1–5, how true is this statement for you (with 5 being most true)? Put the number in the box.

- ☐ Do you think you're a "work-a-holic"?
- ☐ Do you often make to-do lists with more than three things on them?
- ☐ Do you keep adding to these lists, even before you complete all the tasks?
- ☐ Does looking at your to-do list give you anxiety?
- ☐ Do you wake up at night with more things to add to the list?
- ☐ Do you find yourself obsessing about all the things you haven't done?

☐ Do you often find yourself rushing through things without enjoying the experience?

☐ Are you aware of "rushing" your children or family members with phrases like, "Hurry up," "Let's go" and "Get a move on!"

☐ Do you often feel like you are breathing so fast that you almost can't catch your breath?

☐ Do you often feel like a failure, because you can't accomplish everything you have set out for yourself to do?

☐ Do you often volunteer and promise way more things to do for others than you have time to do?

☐ Do you find yourself apologizing for things you weren't able to do?

☐ Have you noticed yourself talking rapidly, where people almost can't understand what you are saying?

☐ Has your doctor told you that you have high blood pressure, prescribed anti-anxiety drugs or suggested that you have your heart checked?

☐ Have you actually had a heart attack or an anxiety attack? Do you grind your teeth, have high blood pressure, difficulty sleeping or other stress-related medical issues?

Total ____

PARASYMPATHETIC SHOCK

☐ Do you often feel numb, shut down or disconnected from yourself?

☐ Have friends or family members complained because you seem uninterested in what they are doing?

☐ Do you have difficulty knowing what you are feeling in different situations?

☐ Have you had the experience of "missing out on life" or not really enjoying it the way you should?

☐ Do you seem to sleep more than others?

☐ Do you sometimes "nod out" while attempting to listen to friends, family members or clients?

☐ Do you space out a lot while watching television, being on your computer or playing games?

☐ Do you prefer to just withdraw and be by yourself, not wanting to connect with others?

☐ Do you sometimes feel very confused, like your head is spinning?

☐ Do your eyes feel blurry, not due to any medical condition?

Total ____

A score of 12 or more in either category indicates that shock may be affecting your:

+ ability to accomplish what you want to in your life
+ relationships with those you love
+ ability to truly experience your life on a daily basis
+ awareness levels

How shock is affecting my life:

· ·

Questionnaire from

THE WELLNESS INSTITUTE

Chapter 7

SHOCK AND NATAL ISSUES

Imagine you planned to travel to a foreign country to live with a host family as an exchange student. You wanted to expand your experience, your understanding of other cultures and your knowledge through new teachers. Imagine you had pumped the idea up in your mind. You were excited to do it, even if it took you from your familiar settings. You looked forward to discovering new friends, trying new foods and seeing wondrous sights.

Finally you took the airline flight, the plane landed and you arrived at the home of your host family. And the first thing that happened—even while you only half-understood the language—was that the father greeted you in a violent mood. Maybe he was so angry he was actually hitting his wife or children despite the presence of a stranger. That would certainly set a different kind of atmosphere from what you had expected!

There probably would not be a single day during your time in that house when you felt entirely comfortable. If the father continued to show violent tendencies, your time there would become even more tense. Your body would probably never relax, and the continued state of stress could cause physical problems for you. You might experience a weaker immune system, the inability to digest your food properly, etc. Yes, you would adapt and you would survive, but perhaps not as well as you might have. Not as you had imagined.

FORMATION OF THE SHOCK POOL

Focusing on our foreign exchange story, think about how one instance of anger or violence—or more importantly, ongoing anger or violence—poisoned the atmosphere and created stress, trauma or even shock for the visiting student. Now imagine how such an atmosphere would affect someone vastly younger, smaller, more delicate and more sensitive than a student who has learned how to adapt to life.

We know that children, because they're still growing and developing more rapidly than adults, are more substantially affected by diet and sleep and yes, even the environment. Look how quickly they learn new languages, for instance. So how much more powerfully can we influence a brand new life, still inside the womb, when it is just two cells joining and becoming four, then eight and then sixteen? The embryo, and later the fetus, inside its mother is extremely sensitive to everything the mother experiences—from diet to lifestyle to stress and abuse but also happiness and soothing energies too. In this book, we'll look at the impact of a mother's shock upon the fetus. More specifically, at the impact of the shock pool.

What we call a *shock pool* is a reservoir of unassimilated distress carried by every individual as a personal energy field. The pool stores any shock that a person has had from conception on, as well as the habitual behavior patterns, self-limiting beliefs and disease in the body's organs and nervous system.

For example, if a woman is raped or forced to have sex and becomes pregnant, then her reservoir is immediately filled with intense energy of shock, fear, anger and all the other emotions that go along with being raped. Because the new life in the womb shares one energy field with the mother, we see that this potpourri of victim energy from the child's mother and the persecutor energy from the rapist is also implanted in the womb, into this pool, along with the fertilized egg. In this case, because of the violent energies, the embryo sometimes will *not* implant itself in this environment, but this depends on the lessons of this soul for this lifetime. If the embryo does descend into this shock pool within the mother, it immediately dives directly into this ocean of chaotic emotions.

The womb now becomes the total environment in which this embryo is living, developing and growing. Besides the energy of the conception itself, if the mother is also smoking or using alcohol, drugs or other toxins to numb her pain, this will definitely contribute to the amount of toxicity that the embryo or fetus is absorbing. As you can see, right from the very beginning of its existence, the developing baby may become used to swimming in a shock pool that contains all the energy of numbing rather than of feeling and the energy of frantic activity rather than of gentle movement through life.

In contrast, a baby who is conceived in love and develops in a womb with healthy energy—a womb without drugs, alcohol, fear or shock—learns from the beginning that life is safe and that it is safe to feel. There is much research to demonstrate that the fetus responds to soft music by swimming around gently and will actually become relaxed when that music is played after it is born. Also, Kabbalistic wisdom gives us a detailed description of the requirements for a couple to conceive the most spiritually enlightened soul. Abuse and chaos are absent from the enlightened model.

Getting back to the development of the shock pool, perhaps the mother was not raped but was unaware that she was getting pregnant. It was an unplanned conception. At some point there will be a moment of discovery when the mother realizes that the fetus is actually in her womb. A surprise pregnancy typically results in both parents (and other family members) being shocked at the discovery. We call this *discovery shock*. The mother who is in discovery shock often experiences intense shame, guilt and fear of others knowing that she is pregnant. Before the 1980s, many young girls who became pregnant out of wedlock were shamed and banished to homes for unwed mothers. This was especially true in Christian families and countries where pre-marital sex was considered one of the greatest sins a young woman could commit. In such cases the discovery shock becomes part of the energy of the overall shock pool in which the infant develops.

Another instance of discovery shock and shame is when the mother is married to a man who may have been away at the time of conception. Perhaps during that time he was bravely serving his country in the military or simply supporting his family through a business trip. Suddenly the mother realizes that this pregnancy is going to let the world know that she has been unfaithful to her husband while he was gone. The developing fetus, in this toxic womb, takes on the shame and discovery shock of the entire situation and of the mother specifically. After birth, this has a very real effect on the person's life. In fact, we have worked with many talented and bright musicians, therapists and writers who become frozen when the time comes to express their talents and gifts. This is often the result of discovery shock, because, for them, being "discovered" is often painful and/or shameful, and part of them resists any success in their field. Many people can relate to a sense of unease or perhaps even dread at walking into a crowded room or onto a stage in front of a large audience, or being called on to perform in some way for a group of people; this can be the result of this kind of shock.

Discovery is not the only kind of shock that can affect the shock pool. For any number of reasons—sometimes from the shame of conception (the pattern of using drugs to deal with shock is well documented), but often from problems starting long before—the mother may use numbing substances such as drugs, alcohol and tobacco. The baby is getting a full dose of these drugs through the umbilical cord, which is filled with amniotic fluid. As with any shock, these can lead the fetus into fight/flight or freeze and as with the way discovery shock can rear its head later in life, this shock pool of chemicals in the amniotic fluid can determine how stresses and traumas are handled after the fetus is born. We'll talk more about this in our chapter on addictions.

CONCEPTION SHOCK

So we've discussed the environment in which a fetus is conceived and grown, which is affected by the mother's and father's emotions and beliefs. But there are other shocks that can take place from the perspective of the fetus itself, and this begins at the very point of conception.

Conception is preceded by tremendous force and chaotic activity as the sperm rush in, millions of them competing to be the one sperm to fertilize that egg. And this can lead to what we call *sperm shock*—a sympathetic shock, which you know by now involves movement and activity. It is the fight/flight mode that goes unresolved. So many times, you see people sit there and tap their fingers constantly, move their feet restlessly without stopping or talk incessantly without the normal back-and-forth of conversation. This can be the result of sperm shock.

On the other hand, the egg is in a more passive, non-moving state—more of a "freeze" or parasympathetic state—when all these sperm come rushing in on it. If this causes an unresolved shock for the egg, we call this an *egg shock*. It has felt invaded with a need to protect itself, and this sort of parasympathetic shock can lead to results later in life where someone just reads a lot and has to withdraw, curling up in his or her own little nest as a kind of protection.

In neither case is there a conscious sense of hyperactivity or being attacked the way we might have later in life with a fully developed mind and self-awareness, but the energy of these experiences is still there and can still have a lasting, shocking impact.

INDWELLING SHOCK

"Indwelling" or "embodiment" describes the mutual commitment between body and soul to make a life here on Earth. The terms are taken from Donald Winnicott, a British child psychiatrist who observed that infants only become integrated and personalized, or "called into existence," as they come to experience linkages between self and body and body functions.[1] If the linkage between body and soul fails, then death results (e.g., miscarriage, vanishing twin, stillborn, SIDS) or a serious disconnection of mind and body occurs (e.g., depersonalization, mind-body disintegration or disidentification with the body).

If the body is less committed than the soul, there may be medical issues and somatic complications, yet a strong will to survive even "against all odds." If the soul is ambiguously committed, there may be failure to thrive which cannot be explained medically. In either case, the individual suffers from severe, chronic shock that is deeply embedded in the autonomic nervous system. Conversely, when the body and soul mutually agree to move forward as partners in embracing life, each feels contained and protected due to the security of knowing "we're in this together" and "you've got my back."

IMPLANTATION SHOCK

Following the conception experience is implantation, which happens within two weeks of conception. So now the egg and sperm, united, are trying to find a safe place to implant on the wall of the mother's uterus. As in any stage of life, this new life needs to feel safe and welcomed. Yet for reasons we discussed, the embryo may feel unwelcome. Maybe the mother is afraid of being pregnant or of giving birth to a baby, maybe it's not a good time, maybe she is just a nervous person. So the wall where this embryo is trying to implant may feel tense and tight and cold, contaminated and toxic, barren or engulfing—an unwelcoming scene. This can cause a shock of its own, what we call *implantation shock*.

Themes of the implantation experience are creation, survival and the life-death struggle, because failure to implant successfully is to die. It is also during this phase of development that some individuals encounter the spirits or energies of previously conceived lives that have passed through this womb; particularly siblings that have been miscarried or aborted. Many people experience twin loss as well. A surprising percentage of conceptions are multiple, while only 10 percent of births are twins, leaving many twins lost within days of their multiple conception. Most of the deaths of a twin occur in the implantation time period: "Using these data on twin gestations, if two sacs are identified sonographically, loss of one twin can be expected in 27.1% of pregnancies achieved after assisted reproduction and in 40.5% of spontaneous pregnancies; if two embryos are seen, the loss rate is 38% in pregnancies achieved after assisted reproduction and in 7.3% of spontaneous conceptions."[2]

TWIN LOSS SHOCK

This is a theory that some of us began life as a twin and our twin ceased to exist so early in the pregnancy that no one knew. But we knew. We felt the profound connection between two souls who share a womb and we felt bewildering grief at the inexplicable loss. Such a loss can establish a lifelong, deeply unconscious pattern of feeling like something vital is missing in life and it can have us endlessly seeking to find it, to replace the lost twin. We call this the *vanishing twin*.

James, a man of forty, had a history of many short-lived relationships with women. He seemed to be looking for someone to help him feel complete, but soon after falling in love with a woman he began finding fault with her. When he made his growing dissatisfaction clear, as if to say, "You are not the one," the woman felt hurt and betrayed and she left.

In hypnotherapy age regression, James went back to very early in his womb experience, within weeks of conception. He realized that he had a twin in the womb with him and he felt intimately connected and complete. The fetus that was his sister did not survive, however, and he experienced profound despair at the unfathomable loss. In the session, James grieved the loss of his twin that he had never consciously known about. He felt that he was able to contact that soul in the spirit world and make peace with his huge sense of loss. The pattern in his adult relationships of endlessly trying to recreate that feeling of sharing the womb with a twin became crystal clear. And he discovered over the coming months that grieving for that previously unknown prenatal loss allowed him to be fully present in relationships. He no longer had the gnawing sense with his current girlfriend that "she was not the one."

INDIVIDUATION SHOCK

After five to seven days of being completely absorbed by the mother in the uterine wall (in implantation), i.e., about two weeks after conception, the embryo begins to grow back out of the uterine wall, separating from the mother's flesh. This separation can bring relief and a sense of freedom and accomplishment, but it can also initiate a profound sense of alienation, rejection and loneliness.

Because 60 percent of fertilized eggs die during implantation, and another 40 percent of the remaining embryos die during or after individuation, the struggle for the embryo is one of life or death. In a hostile or ambivalent uterine environment, it may experience a sense of impending death, carrying a "death imprint" that contaminates the impulse to move forward in life.

We should point out that several elements from this time of individuation can persist in later stages of development: feelings of rejection, confusion, foreboding, engulfment and a sense of impending death. We find these recapitulated in later stages of prenatal life, in the birth experience and in the struggle for balance on the continuum of security/exploration and of attachment/individuation for infants, toddlers, children, adolescents and adults.

NEED SHOCK

Because safety is such a primal need for us all, implantation shock is a kind of *need shock*, though this topic goes far beyond that one event. This is a complex phenomenon that we'll greatly simplify here, and the easiest way to define it is as the shock caused by not having one's needs met, or by having them met in a tainted way. It often begins in the womb and is reinforced over and over again throughout life. An example is a mother who starves herself during pregnancy for a variety of reasons. It may be an intense fear of getting fat (eating disorders) or perhaps she starves herself and her baby due to poverty or lack of proper nutritional awareness. This young mother may starve herself in an attempt to hide the pregnancy as long as possible due to feeling that this was a "shameful" conception. In any of these cases, the fetus begins its life with nine months of starvation, not getting the nutrients needed for optimal development.

As with all the shocks we discuss, this fetus may go into need shock in two different ways. The first is sympathetic shock, which involves raucous kicking and uncontrolled, frantic activity. The second type of shock is parasympathetic shock, when the fetus becomes numb and frozen. Many times people think of the baby as "calm" and "content" when in fact it is frozen with shock. As we've discussed before, both types of shock are designed to numb the intense pain being experienced—in this case, the pain of the most basic needs going unmet. From a psychological perspective, this fragile young soul quickly learns to ignore his or her own needs as well as the needs of others, because there is too much pain in trying to have those needs met. We'll discuss this subject more fully in the next chapter, in the context of the nourishment barrier.

PRENATAL TRAUMA IMPACTS

In the previous chapter, we spoke about the cortisol and endorphin levels that surge during trauma and the impact these have when they linger in the system rather than being released. Given this, it's important to understand how a fetus responds to a mother's stress, trauma or shock. When the mother's stress hormones kick into high gear, they don't simply cross the placenta and affect the baby in this way, but actually trigger the fetus to produce more of its own stress hormones.[3] What's more, these stress hormones persist longer in the fetus's system than in a child or adult.[4] This means that the memories and learned helplessness are embedded more deeply, and at a pre-verbal, cellular level. After all, the repertoire of survival skills is only as good as those skills that were acquired up to the time of the trauma and the fetus has not developed anything beyond pre-verbal.

Because trauma has such a powerful effect on the fetus, it can actually be fatal. Dissociation is used at the earliest stages of development to defend against intolerably painful experiences.[5] The passive defense of parasympathetic dissociation in prenates and newborns may even, at the extreme, account for death. Infants born of unwanted pregnancies are more than twice as likely to die within a month of birth as wanted infants.[6]

There is growing evidence, however, that stress affects the fetus differently depending on when it occurs during the pregnancy. Janet A. DiPietro and associates have published research challenging the assumption that stress in mothers during pregnancy (specifically from twenty-four to thirty-two weeks gestation) is always harmful.[7] Their work indicates that babies born of mothers who reported elevated stress during this part of their pregnancy showed no restricted growth, birth defects, temperament differences or behavior differences. During this period elevated levels of cortisol "could be enhancing the development of organs before birth."[8] Other research indicates that maternal stress between twelve and twenty-two weeks gestation may indeed be related to a variety of negative outcomes for the baby, including greater likelihood of developing ADHD...whereas anxiety at thirty-two to forty weeks is not.[9]

BIRTHING SHOCKS

Shock from the birth process is an enormous topic that we discussed at length in our book *Longing for Belonging*. There is an astonishing amount of research and evidence on how the shocks present in the process of giving birth correlate with the struggles a person will have later in life, whether with addictions, sense of self or the ability to move forward in the face of challenging obstacles.

One stark example of this is documented in a study of adolescent patients with a history of more than five suicide attempts each, in which the attempts were always at the same time of year. The researchers determined that the suicide dates of four patients corresponded to the month in which their mothers had tried to abort them. The adolescents had no *conscious* knowledge of the abortion attempts that they were *unconsciously* acting out. The adolescents had even used a method of suicide similar to the method of the abortion: chemicals or instruments. After discovering that their suicide attempts were seasonal intrusions of prenatal memory, the patients were free of the suicidal compulsion. They never attempted suicide again, even when their "anniversaries" recurred.[10]

These birth shocks can include apparently natural challenges that may have causes of which we're unaware, but can include events like having the umbilical cord wrapped around the baby's neck, being in a difficult position for the birth and/or being unable to pass through the birth canal, having the help of a C-section or forceps at birth (giving the newborn the sense that things will be done *for* him or her in life) and so on.

Anesthetic shock is another important component that parents and doctors should take into consideration. Prior to anesthesia, the baby feels connected to the mother and they are involved in the birth process together. The baby usually experiences a strong connection and bonding with the mother, the baby's partner in birth. Then suddenly the mother receives the numbing drug appropriate for her adult weight, which is actually a massive dose considering the weight proportion of the baby. As a result, this infant experiences numbness, cold, disconnection and abandonment. This moment is significant in the development of trust and belonging, as the mother and baby bond is instantly compromised with the onset of this numbness and separation. The shock is often complicated further when the baby isn't placed immediately onto the mother's stomach and given the opportunity to follow nature's call to move toward the breast and begin feeding, receiving important nutrients and hormones to ensure survival and bonding.

After all, the "delivery self-attachment" is every newborn mammal baby's instinctive and innate ability to find its mother's breast, latch on and suck.[11] The human newborn, if placed on the mother's naked belly immediately after birth, begins the self-initiated journey to the breast within about twenty minutes, and completes it within about fifty minutes. According to Dr. Ray Castellino, "Delivery self-attachment is an integral part of the bonding and attachment process," and "the completion of the delivery self-attachment sequence at birth will have long-lasting positive effects on the baby's neurological, somatic, and psychological development."[12]

Immediately upon birth, the baby enters a prolonged quiet but alert state of consciousness, averaging forty minutes duration. In this *quiet alert* state, babies look directly at their mother's or father's eyes and face and can respond to voices.[13] During this special time, in the state most conducive to eliciting the mother's bonding, motor activity is suppressed and all the baby's energy seems to be channeled into seeing, hearing and responding.[14] This period is a "sensitive period" for the installation of a personal relationship with the baby's mother. This is the most crucial time in the development of a healthy mother-child connection.

Unfortunately, in modern delivery the baby is too often born into a cold environment (it was used to being in the womb at nearly 100 degrees while parents and hospital staff prefer the comfort of 70 degrees); the umbilical cord is promptly cut while blood is still flowing through it (another shock); then the baby is whisked away, given drops in its eyes, cleaned up and clothed before being handed to its mother (where there will be minimal skin contact). Yes, a neat little package, delivered conveniently, but not at all in a way that prevents shock or promotes bonding.

Besides all these frantic events during a normal birth, there are also emergency moments when shocking things are said that can also have a lasting impact. For instance, sometimes doctors make disturbing announcements in the delivery room. We have heard reports of doctors proclaiming things like, "This baby is killing the mother. Get ready for emergency surgery (C-section)!" or "They're both going to die and we must try to save at least one of them. Call in the father and let him make this choice!" Such shocking proclamations along with the accompanying frantic behavior put a huge amount of sympathetic shock into the womb and the shock pool that the baby is still swimming in prior to delivery.

As this child begins school, he may be diagnosed with Attention Deficit Hyperactivity Disorder. Even earlier in life, the infant may have what doctors call colic. This can take the form of nearly continuous crying, screaming and discomfort. The medical profession really doesn't understand it but, in their attempt to comfort the parents, they come up with this name and a treatment. They will often say that the baby is allergic to the formula or even to the mother's milk! They will try different things to quiet and comfort the baby, often to no avail. This is because conventional medicine is simply unaware of the shock pool that this baby was born from and to which the infant is still reacting.

Not long after birth, there is occasionally the tragedy of Sudden Infant Death Syndrome. While this is another complicated topic, its cause can again be traced back to the toxic shock of the womb. The incoming soul may have realized on a deep, unconscious level that it has made the wrong choice about being born here and now into this family. The infant may have decided to leave Earth before things get worse. We realize this concept may be challenging for some readers, but perhaps more plausible as you continue to reflect on how deeply we are affected both psychologically and physiologically by trauma and shock. In any case, after thirty years of psychological, soul and energy healing work, we have found that the desire by a new infant to leave like this is quite common, although not necessarily acted on. In this event, the child may live but with a debilitating ambivalence about living, a predicament we call *resistance to life*.

We are only touching on these complex topics, because this book isn't devoted to prenatal and birthing issues but to shock itself, and these are simply illustrations of moments in which shock can take place. In our next chapter, though, we'll take a closer look at need shock and the psychological barrier we set up to deal with need shock: the *nourishment barrier*.

HUMAN NEEDS

What are the basic needs of human beings when we are born?
  A. To breathe
    1) How would our need to breathe be unmet?
      a) Cord wrapped around baby's neck
      b) Difficulty getting out of birth canal
    2) Anesthetic causes lack of power
    3) Doctor is late, mother told to hold baby back
  B. To be loved
    1) What are the ways we, as newborns, know we are loved?
      a) Being lovingly held immediately by mother
      b) Being softly talked to
      c) Being touched
  C. To be nourished
    1) What are the ways to be nourished?
      a) Breastfed (loved and nourished)
      b) Bottle fed (can be both)
      c) Wholesome, non-toxic environment (physically and emotionally)

What could happen if these basic survival needs are not met? There are three reactions to need shock:
    1) Fight (sympathetic shock): kicks, thrashes, cries
    2) Flight (sympathetic shock): running away, hiding

3) Freeze (parasympathetic shock): very quiet, eyes stare, no real contact, no smiles

Some possible consequences to the baby when basic needs are not met:
1) Baby cries all the time (sympathetic shock)
   a) Baby can't seem to be comforted
   b) Doctors call it colic or milk allergies
2) Baby seems quiet, rarely cries (parasympathetic shock)
   a) People marvel at what a good baby this is
   b) Caregivers tend to be more demanding of the child
3) Difficulty bonding often called attachment disorder

How can this need shock affect later relationships?
1) Difficulty knowing what one's needs are
   a) Difficulty asking for needs to be met
   b) Frustration, anger and resentment build up for seemingly no reason
2) The person physically goes into need shock when needs are not met
   a) **Sympathetic (active) need shock**
      1) Becomes demanding, resentful, anxious and fearful
      2) Begins to blame the other person
      3) Becomes angry, often physically and emotionally abusive, yelling and shaming those closest to them
      4) Overtly criticizes, judges and uses put-downs
      5) May use children, other family members or friends to manipulate or "team up" against the other
      6) Threatens leaving or going to see a lawyer (divorce)
      7) Anxiety disorder

   b) **Parasympathetic (paralyzed) need shock**
      1) Says nothing, but fumes quietly inside
      2) Becomes sick or has accidents to manipulate a caring response
      3) Quietly criticizes, judges and wants to "get rid of" the other
      4) Internally plans on leaving or getting a divorce
      5) Retreats into books, computer, sleeping, addictions, depression, amnesia

Neil's Story: Discovery Shock

When we release the shock that has kept us frozen in the past, everything around us changes. The story of Neil, a gifted therapist, musician and teacher, illustrates this principle. He has been reluctant to express his gifts to the fullest. For example, he kept his practice small, worked for other professionals and did not facilitate groups. He wrote beautiful music and played the guitar, but only for himself or a close friend or two. He was invited to become a professional trainer but always seemed to put this off. The manifestation of his self-loathing and attempt to hide his gifts came when one of his very disturbed clients reported him to his professional board for alleged misconduct.

Co-workers and his attorney privately reviewed the client's claims of misconduct. They found that Neil had kept excellent records and had treated this disturbed patient with the utmost respect and with the highest of clinical skills. His integrity was impeccable and there was no way that the client would win this case. It was expected that she would soon just drop it. However, that did not happen.

Neil was unable to accept the evaluation from his lawyer that he was innocent and he was filled with fear. He experienced anxiety attacks, nightmares and spent many sleepless nights tossing and turning. During the daytime, he felt numb and often couldn't go to work. He was in the throes between parasympathetic shock and sympathetic shock, where he would pace the floor, do tons of research about similar court cases and engage in other frantic but unproductive behavior.

Dreams are often a road map with signs that point to potential solutions for one's dilemma. In his dreams, night after night, Neil was facing his accusers, the judge and the jury, who were all finding him guilty. This became the shock state in which he was stuck. It is called *discovery shock*. His fears always went back to the idea that, if he was seen or discovered, he would be found to be guilty, responsible for wrongful acts and disgraced!

As we gathered information on Neil's life and family, we found out that Neil's mother, Susan, first discovered she was pregnant with him in the second trimester of pregnancy. Susan was a fourteen-year-old girl who had been raped on a date and got pregnant without realizing it. She came from a Christian family that didn't believe in sex before marriage and thus had given her no information about her body and especially about sex. After Susan had not menstruated for four months, her mother finally took her to the doctor where they discovered the horrifying news that she was pregnant!

Upon being told she was expecting, Susan went into shock, as did her mother (Neil's grandmother) and the whole family, and our research indicates that discovery shock, as we call it, was most probably directed into the uterus and transferred directly to Neil, the developing fetus. He was swimming in a deep shock pool filled with shame, self-loathing and hatred. And the message he received was that *he was the source of this shame* for the entire family.

Susan, Neil's unwed mother, spent her entire pregnancy in a state of depression as she was continually shamed, ridiculed and verbally punished for what she had done. Her family did not believe in abortion, so there was no choice but to deliver this unwanted baby. As the developing fetus in this hostile womb, Neil was filled with self-loathing, disgust and a strong desire never to be seen or recognized. The unconscious conclusions he made about himself were: "I'm despicable. I'm a worthless piece of trash and I deserve to be punished." The unconscious decisions he made were to be invisible, to disappear so that he wouldn't bring pain to those in his life. As Neil grew up he concluded that it would be much safer if he could just hide and never be seen. These unconscious decisions, having been made very early, were still activated later in life and were perhaps the underlying reasons that drew this lawsuit to him.

The ensuing court battle between Neil and his disturbed client raged on for over a year. The client was not willing to drop the case and there were many continuances for various reasons. Ongoing negotiations and further examinations of the evidence only served to extend Neil's agony. He remained sure that when the case came to trial, he would be publicly humiliated and lose everything. Even though his friends, family and lawyers continued to counsel him that he had done nothing wrong, he could not hear any of it since he was still drowning in the shock pool of shame and unworthiness.

During that year, however, we continued to work with Neil, helping to treat and release the shock through hypnotherapy and a powerful group psychodrama. He was regressed back to the womb to realize that none of this was his fault and that he did nothing intentional to harm his mother or her family. As he released the shock and trauma, he began to climb out of the shock pool and was able to make new, conscious conclusions and decisions for himself. His newest conclusion was, "I am an innocent child of God and it is safe to let my light shine." Another was, "I am an instrument and I help others to heal."

We have seen over and over again that when people do deep healing work on the inside, things change on the outside. Neil is a very powerful display of that principle. The court case went on for so long that it actually gave him time to do the healing work that he required.

Finally, the case was scheduled for a court hearing one week after his powerful psychodrama session where he healed the very last bit of discovery shock. We received an amazing e-mail message from Neil stating, "I was all dressed up in my suit for court when I received a text from my attorney saying, "The plaintive has dropped the case! You are indeed innocent!"

Chapter 8

THE NOURISHMENT BARRIER—THE SHOCK RESPONSE TO TOXIC INTIMACY

The *nourishment barrier* of which we spoke in the last chapter is a concept that we strongly believe explains a common problem in society, where we *say* that we want emotional intimacy yet we push it away. As with any of the shock responses discussed in this book, this happens because we were literally programmed by shock to push away that intimacy. Consciously we want it; unconsciously, we believe that the intimacy is a threat to our survival, so we spurn or sabotage it.

This is a terrible fate for our conscious selves. We see others enjoying intimacy. We want it for ourselves. We cannot understand why we run from commitment or otherwise keep others away. And it's one more reason why therapy can be such a game changer for those unable to alter their life patterns on their own.

The nourishment barrier affects more than just our ability to nourish ourselves emotionally. It also affects our ability to nourish ourselves physically. Both come back to a common cause, where accepting nourishment came with a heavy price, because it was quite literally toxic, making it impossible for someone to get nourished without also suffering from a toxic load.[1]

Physically, we can see this with a fetus when the mother is polluting her womb with alcohol or nicotine, or even with rage or depression. The fetus has no choice but to accept the resulting toxic load and this leads to need shock, as we discussed previously. In a similar way, when children are fed foods that are more artificial than they are nutritional, the same dilemma exists, even if the child has no concept of the toxins being consumed, because it is the nervous system that registers the shock.

Emotionally, a child whose mother is suffocatingly overbearing is forced to accept her toxic invasiveness in order to get any emotional support from her at all. A child whose father confuses intimacy, love and sex and thus perpetrates incest with the child takes on her father's love at great expense and is vulnerable to all sorts of unhealthy future sexual interactions.

Part of these children's psyches knows, then, what comes with nourishment, whether it's physical or emotional. They know the price and know that they must pay it, even while trying to avoid the burden. So this is when they begin to set up a psychological barrier between what's needed to feed them physically or emotionally and what they will allow themselves to have. For instance, they may avoid intimacy in their relationships or become compulsive about perfumes, smoke or incense in their environment. They carefully yet unconsciously arrange their world so that nourishment is never within reach, or alternatively that the only nourishment within reach matches the dysfunctional (toxic) prototype.

In the latter case, they are seeking the familiarity of toxins they've become accustomed to as *part* of their nourishment; the two are inseparable in their minds and they cannot take nourishment that is *not* contaminated with mental poisons. They may actually avoid less polluted opportunities for nourishment. For some, life may not feel real without large doses of emotional toxins, so they seek high drama, personal danger and polluting habits or addictions. Indeed, according to psychologist and psychoanalyst Michael Eigen, "Emptiness and violence can get so mixed up with nourishment that they can come to substitute for it. In a way, noted psychiatrist Sigmund Freud conveyed this by asserting that every psychic act combines life and death work. If life and death drives fuse, death might seem nourishing, because of its fusion with life (as life might be frightening because of its fusion with death)."[2]

Either way, these people have been strengthened, in a sense, by tolerating a steady diet of toxins. They have learned to endure, to make the compromises necessary to eke out a subsistence level of nourishment. In doing this, they have refined the defenses of hyperarousal and hypervigilance on the one hand, and the parasympathetic mechanisms of shutdown, avoidance and dissociation on the other. Both sets of defenses are largely determined by right hemisphere systems in the developing brain.[3] The individual's nervous system carries the tension of incompatible defenses; shock is the *physiological* result. Psychologically, the person is stranded in the "no man's land" of impasse and ambivalence, resigned to a life not fully lived. We might call them *as if* people.

THE *AS IF* PERSONALITY

Hélène Deutsch, a well-known psychoanalyst and colleague of Sigmund Freud, discussed a type of patient she called "as if," "in which the individual's emotional relationship to the outside world and to his own ego appears impoverished or absent."[4] The patient himself appears to be unaware of this absence, though he may complain of feelings of emptiness. Deutsch explains her use of the term "as if," observing "the inescapable impression that the individual's whole response to life has something about it which is lacking in genuineness and yet outwardly runs along 'as if' it were complete."[5] Deutsch emphasizes that such personalities are "intellectually intact, gifted, and bring great understanding to intellectual and emotional problems."[6] However, she states that "although they produce good work, it is based on imitation rather than true creativity, just as in their affective relationships there is a lack of true warmth."[7]

"As if" individuals are unable to trust others, since they expect toxins to accompany the emotional connection or emotional nourishment of engaging with them. They are also unable to trust their own real selves, having abandoned that long ago. Their survival strategy requires creating and trusting in the "as if" self by separating the real self from its (noxious) experience. They trust their "as if" imitation of a self, because it has done relatively well in the world, but this is not their "true self," from which their highest ideals, creativity and ability to love must come.

So how do people avoid nourishment which is available to them but that they unconsciously need to push away? Or alternatively, how do they arrange to receive nourishment only when it is contaminated with something toxic in order to stick with what's familiar? They unconsciously erect a barrier around themselves to keep out healthy, nourishing experiences and to magnetically draw to themselves the toxic experiences that feel so familiar. Ron Kurtz, originator of the Hakomi psychotherapy modality, calls them *nourishment barriers*.[8] These self-defeating patterns are deeply embedded in the unconscious, so they are acted out in every aspect of one's everyday life, especially within one's most intimate relationships.

What we've discovered through our thirty years of practicing hypnotherapy with thousands of people is that we draw conclusions about who we are through the experiences that we have. This process begins from the moment of conception and continues throughout our lives.

For example, if a young, developing fetus experiences that it is the "wrong" gender for the parents, it may draw certain conclusions such as: "I'm not who they wanted. There is something wrong with me." Or, "I'm unlovable. I'm not safe here." That unconscious conclusion is then placed in the *personal programming file* for that child and will be used throughout his life unless it is changed, preventing vulnerability in intimate relationships. He erects a nourishment barrier to fend off nurturing, intimate relationships in order to avoid the pain and shame of being confronted with what he anticipates to be the price of accepting that he's unlovable.

That kind of conclusion is almost always accompanied by decisions telling us how to behave—decisions that are compatible with the conclusions we've established about ourselves, whether or not they're accurate conclusions. If someone concludes that she's unlovable, she might decide that she must be "a very good little child," to try drawing the love that she knows will be so difficult to get. This is a completely unconscious decision in order to try to get the love that every human being needs in order to grow and develop properly. Another important need of every human and animal is self-preservation or safety. So if the fetus or child concludes that "I'm not safe here," her decision may be to disappear or to run away to the circus and find a protector.

Safety represents preservation of the species and is the most basic need of all animals. When a safe environment is not created for a very young, vulnerable being, fears, anxiety and shock often develop right from the very beginning of existence. Love is another one of our basic needs—for humans, most domesticated animals and other mammals. So when we look at basic needs, love is the next most important form of nourishment after safety in order to grow, develop and thrive.

One common inner program that we hear is, "there's not enough." If you listen carefully to yourself or to others, you may often hear the words, "I don't have enough..." There are many unmet needs that can follow this statement, such as, "I don't have enough nourishment, food, time, energy or money." Or, "We can't afford that, we don't have enough savings." Or, "No, I can't help you because I'm too tired. I don't have enough energy." Or, "I'm so busy, I just don't have enough time to..." These are common phrases that we hear ourselves and others saying over and over again. This fear of *not enough* often begins in the womb where there may not be enough safety, love, connection, nourishment or oxygen for the developing fetus. So we are embedded with this concept of not having enough and it continues on a profoundly unconscious level for a lifetime.

Some examples of *not enough nourishment* for the developing fetus could be a mother who is terrified of gaining too much weight and so is starving herself (and the fetus) during the pregnancy. In our last chapter, we discussed several reasons why a mother might not want others to know she's pregnant, so she might try hiding it in this way. During the 1950s and for the next fifty years, doctors put a large emphasis on low weight gain for women during pregnancy. Young mothers were weighed every week and given frightening lectures about the dangers of too much weight gain during pregnancy. Accordingly, some mothers became anorexic and their developing fetuses felt like they were starving.[9] Need shock drove the creation of defenses since the babies' basic needs for nourishment were not being met. In cases like this, eating disorders and other self-injurious defenses developed later in life into barriers to receiving exactly what the individuals most craved, yet were resigned to live without. Sometimes an individual even carries deprivation as a "badge of honor," validating that he/she is unselfish and humble.

So we look again at the unconscious conclusions the fetus may have drawn from this kind of situation: "My needs won't be met" or "I'm a burden," for instance. These are conclusions that then cause programming for future life choices, and later decisions could include thoughts like, "I won't even ask for what I need," or "I don't have any needs." As we mentioned before, some programming can include the opposite also, such as, "I'm going to grab whatever I need," or "I'll scream and cry so they can't ignore me."

In order to understand the nourishment barrier, it's vital that we understand how human programming is laid down in the unconscious mind. Let's begin with the theory that people are able to create a wall or barrier around themselves, giving the message to others: "Stay away! Don't come any closer!" Maybe you know someone like that. What kind of subliminal messages do you think might get that sort of statement out to other people?

Dr. Stephen Porges suggests in his Polyvagal Theory that facial expressions speak loud and clear for us. We can make a baby cry just by looking at her sternly or angrily. Everyone is looking, first of all, to feel safe. We need reciprocity in our connections in order to feel safe, to trust. We need to feel validated or recognized before we allow ourselves to be vulnerable with another human being. And so, we look into another's eyes to see if there is love, anger, hatred or fear...or even shock and disconnection in the other person.[10]

When we first meet someone, our unconscious mind, our emotions, our instincts all know if this is a person who is drawing us closer or pushing us away. We pick up a multitude of cues before the first words are even spoken! Facial expressions are among these cues.

Vocal intonation is another important way we communicate with others. If we hear soft, gentle tones in someone's voice, we may begin feeling safe with that person. We may then be drawn closer so that we can listen to the words themselves. On the other hand, tone may also help us to pick up on danger: shrill tones may convey fear while deeper, louder tones may convey anger.

When danger is present, the prosody (rhythm, stress and intonation) of the voice communicates even if we speak another language. Low tones communicate predatory energy, perhaps anger. It comes naturally to use a higher-pitched tone of voice when speaking to a baby or a pet. So these are other cues that people pick up on when someone, even unconsciously, has built a wall to keep others out.

PRENATAL DEVELOPMENT OF CAPACITY TO RESPOND AND REMEMBER

We should be clear that these cues are not just something people pick up on as adults, having learned them through years of living. In fact, we have the capacity to differentiate these intonations in the womb. Prenates as early as twenty-six weeks learn intonations, rhythms and other speech patterns of the mother's voice, demonstrated in matching spectrographs.[11] Four days after birth, infants can distinguish language from other sounds, prefer their mothers' voices to that of other females and prefer their mothers' languages.[12] They discern a language by its intonation and rhythm,[13] and have registered their mothers' voices during the third trimester of pregnancy.[14] By the time of birth, a child has already learned neural patterns of language, including the emotional context for phonological rhythms, tones and sequences of his mother's speech. That is to say that at birth, French infants already understand that their language is syllable-timed, English infants understand that their language is stress-timed and Japanese infants understand that their language is mora-timed (a mora is a unit in phonology that determines syllable weight, which determines stress or timing in certain languages).[15] These prenatal experiences are learning experiences and are recorded in memory.

This kind of learning and memory requires some form of sentient awareness, and we know that memory of prenatal experiences is present immediately after birth. For example, newborns prefer a lullaby their mothers sang to them in the womb to an unfamiliar one sung by their mothers.[16] After birth, babies prefer to hear stories that were read to them in the womb rather than unfamiliar stories.[17] Newborns of mothers who consistently watch a particular television soap opera during pregnancy respond, when played the theme song after birth, by stopping crying, becoming alert and changing their heart rate and movements.[18] The newborns do not respond to other, unfamiliar television tunes.

The point here is that the unborn human develops the capacity to respond to the environment almost immediately upon conception, as we explained in our last chapter, and this is why it's possible for shock to take place any time from conception onward. As we continue to develop, shock has a more intricate framework within which to settle. The central nervous system's limbic system, for instance, isn't present at conception. But it's partially mature at four weeks of gestation and is fully formed by the third trimester of prenatal life.[19] The limbic system records the emotions and behaviors needed for survival, and is critically involved with the storage and retrieval of memory.[20] The cerebral cortex, the highest level of brain functioning, has been found operative by thirty-two weeks of gestation, although it is far from fully functional.[21]

With the capacity to respond comes the ability to store experiences in memory for future use. Research supports the capacity of the prenate to store very early traumatic experiences in the *bodymind* (Candace Pert's terminology), expressed permanently in psychosomatic conditions.[22] This capacity to respond and remember carries with it, by definition, the ability to make decisions and choices, so you can see the connection here between a traumatic event to which we can respond and the role it plays in our unconscious decisions (shock responses) later in life.[23]

Neuroception is a term used for our nervous system's attention to what is happening in our environment. We suggest another mechanism through which we pay attention to the environment: *neuroperception*, one that is available even to the developing fetus in the womb from the moment of conception.

The embryo can't think or speak, but can perceive through the nervous system—it can *neuro-perceive* that this womb is receptive, loving, inviting and thus a safe place in which to grow. Perhaps it is through the vagal nerves that the embryo gets the "go ahead" to continue its journey through the fallopian tubes and to implant in the uterine wall. Another choice point is that of leaving the security of being burrowed into the mother's uterine tissue. It is a huge risk for this tiny being to trust the safety enough to "let go" and fall into the great space of the mother's uterus. If the embryo is safe enough and neuro-perceives that this will bring him/her into union with life itself, the journey that comes with the "embryonic fall" will happen.

However, in another instance, a fertilized egg may neuro-perceive an unsafe uterine wall that is rejecting or filled with fearful neuro-receptors. So all along this journey there are neurological choice points about whether it is safe to embrace life or whether it is necessary to hold back from full participation, to expect and adapt to toxic conditions and to erect a protective barrier against the world. This is the beginning of our karmic journey into life itself.

THE NOURISHMENT BARRIER AND THE VAGAL PARADOX

The Vagal Paradox provides the mechanism for the nourishment barrier.[24] The vagal parasympathetic response puts a "brake" on sympathetic activation when fight or flight is attempted and found to be useless; it reverses course in the nervous system and begins feigning death as a last, desperate bid for survival. Such a drastic shutdown mode is dangerous, however, because the sudden, overwhelming influx of parasympathetic dominance can be lethal. Imagine travelling at sixty miles per hour in your car and slamming on the brakes as hard as you can. That's one way to think of it.

The "paradox" in the Vagal Paradox is that this braking system is, as we've said, dangerous. And yet, it is also the same brake that allows us to be vulnerable to others when we deem it safe to be so. Therefore, it is both a dangerous and beneficial system for us to have.

One example is that, through sensory perception, a fetus may go into hyper-vigilance and create death feigning or parasympathetic shock, i.e., freezing. Perhaps this could account for what we know as a miscarriage or the "vanishing twin" phenomenon. Often there is no medical explanation; the Vagal Paradox may explain it.

Looking at some of the physiology involved, the brain and nervous system begin primitive development three weeks after fertilization, and by week seven have formed the telencephalon, i.e., the embryonic structure from which the mature cerebrum develops. The developing heart begins to beat in a regular rhythm by week six. By its seventh week, the developing embryo converts the yolk sac, which provided primitive self-nourishment and functioned as the developmental circulatory system of the human embryo, into an umbilical cord.

Once the embryo connects to the mother's placenta through the umbilical cord, it becomes dependent on the mother for blood circulation, waste disposal and nervous system activation. What is coming through that cord to nourish and feed this fresh young life? It may be pure love, which produces the same hormones as when the new mother gazes lovingly into the eyes of her newborn. For this reason oxytocin is called the bonding hormone: "Mother and I are one." This is the perfect neurological and hormonal environment to support healthy life.

However, if the visceral attachment is contaminated with fear, anger, jealousy, betrayal and shame, the embryo may go into shutdown mode, which we call (parasympathetic) shock. When frozen, it may not be able to take in any nutrients. This may be where, for some, the nourishment barrier is formed. This barrier, just as in the death feigning of a threatened animal, is neurologically constructed to protect the fragile embryo from being poisoned. However, ironically, just as in the Vagal Paradox, this barrier may kill the developing baby or hamper its proper growth.

Alternatively, hypervigilance may begin in this early stage of development, resulting in a much more active defense leading to sympathetic shock.

Once the embryo drops into the uterus of the mother, the interdependency begins. Now the fragile young soul must rely on the physical, emotional and spiritual health of the mother and her environment to support new life. As noted previously, we now believe that a surprising percentage of conceptions begin as twins, with one of these embryos perishing so early in the pregnancy that it happens before even being discovered. We will return to this later. We call this *twin loss* or *the vanishing twin*.

As time goes on, the fetus develops more sensory awareness. Different sounds and tonal vibrations, as well as ever-present emotions, convey the relative prevalence or lack of safety. If the frequency of the sound waves is low, such as from anger and fighting, the fetus may be influenced by the primitive reptilian vagal nerve response. And just like a reptile in danger, the digestive system of the fetus may begin shutting down as a protective mechanism. The primitive reptile, such as an alligator, will cut down on metabolic demand so as to preserve energy in the face of a survival threat. In this situation of perceived danger, the primitive reptile will also defecate so as to clear out the digestive system and thus *preserve all energy* in preparation for a possible battle. However, if the perceived threats are continuous, what begins as a primitive way to protect from danger may end up shutting down the functions of the fetus (just as for the alligator) to a level from which it cannot recover. This is how the vagal brake response can become fatal.

This tactic of defecating in the presence of perceived danger may explain the curious situation medically defined as a "meconium birth." There are times when the placenta becomes filled with the baby's own feces due to a rupture of the bowel. This primitive neurological response could explain how the paradox created by the nourishment barrier is protecting the baby from a "toxic womb" (defecation in order to preserve energy for defense) and then how this protective mechanism becomes just as toxic as the perceived threat. In certain situations, the fetus can die from ingesting its own feces.

DEVELOPING A SEPARATE IDENTITY

There is no sense of self, identity or autonomy for the prenate. Rather, it lives in an undifferentiated state, identified with its environment, absorbing the mother's emotions and belief system as its own.[25] There is no defense against "negative" experience, i.e., the fetus is receptive and reactive to all experience, incorporating it into its growing blueprint of core beliefs.

The fetus does, however, eventually develop primitive defenses or learned responses in reaction to its experience. In the process, it develops the beginnings of a self separate from the mother. The prenates in fetal expert Alessandra Piontelli's study developed characteristic ways of being, e.g., contentious or passive or loving, in response to their environments.[26] As early as thirteen weeks gestational age, the fetus is showing individual behavior and personality traits that continue on after birth. Piontelli observed four sets of twins by ultrasound periodically over the course of the pregnancies. Each set of twins seemed to manifest a unique relationship together: one set was loving, another contentious and another was passive. One pair consisted of a brother who was active, attentive and affectionate, and his sister who would passively follow his lead. The boy in this pair kicked and wrestled with the placenta, actively pushing for space and looking disgruntled. However, at times he would reach out to his sister through the membrane separating them, caressing her face or rubbing her feet with his. His sister would reciprocate when he initiated contact.

Piontelli conducted follow-up observation of the four sets of twins through age four. She found that behavior after birth for each child, and in the relationship between each set of twins, continued remarkably unchanged. The twins just mentioned continued to be affectionate with each other. At one year of age they would play together, touch, hug and kiss. The boy was self-starting and independent and the girl passively followed his lead. The other twin pairs exhibited the same contentious behaviors and the same passive, non-interested relationships at one year of age as they had in the womb.

Another example of prenates' responsiveness is a study, "Early developmental stress and later behavior," conducted in 1963 and published in *Science* before nicotine was determined to be unhealthy for the unborn, in which pregnant habituated smokers were forbidden cigarettes for several days.[27] When the women were allowed to resume smoking, prenatal monitors detected immediate stress reactions *before* the mothers had actually lit the cigarettes. Although the mothers' thoughts and physiological anticipation were positive and pleasant, their fetuses' reactions were distressed and negative. The prenates had an experience separate from the mothers', the

fledgling beginnings of a separate self. Not only were the prenates reacting
with a personal point of view (distressed) rather than simply absorbing the
mothers' experiences (pleasure), they did so reacting to their mothers' *antici-
pated* experience rather than an already accomplished one.

We can see, then, that as the fetus develops this separate identity, it
begins to assess the safety or danger of its situation and, if needed, its nervous
system will begin to set up this natural defense called a nourishment barrier. It
will begin the process of living on the bare minimum so as to not overwhelm
itself with the poisons it knows or believes to be in its environment.

THE NOURISHMENT BARRIER AND BIRTH

When the fetus becomes exhausted from the ever-present effort of defending
against poisonous toxins, it may shut down and move into freeze mode: parasympathetic shock, paralyzed with fear, triggered through the vagal brake.
The defenses shut down and can't seem to be retrieved. The fetus may become
trapped or strangled by its very source of nourishment and the nourishment
barrier may begin with a toxic or tangled umbilical cord, which carries the
nutrition for life but also the hormones of danger, fear and threat. The frantic
sympathetic shock response to the toxins or lack of oxygen may cause the
fetus to flail and may actually end up choking the desperate fetus.

When the baby has matured to the point of being ready to move out of
the womb, there may be several signs of this vagal brake response happening
even before birth: the cord wrapped around the baby's neck, meconium poisoning or lack of oxygen (a "blue baby").

On top of all these potential building blocks of the nourishment barrier in this tiny fetus, there are many hospital interventions that may add
to the difficulty the fetus is encountering. We discussed some of these earlier. Among them are the administration of some drugs and anesthetics, the
use of forceps, Caesarean delivery, etc. These obstetrical interventions can
be necessary and even life-saving. However, they are sometimes used due
to impatience or for scheduling convenience. Currently in America, about
one third of births are performed as Caesarean sections, many of which are
not medically necessary.[28]

Among other things, the nourishment barrier is complicated by the
chemical Pitocin, a synthetic form of the bonding hormone oxytocin, which

stimulates powerful contractions. The baby's experience of contractions is intended as a welcome, nourishing means of moving through the birth canal and out into the world. But the Pitocin-enhanced contractions can be experienced as violent by the baby (and the mother, too). So the natural process of laying the new baby on the mother's tummy so that it can crawl up to find its own source of nourishment (her breast) has been blocked (the barrier) first by the drug Pitocin and then by the practice of having both mother and baby anesthetized at birth to deal with the pain of the violent contractions. The anesthesia produces a mother who is too sleepy to breastfeed and a baby who is too drugged to nurse. Combined with the lack of oxytocin, the mother-infant bonding does not happen at the most critical time for bonding and creating a basic sense of safety, which is in the first thirty-six hours of life.

If the baby, for whatever reason, has been in a toxic womb and began to construct this nourishment barrier, it certainly may continue to be maintained and reinforced in a variety of ways once the baby begins its life journey outside of Mom. We have many clients who have experienced horrendous sibling abuse in families where there were just not enough resources (time, money, food, energy, love) to go around. Just as when a bite of food is dropped in the middle of a starving pack of animals, the attack begins.

CAN THIS NOURISHMENT BARRIER BE DECONSTRUCTED?

The baby who is being held by the mother while being fed, face to face, experiences and understands safety cues better than a baby who is just left in the crib with a bottle propped up by a pillow. The sensory experience of receiving nourishment while at the same time seeing the mother's eyes, feeling the love, smelling her familiar smells and feeling her loving touch can remove any barriers to nourishment that may have been previously constructed. Another important sensory experience, according to Stephen Porges, is that of hearing the mother's sounds and the intonation of her speech—the prosody of the voice, as we discussed earlier.[29] If the mother is speaking sweetly, lovingly and perhaps even singing a lullaby, this tone facilitates safety. As we've discussed, the baby does not have to understand the words at all to get the message clearly.

Dr. Porges teaches that the social engagement system of the baby with face-to-face interaction can dampen down the defensive states, such as the nourishment barrier we have been discussing, to create enough safety to promote a loving connection. So even though the baby may have had a difficult beginning, this can definitely be repaired, the sooner following the trauma the better.

Erecting a barrier against receiving nourishment is an innate instinctual response to nourishment contaminated by trauma. Studies show that animals subject to a state of over-excitation and danger (the human equivalent of which is a state of stress) will ignore their need for food for abnormal lengths of time.[30] After the threat is lifted, the animals will engage in bulimic episodes of gorging. The researchers suggest that stressful feeding episodes in the infant's first year of life create sympathetic circuits of anxiety embedded in the amygdala, becoming a long-lasting association between feeding and stress. Because the association is formed at a pre-verbal developmental stage, however, it remains an "emotional memory," dissociated from any capacity to cognitively understand or control.

Following trauma or prolonged stress, these emotional memories or sense memories may remain "encapsulated." This means that ongoing experiences believed to be similar are unprocessed and unmediated by the hippocampus and frontal cortex, which would give them context and meaning and allow for a conscious decision to change.[31] Dissociated from conscious awareness, arrested at a primitive developmental stage, these memories or behavior patterns—shock states—persist throughout life.[32] "Owing to the sub-cortical nature of this memory encoding, these memories are apparently extremely unresponsive to verbal communication and may often prove persistently resistant to orthodox verbal psychotherapy."[33]

An experience of stress or threat while eating, as opposed to a sense of security, may be a major determinant of eating disorders. As with the animals subjected to danger or threat mentioned above, food intake is reduced in the presence of others because the presence of others is perceived by many eating disordered patients as a threat. Thus binge-eating or bulimic episodes occur when alone, often at night, which is perceived to provide safety. This is a classic example of erecting a barrier to healthy nourishment as a defense against the expected toxicity in receiving it.

Emma's Story: Toxic Womb and Umbilical Shock

Another example of the long-lasting impact of toxic nourishment and the individual's erecting of a nourishment barrier is conveyed in the story of Emma, a young woman with whom we have worked. Emma is a heavyset thirty-five year old who has been trying desperately to get pregnant for the last five years. She has had a series of miscarriages, which continue to cause her a great deal of physical, psychological and emotional pain. She also has an increasing amount of shame unconsciously that something *must be wrong with her,* even though her doctors say she is healthy enough to have a baby. After the miscarriages, she and her husband decided to adopt. When all the papers were signed and the baby was born, at the very last minute the birth mother changed her mind. This was another huge disappointment for Emma, who saw it as one more time God must be punishing her.

In a hypnotherapy session, she returned to the time of her conception when her mother already had five nearly-grown children. The most recent prior pregnancy, however, had resulted in a baby being born and only living a few weeks. This caused Emma's mother a great deal of grief, guilt and shame. After her infant's death, Emma's mother went into shock and had difficulty connecting with any of the children or her husband. She was told by doctors that she could not have any more children. She was extremely depressed, withdrawn and isolated. Later, she became pregnant with Emma, a so-called "change of life" baby. This was another shock to her and she was so distraught that she considered having an abortion.

That was the beginning of the nourishment barrier for Emma as a tiny developing fetus in her mother's womb. On every level, the mother did not want this baby, so her womb became emotionally toxic rather than nurturing. The emotions and thoughts of wanting an abortion, that is, wanting this baby dead, sent shock waves to the fetus. Hormones were released that became toxic to the baby and, at the same time, her mother was ingesting chemicals to numb her own pain. She was drinking alcohol, smoking cigarettes and taking pain killers and anti-depressants. Only since the 1980s have pregnant women been educated to the fact that whatever they put into their bodies could affect the developing fetus. Nevertheless, some women still prefer to numb their pain rather than tolerate unpleasant emotions during pregnancy, regardless of how it may affect the fetus.

During her time in the womb, Emma continued to feel the stress that was going on in the family, carried to her through the umbilical cord. One of her siblings was being sexually molested by a brother-in-law, causing more distress to family relationships and certainly less ability to focus on the growing fetus in the womb. Each day, as the stress continued to grow, little Emma was tossing and turning in the womb, which caused her to get tangled up in her own umbilical cord—the cord that was supposed to keep her alive and fed. Because of the tangled cord, Emma had difficulty receiving any nourishment, which in turn caused more frantic flailing by the fetus. The cord that was supposed to be feeding her now was killing her. When Emma was born, she had the cord wrapped around her throat, causing her to be a "blue baby" who nearly died of asphyxia. This is a clear example of how the nourishment barrier is erected in the womb as a defense against toxic nourishment.

As a small child, Emma knew she had to be very good—perfect, in fact, in order to reside in this already-troubled family. In hypnotherapy, she became aware that she had to take care of her mother's needs and to try to make her happy. This became an impossible task since her mother, in shock, was totally disconnected from the baby and emotionally unavailable. There was no holding, no eye contact, no breastfeeding and certainly no feeling of being loved and wanted. Emma was cared for by an older sister, who propped the bottle up in the crib and often left her there for hours in dirty diapers, hungry, cold, wet and screaming. After a while, the screaming stopped as Emma went from sympathetic shock (active/screaming) into parasympathetic shock (numb/frozen). Too often, families then label this as the *good little child*, when actually the baby has given up and has withdrawn into a deep state of shock. "See how good she is? She never cries!"

This is how the nourishment barrier produces need shock. The earliest and most basic needs are not met, beginning in the womb. When the cord becomes wrapped around the flailing baby and the fetus is deprived of nourishment, sympathetic shock is the initial response. Powerless to influence the dire predicament, the fetus then goes into parasympathetic shock. Then, when it is time for the birth, the fetus cannot get through the birth canal on its own volition and the delivery requires Pitocin to initiate contractions. This pattern of a stressed baby flailing in the womb often continues when the baby is in the crib and it may possibly become a victim of SIDS (Sudden Infant Death Syndrome), for which doctors as yet have no proven medical explanation. Emma's older sister had a baby that died of SIDS when Emma was only three—another lost baby in a broken family where they were all suffering from toxic nourishment and severe need shock.

As you can see, need shock and the nourishment barrier go hand-in-hand. An example is the young child who screams frantically at the smallest frustration of not having what she wants. Doctors often call this colic or food allergies when the young baby screams and screams for no apparent reason. We may be unaware that this is just a continuation of the toxic nourishment barrier experienced in the womb. In the *Diagnostic and Statistical Manual of Mental Disorders (DSM)*, published by the American Psychiatric Association, this child is often diagnosed with Reactive Attachment Disorder. In adults, the same symptomology is diagnosed as Borderline Personality Disorder. Whatever it is called, the patterns are similar. The individual has a real or perceived need, expects that the need will not be met and then goes into panic (sympathetic shock) when it isn't. This becomes a self-fulfilling prophesy as described in one book about borderline personality disordered people: *I Hate You, Don't Leave Me.* The words "I hate you" imply that the baby already expects that the parent will not meet his or her needs, followed by the silent pleading of the needy infant, "Please don't leave me." This is a powerful phrase, showing the conflict faced by those with a nourishment barrier, where they will deny themselves something that is needed even while losing themselves by obsessing over it.

....

Hector's Story: The Nourishment Barrier and Emotional Eating Patterns

People with eating disorders often grew up in emotionally toxic home environments, where love was contaminated with abuse, fear, guilt trips and shaming, or love wasn't even available.

Hector, a thirty-two-year-old, came to us to lose weight. He was very obese and had tried every diet program he could find. Nothing seemed to work or last for more than a week or so. He was discouraged and depressed about this, especially since he wanted to find a girlfriend and hopefully a wife.

His doctors were also worried about him and had suggested a stomach bypass operation, which he didn't want.

Hector began by telling us about all the accidents and near-death experiences he'd had during his young life. Many of these accidents were in cars and one was on a motorcycle. He also confessed to trying to end his own life several times. We pointed out to Hector that his compulsive eating was another, more subtle suicide attempt. He somberly nodded his head in agreement and shame.

Hector told us he'd been in a serious accident recently in his beautiful new sports car, of which he was very proud. Immediately after the accident, an ambulance rushed him to the hospital where it was found he had a broken leg and other fairly serious injuries. When his parents found out, they blamed him for the accident (without checking the police report), assumed that he had not even gotten auto insurance yet (which wasn't true) and were furious that he would now be unable to work for several months. They seemed to be more upset about the financial considerations than about his condition. They also accused him of paying too much attention to his girlfriend—who they assumed was sitting next to him—instead of to the road, and believed this had caused the accident. He told us this was all untrue and was typical of the negative assumptions they had always made about him, comparing him to his siblings who they thought were angels. No matter what the facts were, he always felt that he had received nothing but anger, shame and blame from them, especially from his father.

In Hector's psychodrama work, there seemed to be a consistent connection between lack of food and lack of money. Hector came from a working-class family where he received the message at a very young age that only rich people eat pizza, ice cream and Coca Cola, and that he couldn't have food like that. His father shamed him for wanting "the finer things in life," especially when it came to food and drinks such as pizza, soft drinks and wine. As is often the case in family feuds, the victim triangle (see *Breaking Free from the Victim Trap* by co-author Diane Zimberoff) is formed even before the child is born. Hector had been placed on the family side with his mother and her mother. In short, Hector was assigned the role of *the victim in the family*, the one the father would always blame, punish and shame.

The father, in his role as persecutor, used Hector as a pawn in the game of war he played with his wife and her live-in mother. The grandmother felt sorry for young Hector and rescued him from his angry, often violent father by comforting him with the foods he loved, like pizza and ice cream. So the food and drink, as is often the case, became a substitute for emotional satisfaction and a way to numb the pain of emptiness, loneliness, fear, guilt and shame that Hector experienced on a daily basis.

In his psychodrama session, after exploring his feelings in the hospital following the accident, we regressed Hector back to a younger time when this victim pattern began. We used the feeling bridge of anger, shame and hurt as he regressed to the age of six. He described being in the family living room where his parents were fighting and his five other siblings were crying and fighting too. He felt a big, empty hole in his heart. In this chaotic scene, his mother was hurt and crying, because the father was drinking and going out with other women. The mother was so focused on her own unmet needs for love and attention that she was completely oblivious to the needs of her children. She felt so distraught that she became nearly crazy and at that time, young Hector took on the burden of trying to make her feel happy. The unconscious conclusion he made about himself was, *I'm not important. She can't even see me. My needs will never get met.* The decisions he made in an effort to get his needs met were, *I'll give her the love she needs. I can get her to love me and to see me if I become the man of the family.* So as a young child, Hector took on the burden of rescuing his mother in an attempt to fix the family chaos and perhaps to get some form of safety, nourishment and love from her.

In our therapy sessions, we often notice when a certain part of a client's body is moving or when the hypnotized person puts his or her hands on a specific area. Then we ask in these sessions for different parts of the body to speak, in the classic Humanistic Gestalt tradition of therapy. We ask the body parts to describe the deepest unconscious feelings. These emotions are held in the body and will always speak an even deeper truth than the person himself may be aware. This technique is especially effective for someone in the hypnotic trance state, because there is heightened awareness of somatic experience and less self-censoring inhibition.

At one point during his psychodrama session, we noticed that young (regressed) Hector had his hands on his heart. We asked *his heart to speak* and his heart told us, "I am lonely. I feel my mother's pain and I want to take care of her, but I don't know what to do for her." We could feel the deep emptiness and pain of this young boy, confused and unable to figure out the solution to this family dilemma. Then his hands moved over his big belly and we asked him to give this a voice. The belly said, "I'm so heavy. I am all the weight you are carrying around. You are trying to take care of the whole family. It is too much weight! Too heavy. A big burden. I can't carry it anymore."

Then we noticed Hector's hands as they moved up to his shoulders, which he was rubbing. We asked him to let his shoulders speak and they said, "I feel so heavy. I feel trapped here. I am a kid and I just want to go out and play. I don't want to be inside this house any more. I feel stuck here with my mother. I don't want to feel this burden of having to take care of my mother. I don't want to worry anymore. I just want to get out and be a carefree young boy."

From our years of pre- and perinatal psychology work, we recognize that words such as *trapped*, *stuck* and *want to get out* are often indicators of some unresolved womb experience that may be the source of an issue. We do not, however, suggest anything about this, but if a client uses these words we ask the person to go back even further in his life to the origin of the feelings.

As Hector regressed to the source of this weight, this burden and this feeling of being stuck or trapped, he found himself in his mother's womb, which he described as poisonous. He started making faces, saying that he was choking from the smoke (her cigarettes). He started rolling around and yelling, "It's killing me in here. I'm dying! I've got to get out. It's too hot and I can't breathe. I'm choking!" We noticed his neck becoming red and he began pulling at something around his throat saying, "You're choking me. I can't move. I can't breathe. I've got to get out of here." We asked him what his conclusion was right there in the womb. He said his conclusion was, "I'm stuck and I don't deserve to live." His decision was, "I might as well give up and die." This is a classic example of the nourishment barrier, where the mother's fears about having another child, and her inability to properly nurture her baby, result in that child's approach-avoidance reaction to toxic nourishment when it is offered.

Hector continued to talk to us of his birth experience and we noticed his feet now moving rapidly, trying to push him forward. This is a body memory that most humans have of pushing their way out of the womb. We brought Hector close to the wall in the therapy room so he could push his way out of the womb with his own power. We call this a *corrective birth experience*. Then we asked who he wanted to hold him as he created his new, more powerful birth experience. He wanted it to be his grandmother. So we had the group member who was playing the role of his grandmother in the psychodrama catch him and hold him in her loving arms.

Then we noticed Hector's hands had moved again to his heart as he was being held. We asked him to give his hands a voice as they spoke to his heart. They said, "Don't worry, we will take care of you. Your mom is safe. She just made a mistake, but it wasn't your fault." He now had a beautiful, radiant smile on his face and said he saw angels and the Virgin Mary before him. Mary told him, "I am your real mother. I will protect you and keep you safe." At this point he had a joyful look on his face as he stated his new conclusion: "I feel all the love is right here in my heart. Something was blocking me before but now it is gone." His new affirmations were, "I can breathe. I'm free. I connect. I am love and I am loved."

We asked him what new decisions he had made about himself and he stated, "I now release the burden of heaviness from my body, mind and spirit. I now choose to heal."

Hector's story is a clear example of the beginning of what is termed *need shock/need shame*, which often develops in the womb. This baby struggled in the womb, realizing that not only would his needs not get met, but that he would have to bear the heavy burden of taking care of his mother's needs in hopes of getting his own needs fulfilled.

Hector was being raised by parents who themselves were emotional children. His parents were so overburdened and stressed that he and the other children were often shamed for having any needs at all. Hector had memories of being yelled at for having a dirty diaper and shamed for having wet his pants out of fear. The continual practice of basic needs being shamed often puts the child into severe need shock/need shame. But fortunately for all of us, through these regressive techniques, we can reach back to the early programming we're operating from and change our lives for the better.

Chapter 9

HOW SHOCK CALCIFIES ADDICTIONS

Our bodies are biologically programmed with certain needs including breathing, eating, drinking and sleeping. Luckily, the body provides signals telling us to engage in these activities for survival.

Moreover, the body responds to changes in the environment to tell us to engage in these activities differently, once again with the wisdom of a vehicle that wants to survive. Because of this, we crave different types of food as the weather changes and we may find ourselves sleeping more in response to shorter winter days. If oxygen levels are low, we may breathe more rapidly; if we have depleted certain nutrients because of stress or poor diet or a toxic environment, the body may begin to crave foods with those nutrients.

Because these are responses to keep the body alive and in the best condition possible (given the circumstances), we consider these behaviors and the body's signals for these behaviors highly beneficial. While you might say the body is "addicted" to food, we don't use this term or suggest that hunger signals, for instance, are a problem.

All human beings also have a number of honest, healthy psychological needs. At the core of all these is group belonging and love. This isn't just about a feeling. Once again, it's about survival. If we weren't driven by our basic psychology to connect with others, we probably wouldn't have survived as a species. We rely on one another for safety and for job specialization (right on back to hunters, gatherers, home keepers and other basics).

We've talked about how we can be tricked into perceiving needs that aren't there or trying to fulfill actual needs in ways that don't fulfill them at all. When we're stressed and enter heightened sympathetic or parasympathetic states, the body responds in any number of ways. If we successfully shake off that stress when an event has passed, our natural biological signals return. In the case of shock, though, when we fail to shake off stress or trauma, these sympathetic and parasympathetic states remain active and continue giving signals to the body long after they've stopped being useful.

We've pointed out that these nervous system responses are important to our survival when they're needed. They are the best responses to less-than-ideal situations and don't cost us much when used temporarily and then put to rest afterward. When they become stuck, when they keep running the show, it's no longer the physical needs of the body determining when we eat or sleep or telling us that food is actually dangerous. It's no longer a healthy psychology telling us to connect with or run from certain people. Now it is the resident shock—our circus partner—giving us unhealthy directions that we cannot ignore, because it feels as if our survival depends on it. While it is not "addiction" when the body or psychology really needs something, it *is* addiction when we misunderstand our needs and improperly try to fulfill them. We call it addiction when we're attached to a substance or action that doesn't help us survive. It is also addiction when we use substances to meet basic needs. An example is when our deep longing is for closeness and connection and we use comfort foods to try to fill up the inner emptiness. We call it addiction when our craving is to be loved and to belong and we use tobacco, alcohol or drugs to numb the pain of inner emptiness.

If a small child who has never had any is given some ice cream, there's a good chance she'll love the ice cream, because it is sweet and we are biologically attracted to sugar since it provides a lot of immediate energy. Moreover, children are especially attracted to sweets because of their additional need for calories when growing. So her attraction to the ice cream would only be natural and biological. There's a good chance she'll want more ice cream if it's available.

This biological attraction is something she would be able to control if she chose to. So she grows up; she begins learning about nutrition; she determines that ice cream overall *isn't* good for her body and that there are better ways to consume sweets in moderation. Perhaps she determines that she will make exceptions on special occasions because her understanding of health suggests that this won't harm her body. With this information in place, she could change her actions.

Now information about breathing or sleeping or eating won't get her to stop these activities, because they are in fact biological imperatives. But the ice cream is not an imperative, so she can stop consuming it if she believes she should.

Yet some people could not stop eating the ice cream—or perhaps more broadly sweet foods or even more broadly food in general—if it was, for them, what *seemed* to be a biological imperative; if they associated food or sweetness with something that actually *was* an imperative (biological or psychological). This is an instance where we no longer have control through rational choice. We are controlled by the perceived need as if it's an imperative when it's really an addiction, numbing the pain of what is unavailable to us or the pain caused by past trauma.

So when this adult cannot stop eating sweets, it is her frightened child within who is ordering comfort food off the "children's menu"—not her rational, adult self who has a much more expansive menu to choose from but doesn't. The adult has yielded control to the child within by being in an "auto-pilot" trance state of shock. And this state has become so habitual and the person's physiology has become so habituated that it is a "new normal," and she is no longer rational or consciously aware of all the choices available.

The state of shock is like the effect of a powerful drug on the body's nervous system. Over a lifetime of using shock to attempt to numb the pain of unmet needs, the nervous system develops this "new normal" in which either the sympathetic or parasympathetic branch is dominant in an unbalanced way. The person who rages has a sympathetic branch with a voracious appetite. When the body's natural rhythm begins to assert itself with quiet restfulness, the sympathetic branch needs a "fix" to reassert its dominance just like a junkie needs a fix to avoid getting sick. Some event in the person's life provides the spark that ignites his rage and the new normal is reestablished in his nervous system. The triggering event itself is merely a convenient catalyst; the rager's reaction to the trigger is determined mostly by his unconscious need to maintain the state of shock.

The person who is depressed has a parasympathetic branch with a voracious appetite and needs deflating and demoralizing experiences to feed it.

When the body's natural rhythm begins to assert itself with excitement over a promising possibility, the parasympathetic branch needs a "fix" to reassert its dominance. She will find some discouragement or defeat to send her spiraling down into depression, and the "new normal" is reestablished in her nervous system. Or she will overeat, smoke cigarettes or drink alcohol, which activates the parasympathetic branch. Her body is attempting to maintain equilibrium at the level of the new normal, the state of shock.

On some television programs dealing with psychological problems, such as *Dr. Phil* and *Dr. Drew*, we sometimes see an episode wherein people are concerned that someone has an addiction and the assumed addict tells them, "I could quit if I wanted to." The question is, could he really quit? If he could, then he's making a choice about his actions. If it's obviously harmful to himself and others, however, there's a good chance he's doing this thing for some unconscious reason, perhaps responding to something that happened long ago. In this case, he's likely deluding himself—maybe he can stop for a period of time, but the need will build up in him as an imperative. And he'll either return to the habit or replace it with another habit that feels, psychologically, like it's meeting the need even though it is just a numbing agent.

We've been discussing some of the rampant addictions we see in our society, like addictions to sugar (alcohol turns immediately into sugar in the body and thus is also a sugar addiction) or food in general. The same addiction can be the result of different shock experiences—we're not proposing that a single shock is at the root of all sugar or food addictions or any other kind of addiction. However, someone might associate sugar or food with a way to sooth shock, to cover up his or her pain.

Babies are sponges for the events around them and the energy of those events. Our chapter on conception and birth conveyed that there are many traumas and shocks that can affect infants in their earliest days, and you can imagine that feeding time is a welcome escape from the unprotected feeling of shock. Here they may find welcoming, protective arms; may feel a calm heartbeat; may be able to look into caring eyes. If this is the case, then food can become associated with protection and escape from pain. Specifically, the sweetness of breast milk or the corn syrup or other sugars in prepared baby formula could equally carry this association and trigger later desires for sugar that aren't just about growth of the body, but about protection from shock.

A sugar addiction later in life can take all sorts of forms, but think about alcohol, which quickly coverts to sugar in the bloodstream. Yes, there can be many reasons for an addiction to alcohol, but here is one of them that you might not immediately think of or make a connection to.

What we want to remember is that these addictions are responses to trauma or shock and, because of this, they can be triggered at different times in our lives when circumstances have us reliving an event in some way. As we've talked about, in some cases we never let go of these sympathetic or parasympathetic states and may have ongoing addictions. In other cases, they can ebb and flow with our triggers.

When Diane, one of the authors, realized she wanted to lose some weight, she thought about the fact that she was rather addicted to a particular cold, sugary drink. As she thought more about why and when she started to drink so much of it, she realized that it was after a shocking tragedy within our family that she began really drinking the substance. This was an unconscious response to a family member being murdered by another family member. So something was triggered that caused her to begin drinking these sugary drinks, which was a response she's had throughout her life due to an underlying sugar addiction.

Diane visited her naturopath, who asked her, "What is it about these drinks that really drives you?" That's when Diane realized that, when we treat shock, a lot of times we ask our clients, "Do you want cold or do you want hot?" And we either give them a cold pack to put on their neck or something warm. Typically when we're treating shock, a person who has sympathetic shock (agitation) wants something cold and someone with parasympathetic shock (lethargy) wants something hot. Diane was looking to a cold drink each day—something she just couldn't give up. So she realized that this was a way she was unconsciously trying to treat the agitation of sympathetic shock. Unfortunately, this puts you in more shock. Diane would sit there almost in a trance as she had her drink, similar to how people smoke a cigarette and stare off into space.

A lot of people eat like this—basically in a trance, zoning out and simply pushing food into their mouths. They're not conscious of the food or the taste or how their body feels about the food, but are really just feeding some other perceived need. A lot of these behavior patterns are connected to shock, so in order to lose weight, Diane realized that she had to stop drinking this addictive drink and had to stop eating in a trance state. By paying attention to her actions, along with her own therapeutic work to resolve the unconscious motivations, she was able to change them.

EXAMPLES OF SHOCK AND ADDICTION

It will help to understand how shock leads to addiction by reviewing a few examples. These are only possible scenarios leading to addiction and apparently similar addictions can have various causes and therefore need to be treated differently.

If we go back to our earlier discussion about conception, you'll remember that we spoke of *sperm shock*. All the sperm compete for one egg and there is a lot of activity, a lot of competition ending in the explosion of the sperm head when it connects with the egg. When there is shock involved in this stage, you often see the result in people who sit there and tap their fingers or feet all the time. People with this kind of sympathetic shock are anxious and they move a lot. People dealing with this shock may look to drugs like uppers or they may drink a lot of coffee or other caffeinated drinks. They may also be addicted to work, drama or chaos. The shock is driving the person to use substances or behaviors to feed the dissociation, and because the underlying impetus feels like life-or-death, it soon becomes an addiction. Treating it would require slowing down, cooling down and calming down.

The *egg shock* that can occur at that time, conversely, is passive. The egg is sitting there waiting for something to happen, overwhelmed by the surrounding activity. It may feel invaded and like it needs protection from the sympathetic shock. You may see symptoms of this in those who bury themselves in reading or anything solitary, withdrawing from other people, looking for a safe place to be. This becomes an addiction because, again, it feels like a necessity for the person. It is more than just an enjoyment, because they feel physically uncomfortable, indeed threatened, when not in these protected situations.

Within two weeks of conception the moment of implantation comes and here the fertilized egg or embryo is searching for a welcoming environment, but the womb may not be all that welcoming and this can cause *implantation shock*. The mother may be afraid of being pregnant; it may just not be a "good time" to be pregnant; maybe she is just a nervous person. But the embryo gets this tense, cold, unwelcoming scene that creates a shock. Or the uterine wall may reflect the mother's engulfing need to control others and the embryo may then feel the unwelcoming shock of suffocation.

Well, that embryo wants to be welcomed and that child, when born later, will want to be welcomed, and you see the results so often with this *need* to please those around her. This is where we get addictions to codependency, to needing acceptance, to wanting to find a connection with someone who obviously (at least to others) doesn't want to connect with us or isn't really capable of being there for us.

We may even find that the embryo moves from place to place, looking for a location in the wall to implant itself and, with each failure to find entry, the sense of impending death increases. From this time of shock, we may see those people who are always looking for something else. You've seen those who stay in one place for a year and then go to another place to find a new job or a new this or that, looking for "geographic solutions." This is again doing whatever it takes to find a place or thing that makes them feel accepted, which on a deep level they never feel. Thus they try to fulfill the legitimate need for acceptance with something that won't ever fill the need as they move from place to place, relationship to relationship or thing to thing. That restless movement is their addiction.

When parents first become aware of a pregnancy, if their reaction is fear, shame or anger, the fetus may well experience *discovery shock*. We discussed previously all the reasons why one or both parents may be upset with the idea of pregnancy, and it hits them in this moment they discover that they are expecting. We tell the story of a man who was at one of our advanced courses and was born seven months after his parents were married. He was born at nine pounds but his parents said that he was born premature. A nine pound preemie? Not likely. Perhaps his parents told him this because they were ashamed of being pregnant before being married, especially in an earlier era when it wasn't so common. And there was no doubt a level of discovery shock when they first learned they were going to have a baby. These days, with our ability to know the baby's gender before it's born, this can even create a second kind of discovery shock if parents were determined or hoping for a baby of one gender and then learn they will have the other.

In cases like this, where there is shame associated with the discovery shock, the individual may, years later, feel panic when she is noticed, such as called on in a class or speaking in front of a group of people. Or the person may engage in shameful addictions—something she is embarrassed by and try to cover up. It could be an eating disorder like anorexia. Here, the person feels shame about her existence so she wants to just keep getting thinner in order to disappear. Unconsciously, people dealing with discovery shock may try to disappear or even attempt to kill themselves to comply with their parents' perceived desire to not have this child and they'll have addictions to help them achieve either goal. We also see sexual addictions here, and these could arise from several aspects of this shock: in response, perhaps, to gender discovery or because we still have a lot of shame wrapped up in the area of sex or even because a rampage of unprotected sex could be part of a suicidal tendency.

Discovery shock is another instance where one may try to please his parents in order to be worthy, to let them know there's no reason to be upset, disappointed, etc. So this person may be addicted to being the best at everything, always performing, actually overcompensating. And this addiction can be exhausting. Also, the overcompensating part may be trying to get bigger to be seen, so behaviors could include acting out, being overly dramatic (a "drama queen") or overeating.

Another cause of discovery shock, which we mentioned in an earlier chapter, comes from finances. Maybe two people want a baby but now is the worst possible time, because they are losing their home or are out of a job. So they're terrified about the pregnancy and that type of discovery shock filters into the womb and the baby takes it in. That unresolved stress—essentially that "lack of money" shock—leads to an ongoing relationship with money in the future, where the person later may always have tension with money and perhaps have addictions to work or hoarding money in an unconscious effort to soothe that initial shock, to feel safe. We know that they will never resolve the anxiety with work or hoarding, but only by addressing the underlying shock.

Now understand that sperm shock or egg shock develop only when, at the moment of conception, there is stress, fear, anger, jealousy, shame, aggression, grief or other unresolved distressing emotions. Imagine the delightful experience of sperm and egg in a conscious conception between two loving partners. In the same way, the uterine wall of a mother who is healthy, non-codependent and eager to conceive a baby will be welcoming, supple and inviting at the moment of implantation. Discovery shock, too, depends on the response of the parents—they may be delighted that they're pregnant and want to contribute to the new being's sense of security and deep belonging. In a similar way, there are many other traumas that never need to occur during pregnancy, leading to subsequent shock, but instead could be replaced with supportive, loving, secure experiences if we understand how influential these earliest experiences are on the baby's lifetime patterns of behavior.

There is not just one level of toxicity that will trigger shock in a fetus; rather, the trigger will depend on other stresses the fetus is dealing with and its own constitution. But let's take the obvious scenario of a *toxic womb*—a woman who is smoking cigarettes. The smoke is bad enough for the woman, but imagine all the energy needed for a fetus to grow into a human child, from two cells to perhaps an eight pound baby in nine months. Tremendous amounts of nutrients, water and oxygen are needed. Each time the woman smokes a cigarette, she is suffocating the baby, and it's all but certain with regular smoking that the regularity of this traumatic intrusion, this suffocation, will cause shock.

As with other forms of shock, this is likely to result either in someone who's addicted to poisonous substances like smoke, because it is familiar to her, or someone who becomes exceptionally sensitive to them, because she is trying to escape from them at every turn—in "flight" mode from the intrusion. Let's take a moment to look at that, because this is actually just the opposite of addiction, where someone latches onto something as a false replacement for an actual need. Here, we're looking at the balancing opposite, running from whatever prevented needsfrom being met.

Corey, who worked for us, was very good at using sage to cleanse our offices. The ancient shamanic tradition involves burning the sage, which sends smoke into the air in a sort of cleansing ritual.

One time before a gathering she had really put a lot of sage into the air. And when Sara, one of our participants, joined us, she said, "Oh, I can't breathe in here." She became agitated. So we decided to explore that reaction, and we took Sara back through hypnosis and she found herself remembering an experience as a small child when her family home was on fire. The parents didn't want to leave, because they didn't want to lose their belongings. They were scrounging around trying to get all their stuff together and this girl was basically suffocating in the smoke and thought she was going to die.

Well, we dealt with that and then during hypnosis returned her to her traumatic infanthood. She found herself actually in the womb and Sara told us her mother was smoking and she couldn't breathe—another connection with her response to the smoke of the burning sage. In this session, she was coughing and choking. It was a powerful moment, and helped us to realize just how directly connected a toxic womb can be to allergies and even asthma. The flight response in the womb continues throughout life—the body keeps trying to flee from and fight against any kind of toxin.

So we worked on this issue with Sara and helped her to cleanse the toxic womb. Sage was hanging in the air once more the next day and she laughed as she realized that it didn't bother her at all. Her extreme sensitivity to the smoke just one day before was gone, because we had dealt with the core of the problem, the shock itself, which had developed from Sara's early suffocation experiences.

Other kinds of shock can occur during pregnancy. Let's focus on the time of birth to show another example. In an earlier chapter we discussed that anesthesia—provided at an overwhelming level for the size of the baby—can cause an incredibly numbing reaction we call *anesthetic shock*.

As we explained, the baby is doing everything he's meant to do, preparing to arrive in this world, and suddenly he is completely numbed with a narcotic dose designed for the mother and far exceeding what someone of his size should get, even if he was *meant* to become numb. When such doses are administered there is little feeling involved in the birth process and a total disconnect from his mother when he enters this world. A disconnect, really, from everything. So there is this sense of abandonment, a sense of being all alone. In the most poignant moment of embracing life, both mother and infant are numb and in shock due to anesthetic drugs given at the hospital.

Addictions for people with this kind of shock can include anything to "wake them up" from the numbness, including certain foods, caffeine, drugs like methamphetamines and adrenaline-pumping activities. Sometimes just to feel something outside the deep, numb feeling, people will even engage in dangerous activities like cutting themselves. This is something that could also be in response to the shock of having the umbilical cord cut too soon, severing the baby from the mother when blood is still flowing through the cord or in response to the surgical cutting of a Caesarean birth. You can see how many shocking moments there can be for a baby and how, when they are not conscious, they can drive similar shock responses.

Conversely, we also know that "familiarity breeds comfort" and although that initial numbing episode perhaps offers an unfulfilling first experience, it is still the foundation of life experience for many, many babies. The numbing drugs became popular in the 1960s among the first generation of American babies born with delivery anesthesia. The anesthetic shock began with the widespread use of ether for births and deliveries in the 1940s. We believe that anesthetic shock may be one of the most prevalent types of shock in society today and that this may partly explain the ongoing popularity of drugs like marijuana and heroin and of dissociative activities such as the over-use of gaming, texting and computers. Alcohol is another numbing drug that can be used in response to this shock, although obviously it's been abused far longer than this form of shock, which again shows that the symptom doesn't necessarily reveal the underlying problem.

We're talking about addictions as ways we attempt to fulfill real needs, but not in ways that actually fulfill them. We might latch onto whatever prevented us from meeting our needs as a point of familiarity—a kind of "freeze response" addiction to the cause of the shock. An example might be a woman who was physically and/or sexually abused as a girl who attracts an abusive boyfriend and refuses to leave him, believing that he will change and provide the healthy intimacy she desperately needs. Another example is that we might run from the cause of our shock in a flight response. This can create an addiction to the opposite of the cause. A child who grew up with a rigidly controlling parent might rebel later in life (probably beginning in adolescence) against any limits or rules, even when doing so is dangerous or self-defeating. In both cases, the adult is not consciously choosing to behave in a self-sabotaging way; it is literally the child within who is choosing. The adult, stuck in an "autopilot" state of shock, is oblivious to the real choices available (such as leaving the abusive boyfriend or complying with a benign guideline).

A NEW MODEL FOR TREATING ADDICTION

In working with a client on addiction issues, we first ask what the *triggering event* was that led to the unwanted, addictive use of a substance or compulsive behavior. Please refer to the graphic on **Shock in the Addiction Cycle**.

"What was it that you experienced *just before* you [ate those cookies, smoked that cigarette, drank that wine or searched on your computer tablet to watch porn, gamble online or play a game]?"

This can be a variety of experiences and may not always be obvious to the client at first. Some common examples of triggering events can be: "I was:

- ...in my office for hours without a break."
- ...at a family reunion, where Mom was yelling and Dad was drinking."
- ...trapped in the house with the kids fighting and the television blaring."
- ...waiting for my spouse to come home, only to be ignored or blamed again."
- ...arriving home from work and my spouse started a fight."

Then we begin asking the clients, from a relaxed state, to drop down into their bodies to understand what they were feeling *during the triggering event* and just before they went for their addictive substance or compulsive behavior. This is best done in a hypnotherapy trance since these experiences are difficult for the conscious mind to sort out when engulfed in shock.

Referring to the diagram, **Shock in the Addiction Cycle**, this triggering event is at the top of the circle.

Some clients may describe being on the *parasympathetic shock side* of this circle, describing feeling bored, trapped, numb, spaced out, exhausted, discouraged, etc.

Others may be on the *sympathetic shock side* of the circle, feeling restless, stressed out, "I've got to get out of here," angry, anxious, etc.

When that resulting experience becomes unbearable, the individual begins to self-medicate with a *substance* or a *compulsive behavior* that activates the opposite nervous system response. When boredom becomes intolerable, an individual moves to initiate some activity to relieve the boredom, turning to a *substance* which offers stimulation such as coffee, energy drinks, cigarettes or chocolate, or to an *activity* such as shopping, compulsive exercise or computer games. Or she goes deeper into parasympathetic shock, feeling discouraged and staying in bed all day. When that becomes intolerable, she drinks coffee or goes shopping, activating sympathetic shock.

Shock in the Addiction Cycle

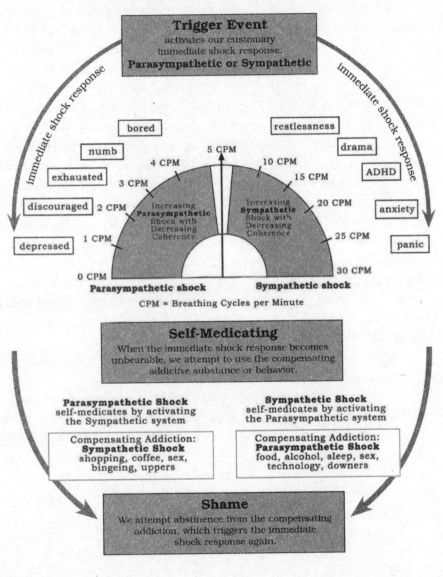

If they are on the *sympathetic shock* side of the addiction cycle, when the restlessness and anxiety become intolerable, they may turn to something to "calm themselves down," such as alcohol, cigarettes, masturbation, bingeing on comfort foods, watching television or porn or playing video games.

We instinctively attempt to treat our own unconscious shock states by seeking the opposite. These self-treatments of our own shock include a very complex set of behaviors that have become so habitual that there is no true conscious thought process involved and thus no real conscious choice. These behaviors have become a deeply embedded defense system locked into our somatic reservoir of behavioral experiences. They have become so automatic that we barely realize we are engaging in the behaviors until we notice some outward sign. Perhaps that sign may be driving drunk and nearly killing someone on the highway. Or one day realizing that none of our clothes fit us since we have gained so much weight. If we continue to remain in shock without treatment, the consequences can become even more dire, such as coughing up blood, having heart palpitations from the frantic sympathetic shock overload or getting diagnosed with diabetes from all the excess sugar ingested. Others may need the wakeup call from their sexual addiction of contracting an STD or, even worse, the AIDS virus. Some clients have had the experience of coming home to an empty house where their spouse has finally taken the children and left due to their pornography, alcohol or gambling addictions, their extramarital affairs or addictive work habits.

Many people in shock don't realize they are in shock and, if they do, would still not know how to find the right treatment for it.

We believe that learning to recognize and treat shock is revolutionary for all therapists, especially those in the fields of treating addictions and eating disorders. By understanding how shock affects us and then becoming aware of pre-and perinatal psychology, new treatment is now available. Talk therapy provides an understanding to some extent, but true healing must address the underlying physiological and psychological shock states in order to eradicate these deeply embedded, addicted behavioral patterns.

The diagram shows the intimate connection between our breathing and our shock state. When a person is relaxed and yet alert, he is probably breathing about five or six breaths per minute. Sympathetic activation speeds up the breathing pattern and at twenty-five or thirty breaths per minute it approaches a panic state. Breathing more slowly, or with more shallow breaths, is characteristic of parasympathetic shock states. Either extreme reduces coherence, as measured by heart rate variability. We return to the importance of breath in managing our energy, devoted to treatment of shock.

You can imagine that this kind of addiction or response to shock can play itself out in any area of our lives. Among the most meaningful to us is our relationships, which effectively paint so much of the quality of our lives. Glenda's story tells more about how shock can feed addiction.

....

Glenda's Story: Shock Fuels Addictions and Addictions Fuel Shock States

Glenda is a woman who came in for hypnotherapy stating that she had lower back pain whenever she was under stress. The back and spine are the main source of support in our lives. According to Louise Hay's book, *You Can Heal Your Life*, the lower back going out often is indicative of feeling unsupported in one's life.

Glenda is a very successful therapist with three beautiful children and a very busy life. She is, however, on her third marriage and is beginning to see some addictive patterns in her relationships. She came in with severe lower back pain, feeling very pressured and overwhelmed in her life. She shared that her husband is a marijuana smoker and has promised to quit but never has. Even though she loves him dearly, he spends his time playing video games or watching television shows, getting stoned and not being emotionally available to her or the children. The children are pre-teens and are beginning to make disdainful comments about their father being "a pot-head." These comments wake him up a bit regarding the example he is giving to his children. As a result, he begins to bargain, saying, "Well, I won't smoke in the house" or "I won't smoke when the kids are around."

Glenda is in agony about this situation. However, she admits that being in relationships with addicts has been a pattern her whole life. Her addictions have fluctuated from food to marijuana, but her main addiction is to unhealthy relationships with men.

Often people in shock states don't really know what they are feeling. They are either in parasympathetic shock, numb and disconnected, or are engaged in sympathetic, frantic, work-a-holic behavior. When asked, "What are you feeling?" Glenda responded, "I feel numb. The only thing I feel is the pain in my back."

We focused first on Glenda's back pain. We asked if her lower back could speak, what would it say? This Gestalt "projective technique" can be beneficial for people who are in parasympathetic states of shock and are numb to their emotions. She told us her back said, "I hurt. I'm overwhelmed. I'm stuck. I'm trying to hold on. I'm trying to fix everything. I hurt and I can't do it all." She then went on to say, "It's all just too much for me. I resent having to take care of everything, while he gets stoned and plays music."

We regressed her to the beginning of this pattern and she traveled back to age five. When we asked where she was, her little girl voice told us she was very excited because it was going to be her very first day of school and she was trying to wake her mom up to take her to the bus. There was a big rainstorm that day and her mother refused to get out of bed. Her mother exclaimed, "Don't be ridiculous, you can't go to school today. It's raining." Glenda was distraught, as she had been eagerly awaiting her very first day of school. She even tried to dress herself, eat some food and go outside in the hurricane-type storm to try to catch the bus herself.

Glenda reviewed much of her childhood, wherein her mother was always sleeping, tired or focused on television shows, completely unavailable to her only daughter. As a young child, Glenda drew the conclusion that, "I'm unimportant and no one will take care of me." With her mother asleep so much of the time, her decision was, "I have to take care of myself." She states that at five years old, she learned to cook, clean, get around on the bus line in a large metropolitan city and also try to take care of her usually "out of it" mother.

We asked this young child what made her mother so sleepy all the time. She stated that her mother stayed up late at night, playing cards and drinking with their neighbor. The fact that her mother was an alcoholic Glenda only interpreted as her mother always being sleepy. She grew up holding onto this myth and never realizing that her mother was alcoholic until this session.

As Glenda related more scenes from her childhood, she began to see her own pattern of being in relationships with addicts who could not meet her emotional needs. There were many situations where young Glenda went into shock when facing adult situations that she as a small child had to fix or handle herself with age-inappropriate responsibility.

As we were processing this, Glenda put her hands up to the temples of her head, stating that she had pain there. Then we regressed her to the source of this pain and she went from age five back to being in the womb and told us she could feel the forceps around her temples trying to pull her out. She began yelling, "I don't want to come out. I know what's out there. You don't want me anyway. You got pregnant by accident and you're too young to have a baby. I want to stay here where I'm protected."

Like Glenda, it is not unusual for clients to regress to the womb in hypnotherapy as this is often the source of shock states, with anesthesia or other toxins. Then we asked, "What conclusion did you draw about yourself?" Glenda stated, "I'm unwanted. I'm just an annoyance to my mother." When asked what decision followed that conclusion, she stated, "I'll just stay in here and stay stuck. I'm safer here rather than having to take care of myself without a mother." There was a deep feeling of sadness in the room as she said this, realizing the dilemma of this beautiful soul, newly arrived on Earth.

After she expressed this, we asked her to look around to see if there was anyone out there who did want her. A big smile suddenly came over Glenda's face as she realized that her father wanted her. She could feel his love and his voice saying, "I've always wanted you from the first moment that we found out your mother was pregnant with you. We will have fun together." Realizing this gave the baby Glenda the impetus to push and get out of the womb. She said, "Get those forceps off me, I'm coming out myself!"

Glenda's pattern of being attracted to loving men like her father, yet who were addicts like her mother, began in the womb and continued all of her life. Glenda was amazed since she had never fully realized that her mother was in shock and an addict in order to numb her own pain of being a pregnant teenager who was in no way equipped to have a baby. Her loving but unavailable husband often uses the same shaming words that her mother used: "Don't be ridiculous!"

Glenda must work on breaking her addiction to emotionally unavailable men who use drugs, alcohol or trance states to withdraw emotionally. The more conscious Glenda becomes through our hypnotherapy sessions, the more she is reducing her levels of shock, and the closer she gets to setting and enforcing meaningful boundaries with her husband.

Chapter 10

HOW SHOCK AFFECTS OUR RELATIONSHIPS

Let's look back at what we've covered so far about shock. As human beings, every part of us tries to stay in balance, in a state of homeostasis. As we're pushed out of balance by stress, the body or our emotional and mental states respond however they must to get back in balance.

In the case of everyday stress that comes and goes, we're generally equipped to maintain balance, but the deeper or more prolonged the stress, the more we need a drastic or prolonged response. Suddenly, what should just be a temporary reaction becomes our way of doing things. It becomes ingrained as a pattern or a kind of programming. Psychologically, we can invite members of the circus to take over our responses if our own personalities aren't getting the job done for us. Physiologically, we can enter a permanent state of alert; permanently hold tension in our jaws or muscles; or have our body determine its own responses when a past shock is remembered through a perception of current events.

Sigmund Freud spoke about this long ago when he talked about the *repetition compulsion* where we have a tendency to reenact what was done to us and what we saw as children. Today's researchers continue to reveal more about how much our unconscious mind is like a video recorder, capturing every scene, every thought and every sensory experience we've ever had.

This has great benefits for teaching us how to survive, but it also leads to this recollection of shock, triggering our automated responses.

In early psychology classes, one of the things a student learns is how the mind makes connections between things, as well as why this is necessary. For instance, if an absolutely perfect circle represents the letter "O" but someone writes an "O" without quite connecting the circle, or without making it perfectly circular, we can still figure out what the letter is. If we couldn't do this, there would be no way to read different fonts or the handwriting of different people.

This ability to connect similar things is so powerful that we can make real leaps in order to comprehend what we're shown. This strength also throws us its challenge: even if a circumstance isn't really like a previous circumstance, we can connect the two. And if we learned as children to respond a certain way to a shocking experience, then any time we connect the present moment with such a past experience (even if it's not really the same), we've already determined how we will respond. Because of this, we might take a perfectly safe situation and perceive it as a threat, thus entering a state of shock and acting not from our true selves but from our programming. As we've seen in previous chapters, this plays out in a number of ways and it certainly plays out in relationships.

One of the ways we see this is with a "need shock," where someone faces the dilemma of either not having their needs met or getting them met at some terrible cost. As a child, Jennifer, a woman in one of our psychodramas, had a mother who ignored her and a father who was abusive. Her needs weren't met and if she spoke up, she got abused by her father. She was really frustrated.

Jennifer described an incident where her mother was talking on the phone and she was trying to get her mother's attention for something but couldn't. Jennifer ended up falling down the basement stairs and cutting herself on glass and there was blood all over the place, which finally got her mother's attention, although it wasn't positive attention. Her mother got angry because Jennifer made such a mess bleeding all over the basement.

So what does Jennifer learn psychologically and even physically here (since this is really a severe need shock leaving a physiological impact)? She learns that the only way to get attention is to create a drama. We see these people often and some of us may have that pattern ourselves, where drama or victimization is a way of life because this was programmed as a way of getting our needs met. So this becomes the way we interact with others, using accidents or illness or chaos or anger to ensure that our need for intimate connection gets met. There is a saying that conveys this: "I'd rather be wanted for murder than not wanted at all."

In a similar instance, people who grow up in alcoholic, violent or abusive families begin to learn that these violent interactions can actually bring the family together, even if it's not in a healthy way. For example, when two family members begin to raise their voices, others in the family are attracted and come around. All attention is focused on those who are fighting. In fact, any kind of chaos can bring the family together, some trying to help or stop the chaos but, in doing so, becoming part of the chaos themselves. Unfortunately, if this kind of thing happens on a regular basis, children begin to confuse the ideas of abuse and chaos with intimacy and may start to use these in an effort to bring intimacy into their own lives.

One of the fascinating things we've also learned is that the unconscious patterns stamped into individuals' minds tend to act as magnets, bringing people together who have been programmed in similar ways. You may have read books or heard people speak about the power of attraction and this works for good or for ill, and those who have been programmed by shock attract others of a like pattern.

Think of how often we see some people repeatedly enter relationships where they are continually being abusive…or being abused. From their own history as children, they may have learned to seek intimacy by playing either role and so they find others who will fulfill the opposite, supporting role. The relationship between recording artist Rihanna and her on-again, off-again boyfriend Chris Brown is one example.

One night in 2009, Chris badly assaulted Rihanna. The photos of that violent night show Rihanna with two black eyes, her lips swollen bigger than her nose and a face that is no longer recognizable. She had been brutally beaten, bitten and punched, according to emergency room records. When interviewed on TV many months later, Chris described the violence that he experienced as a small child when his stepfather beat his mother on a regular basis. His mother was present during this interview and cried uncontrollably when asked if the domestic violence that she experienced could have affected her son's behavior. The guilt and shame were so strong that she couldn't even speak. She cried and shook while her son described these horrific childhood times without emotion. These are both different forms of shock.

Rihanna had similar patterns from her childhood, as she grew up seeing the woman as the victim and the male as the perpetrator. So we observe this magnetism in action. It's no accident that Chris and Rihanna were attracted to each other from the moment they met. As children, they were led to unconsciously see violence as a form of love and this pattern drew them together and had them replay familiar scenes stored in their own personal memory chips on the night of the abuse.

In a *20/20* interview with Diane Sawyer in November 2009, Rihanna offered her graphic account of the fateful February confrontation with then-boyfriend Chris Brown, including the terrifying blankness that seemed to come over him as he assaulted her. She said all she kept thinking was, "When is it going to stop? When is it going to stop? He had no soul in his eyes. Just blank. He was clearly blacked out. There was no person when I looked at him."[1]

During one TV interview, Chris said things like, "I don't remember anything from that night," "I am in shock," "That is not me" and "I feel like I am on the outside looking in at someone else." When you see the pictures, you know how very physically he was there, but—as a soul— he was apparently not. His past shock brought someone from the circus to the table that night, and this circus member took over to the point that the night was all a blur to Chris. This happens because shock can lead to such strong dissociation and literally wipe memory clear from the apparently normal self.

During a court appearance in Los Angeles on February 28, 2014, Chris Brown's rehab facility confirmed that the entertainer had been diagnosed with bipolar disorder and Post-Traumatic Stress Disorder.[2]

Another example of this may be the famous case of O.J. Simpson, who was accused of savagely beating and murdering his estranged wife, Nicole, and her friend, Ronald Goldman. He may be the best liar in the world. However, he may also have been suffering from severe shock due to the severe abuses in his own life. This is *not* to say that a person isn't guilty of a horrendous crime when perpetrated, but rather it is a way to find treatment for victims of physical, sexual and emotional abuse so that they do not become abusers themselves. What's more, it is important for understanding how people can appear so calm during horrific scenes of violence and trauma. O.J. stated over and over that he did not remember that night and thus was convinced of his own innocence. He was always calm and collected and had very little emotion about the night on which the murder of his wife and her friend occurred.

One of the fascinating aspects of how shock affects relationships is the contagion effect. Have you noticed that when a person in a group setting is morosely depressed or is raging loudly about some supposed injustice, others in the group tend to be noticeably affected? Some in the room will shrink away and hide emotionally from the raging person while others will begin to feel their own aggression activated. The rager's shock has resonated with the shock pool within each of these people; some have a sympathetic shock pool and react with activity, and others have a parasympathetic shock pool and react by trying to withdraw.

This shock contagion helps to explain the dynamics of many dysfunctional relationships. When an abusive spouse begins to accuse and shame his wife for some real or imagined infraction, he goes into a trance, leaving his body and entering a role, a habitual pattern of behavior that is no longer rational. He is on "auto-pilot," and his shock triggers hers. She may respond with an equally "auto-pilot" counterattack or she may become submissive. Generally he will only come back to his senses when the trance is broken. If his wife is a typical battered spouse, she will understand that implicitly and will provoke a physical attack to "get it over with." That brings the man back into connection with his body, out of the shock-trance, and he almost immediately begins to apologize and promise never to do it again.

A similar pattern is played out every day on a much less dramatic and violent level in many relationships. Often when a man withdraws behind the newspaper, he has actually withdrawn from connection with his feelings, and thus from the relationship. We might in fact call this a shock posture—an unconscious, habitual, automatic stance of the body that initiates the "auto-pilot" to take over. His wife can sense his withdrawal; his shock then triggers hers. She may now become talkative, or become lost in the mindless activity of compulsively doing chores (sympathetic shock) or she may feel rejected, pout and eat candy as a substitute (parasympathetic shock). They are both now captive to the unconscious shock defense dictated by their own internal nervous systems.

If we trace these habitual reactions back to their source, we find that the patterns were established early in life—in early childhood, in infancy or even in the womb. The pattern began as a reasonable way to defend against the angst of being unwanted, or the terror of being physically abused, or the impossible expectation to be someone other than who you were. Over the years or decades, that pattern has become entrenched in the nervous system itself and the person's reaction to a friend's rejection triggers the same shock response as the initial terror of being unwanted early in life. When someone expresses anger toward you—perhaps a co-worker or family member—you react with the same shock response as when you were physically abused as a child. These are not rational reactions, nor are we even consciously aware of them. They are automatic reflexes, initiated by the instinctual "old reptilian brain." The alarm bell in your amygdala is blasting away, warning your body to prepare for a life-threatening assault. As a result, our relationship with the co-worker or family member suffers, becoming more defensive and insulated and less trusting and intimate.

When these alarm bells sound, we may react from those very young child parts of ourselves that went into shock and made decisions about how to stay safe in the face of threat. These decisions create what Jung called shadow parts of ourselves. However, Jung never addressed the shock pool in which these shadow parts swim. As previously mentioned, these shadow parts are like the blind spots in a rear view mirror. One moment we look into the mirror and it seems as if we have a clear view, no cars in sight. Then suddenly, seemingly out of nowhere, a car appears dangerously close to us! Where did that come from? Similarly in our lives, we may be having a discussion with a partner, co-worker or friend and suddenly "a shadow part" is triggered, reacts to something and jumps out, seemingly without our permission or even awareness! Now we have a mess to clean up that was completely out of our control, like getting sideswiped by an unseen car trying to pass us on the highway. Our shadow parts reside in these blind spots, hidden deep below our conscious awareness. The trick here is for someone to "see" where they are hiding since we often only observe the aftermath of a shadow emergence. This is just like when we have a car accident: without seeing the car hidden in our blind spot, it is very confusing. We might ask ourselves, "Why did that happen; how did that happen? I didn't even see it coming!"

Blind spot shadow collisions are frequently evident in relationships. We had a man, Dan, in our sessions whose shadow parts would emerge through his interactions with others as well as in e-mails. He would characteristically respond to a group e-mail with an angry response to something from out of the blue. One time he was sent an announcement about an upcoming class to which other people responded with excitement and interest in enrolling. Those who weren't interested did not respond at all or simply said, "No thank you, not at this time." The shadow part of Dan responded with an angry tirade, saying, "Why should I take this class? It isn't going to help me and certainly would not increase my income!" Then he went on ranting. Often when we questioned this client later about one of his tirades, he either didn't remember it at all or would just minimize it. "Oh, that's over now, I didn't mean anything by it." This indicates that these shadow parts live in the shock pool of dissociation.

Dan's wife, who had lived with her husband's shadows for years, had learned to dissociate by going into shock herself. As she continued to grow through her own deep work with the Heart-Centered Hypnotherapy, she began to thaw out from her shock state of dissociation, and began no longer to tolerate the appearance of these hostile, demeaning and disruptive shadow eruptions. Through their relationship work, he agreed to honor a signal from her which she could use to let him know that one of his shadow parts had taken over "driving the bus."

In order to bring these shadow parts into the light, we regressed the client to the source of the reaction, the connected feelings and the early decision that was made by a young, uninformed child about how to survive. Going back to the angry responses we'd get, we asked Dan what feelings were triggered when he read the announcement about a new class. He said, "Well, I was very stressed about money that day." Then we regressed Dan back to the source of these feelings of not enough money or resources. In this case, he instantly went back to being five years old, during an economic hardship where his parents were raising several children and they couldn't make ends meet. There was a lot of family stress during that time and Dan wanted to help. He offered his services in some way and was pushed aside by the older siblings with shaming and demeaning words: "Don't be silly, you are a baby, what makes you think you could earn any money for the family?" He ran out and hid in his room, feeling shamed, unappreciated and very anxious that there would be no food for them to eat. The deeper fear was, "We're all going to die." The unconscious conclusion he made about himself was, "I have no value. I'm worthless." The small child's subsequent decision was, "I'll get revenge. They'll be sorry. I'll hurt them the way they have hurt me."

This is when his shadow part developed a tendency to hurt others before they could hurt him again. This shadow part followed him around for all of his life, angrily attacking or reacting to others who he perceived as rejecting his offers to help. This shadow part contributed to many personal conflicts, the loss of business partners and eventually going bankrupt. His healing began when he realized that his inner little boy just wanted to be loved, appreciated and valued. He realized that he had a very soft, loving heart that was easily hurt. Dan learned to put protection around himself and ask his fellow Wellness Institute students and family members for feedback if the angry child shadow part of him emerged without his awareness. The blind spot that had caused collisions so often in his life was now moving into clear sight.

Through hypnotherapy, his wife, Shirley, looked at all the years that she had tolerated his rants and abusive tirades and discovered her own shock pool that was triggered when her husband became angry. A situation came up where they had some very important businesspeople at their home. She was in the kitchen with some of them and Dan came in to discover that something had not been done that he assumed she would do. His shadow part immediately was triggered and he berated his wife in front of the guests. At first Shirley went into her usual reaction which was to dive deeply into the shock pool and disappear. A few of these guests took her aside and asked her if this was the way that her husband typically reacted to her. They were becoming concerned about doing business with the couple if this was going to continue to happen. This gentle confrontation woke her up to the realization of just how instantly she went into shock and the amount of abuse she had learned to tolerate over the years.

In couple's therapy, Shirley brought this realization into their conversation. She was encouraged to stay present in her body by not diving into the shock pool and giving Dan clear messages about how his behavior was affecting her. Through individual hypnotherapy, she became painfully aware that she had also grown up in her own desperate family trying not to notice her father's abusive rage. She began to see how her survival depended upon being the good little girl and making excuses for her father's behavior. As the oldest child, Shirley protected her siblings with childhood defenses of making excuses for him, telling the others that things would be okay and baking cookies to soothe their fears. She soon realized how she had done the same thing with her own children to protect them from their father. She came to understand her shadow parts. She had trained her siblings and her own children to use food, especially sweets, to numb the pain and continue to swim in the shock pool of dissociation.

Shirley has learned, from diminishing her own shock pool, to remain wide awake and to lovingly but confidently confront behavior that is not tolerable to her. This is how shock in relationships is maintained and then healed as long as both people are willing to look at and heal their own behaviors.

We begin to heal our relationships when we bring these automatic reactions to conscious awareness and open ourselves to actual spontaneous response to the person in our life, instead of reacting to him or her as the ghost of past threats. It is helpful to literally say to yourself, and to the other person, "I know you are not my father [mother, abuser, etc.], you are my co-worker [spouse, daughter, etc.]." Just as shock is contagious, so is the subsiding of shock. As I bring myself out of the shock state by becoming more consciously aware and more grounded in my body, those I'm interacting with will also begin to become more present to themselves and to me.

....

Pam's Story

Pam, an attractive, intelligent woman, began her session with us by saying that she was a psychic/clairvoyant. She said she had been working on herself for years. Yet Pam stated that she really could not maintain a normal relationship with a man and had been married and divorced three times. She recently met an attractive man who was drawn to her and invited her out for drinks, dinner and eventually to his apartment. As soon as he began to kiss her and become sexual, however, she froze, felt panicked and had to leave.

She agreed to try Heart-Centered Hypnotherapy to address her issue with men, since she reported having been in every other type of therapy available over the past twenty years and nothing had helped. As we began our work with her, we regressed her to the source of this challenge.

Almost immediately she was transported back to being a young child, just three or four years old. Her grandfather was coaxing her into his bedroom with candy. She felt love for him since he was the only man who paid attention to her. She was his special little girl and she craved the love and attention she received from him. Her father was a doctor and was never home; her mother always had social engagements that kept her from the home.

During the regression, little Pam suddenly began crying and screaming as she felt her grandfather on top of her. She was screaming, "I'm splitting apart. I'm torn apart. I'm bleeding!" Pam then went silent and I knew she had gone into shock. The conclusion that she had made about herself was, "I'm bad, I'm dirty and no one will ever love me." We asked her what behavior she developed after this as a defense, and her answer was "to disappear."

The next scene she related was her mother finding the blood all over her panties and asking Pam how it got there. Pam was crying, saying it was from grandpa. The mother started yelling at Pam, "Don't ever say that again! You're lying, making up stories about grandpa! Don't tell anyone, especially your father. Just be quiet."

In our Heart-Centered Hypnotherapy, we always provide a "corrective experience" where the internal child is empowered to speak all the things the little girl was unable to express. She was able to say, "I'm important and I am lovable. I deserve love and it is now safe to be seen." This reprogramming takes several sessions to complete. In each session it is like replacing the old bricks of a crumbling building. We remove the bricks that are not sturdy enough to support the building (the unhealthy conclusions and behavioral decisions) and we replace them with strong new bricks to support this building that we are reconstructing.

Since Pam had decided she was invisible and didn't matter, her behavioral decision was to never trust anyone, especially people she loved and who said they loved her. The decision she made here about how to behave was to be hypervigilant. She knew that no one else was going to protect her and that, in order to be safe and to survive, she was going to have to protect herself.

Again, be aware that conclusions like these are made from a very young part of a person that has little other information yet about how the world works. In our youngest years, our unconscious minds are basically programmed by the events happening around us and create patterns for how we'll live our lives. Until that unconscious programming is changed, our lives will continue being controlled in this way. And in the case of traumatic experiences, we are programmed to run away when the trauma is triggered in our present moment and then the circus archetype—the bodyguard—arrives to act on our behalf... whether we like its behavior or not.

DISCOVER YOUR SHOCK IN RELATIONSHIPS

Describe a *recent behavior of your spouse, child or co-worker that upsets you.* Examples: you yell at me; you walk away when I am talking to you; you never help with tasks at home; you leave and go places without me; you blame me when you can't find something; you're not on my side when the kids need discipline; you work so much, we never see you; you are not really "present" when I talk to you. Write the description of your experiances here:

a) _____

_____

b) _____

_____

c) _____

_____

d) _____

_____

e) _____

_____

1) Describe *how you react* to the above behaviors (each one individually). Examples: I become quiet and withdraw; I get really angry; I do something to get even; I argue or demand what I want; I talk to a friend to gather support or to get consoled. Write your reactions here:

a) _____

_____

b) _____

_____

c) _____

_____

d) _____

_____

e) _____

_____

2) People often go into shock when they have a disagreement or fight. Some people dissociate by becoming paralyzed with unexpressed fear or anger and rage (called parasympathetic shock). Some people dissociate by becoming preoccupied with a substitute activity (called sympathetic shock). Mark the ones that you experience most with your initials. Mark the ones that you feel your spouse or partner goes into with his or her initials. Fill in the blank lines to personalize the results.

Parasympathetic (passive)	Sympathetic (active)	
___	___	withdraw
___	___	read
___	___	"space out" with the TV
___	___	"disappear" into the computer
___	___	fall asleep
___	___	get a headache
___	___	get sick or hurt
___	___	clean the house
___	___	work
___	___	talk on the phone
___	___	go shopping
___	___	get busy in the kitchen, or garage
___	___	get "lost" in nagging or raging
___	___	become violently angry
___	___	_____
___	___	_____
___	___	_____
___	___	_____
___	___	_____
___	___	_____

3)   People often use a substance or behavior to help them dissociate, allowing them to escape the difficult work of resolving a conflict. Which of these do you use to avoid talking to your partner to resolve the conflict? Initial the ones that you experience most. Mark the ones that you feel your spouse or partner goes into with his or her initials.

		alcohol
___	___	drugs
___	___	smoking
___	___	overeating
___	___	pornography
___	___	computer games
___	___	shopping
___	___	just leaving the house
___	___	fantasizing about other partners
___	___	checking up on your partner
___	___	"cruising"
___	___	_____
___	___	_____
___	___	_____
___	___	_____

4)   Which of the items in #3 are ones you recognize as used by your mother or father (or other significant adults) in your childhood?

Mother	Father	
		_____
___	___	_____
___	___	_____
___	___	_____
___	___	_____
___	___	_____
___	___	_____

      —   —   _____

      —   —   _____

      —   —   _____

      —   —   _____

      —   —   _____

5) Describe in your own words a typical conflict that can develop between you and your significant other or in a significant relationship: their behavior that upsets you and your reaction. Is there a pattern of sympathetic or parasympathetic shock in your reaction? Do you recognize substances or behaviors that you tend to use to dissociate from the interaction? Can you see a connection between your parents' style of interaction and yours?

In our sessions we use hypnotherapy to undo the programming. In Pam's case, we regressed her to the events that programmed her and, with the help of her mature, internal adult, began to change her response. This was the start of Pam's healing. She was able to bring in the loving parent part of herself and nurture her inner three-year-old. She was able to change her inner conclusions and believe, "I am lovable and it is now safe for me to be seen."

In her second session with us, Pam revealed that she nearly died after having a hysterectomy. We should mention that it's very common that women who end up having hysterectomies have been sexually abused as children or raped as they got older. Pam told me she had been raped four times. She also revealed that, after her hysterectomy, she developed a mysterious condition where she was facing death. The doctors could not figure out what was wrong with her medically. After spending thousands of dollars and having to call in a special team of doctors, they discovered that during the operation, some "medical material" had been left in Pam's body and was floating around. They could not remove it as it had become entangled inside her body and seemed to be poisoning her.

At this time, we did an integrative medicine session beginning with the body symptoms and then discovering the psychological and emotional connections. Her female parts, primarily her uterus, felt contaminated with disgust, shame, rage and fear from all of the past assaults. It seemed as if she kept attracting sexual assaults to the point of nearly killing herself (not consciously), until she finally found the deeper unconscious work that could get down below the shock to bring healing. Pam worked diligently to release all of the deep emotions, especially her own self-hatred. We had to help her get down below the layers and layers of shock that occurred with each subsequent trauma.

After this, the doctors were able to remove the material that had been left inside Pam's body and save her life. We also removed the destructive materials of self-hatred and shame to complete the healing.

When we spoke to Pam about her ability as a clairvoyant, she realized that this ability had developed early in life, soon after her grandfather had first raped her. During that trauma, she realized that she dissociated, left her body and was able to look down to see what was happening. She always felt safer outside of her body, looking down and being hypervigilant. Today she is learning to be in her body and experience everything fully, instead of seeing it all as an observer, and to trust that some people really are safe for her to be vulnerable with and to love.

Chapter 11

THE SHOCK RESPONSE TO
CRITICAL INCIDENTS

People who are affected by shock in their lives often have survived traumas of various types. Many of the traumas we refer to in our case examples in this book are early childhood traumas, including parental rejection, sexual or physical abuse, being unwelcome or unaccepted by the family and a multitude of situations experienced in dysfunctional families. But there are many traumas adults face and endure on a daily basis which also result in shock; we will now focus on them. We will examine the shock response to shootings at schools, serious accidents, victims of crime, victims of sexual assault, first responders, combat veterans, traumatic loss of a loved one and natural disasters.

A whole category of critical incident responders working for agencies like The Red Cross and huge companies all over the world have critical incidents within their companies and must respond to the needs of their employees and their families. This includes oil, gas and coal companies dealing with fuel spills, fires, explosions and all types of disasters resulting from the dissemination or use of their products.

A plethora of people in our culture handle the problems that we face on a daily basis. Sometimes they end up bearing the brunt of anger and blame for situations they have no control over. These include airline attendants and ticket counter people, ambulance employees, hospital workers including physicians and nurses, insurance company representatives and many more men and women who are there to serve us and who get blamed, shamed and yelled at when things do not evolve as we had planned.

Who is most likely to develop PTSD?

Although many people who go through trauma will not develop PTSD, some people are more prone to do so than others.[1]

You are more likely to develop PTSD if you:
+ Were directly exposed to the trauma as a victim or as a witness to others being traumatized, abused or assaulted
+ Were seriously hurt during the event
+ Went through a trauma that was long lasting or severe
+ Believed that you were in danger
+ Believed that a family member was in danger
+ Had a severe reaction during the event, such as crying, shaking, vomiting or feeling apart from your surroundings
+ Felt helpless during the trauma and were not able to help yourself or a loved one

You are also more likely to develop PTSD if you:
+ Had an earlier life-threatening event or trauma, such as being abused as a child
+ Have another mental health problem
+ Have family members who have had mental health problems
+ Have little support from family and friends
+ Have recently lost a loved one, especially if it was not expected
+ Had recent, stressful life changes
+ Drink a lot of alcohol or use drugs to regulate your stress
+ Are a woman
+ Are poorly educated
+ Are younger than thirty-five and feel vulnerable

SCHOOL SHOOTINGS AND SCHOOL BULLIES

There are more and more school shootings by disgruntled or mentally disturbed students who did not receive the diagnosis and treatment that could have prevented many of these tragedies. Often these shooters are described as calm, cool and collected. This description is actually a description of their shock state. For example, let's look at the Columbine, Colorado, school shooters. It is now a well-known fact that they watched the movie *Natural Born Killers* over one hundred times before actually committing their horrendous crimes. What the general public often asks is, "Can violence from computer games, television or movies influence violent behavior?" From the point of view of trauma treatment, the answer is yes. If we look at the low blink rate of people in a trance state, we learn that while staring at a screen, such as a television, movie screen or computer monitor, the watcher goes into a trance state and is highly open to suggestion.

Now, that doesn't mean that every person who watches *Natural Born Killers* will become a school shooter. But after watching the movie repeatedly, combined with a specific set of psychological dysfunctions including childhood trauma, bullying and rejection, the watcher can go into a parasympathetic shock state of numbness. This can be especially dangerous when combined with drinking or taking drugs and having access to weapons. The on-screen violence is not the cause of violence—owning a gun is also not the cause—but these are the ingredients in a dangerous cocktail of events and states of dissociation that certainly contribute to the violence. The more that the general public as well as treatment specialists understand shock states stemming from early childhood trauma, the more we can prevent the devastating violence we are experiencing in our society.

A more recent example is the Sandy Hook Elementary School shooting in Newtown, Massachusetts. Adam Lanza shot a total of twenty-six people, including twenty children. Lanza shot himself in the head as first responders arrived. It is still unknown why Lanza committed this heinous act. What shock or trauma existed in Lanza's life to cause this result?

Another common state of shock which contributes to school violence is the rise in bullying. Public figures and school officials often scratch their heads trying to understand why there is such widespread harassment in our schools. Bullying is often perpetrated by students in a group upon another student who is different in some way from them. The bullied student may be new to the school, may be an outstanding student or have some physical characteristic the others don't understand. There is a particularly disturbing case of a young, very intelligent student who was found by her mother hanging in her closet. She had committed suicide after silently tolerating years of teasing, shaming and threats by a clique of other students.

These bullies often learn this behavior in their own families. They may have grown up with a parent who shames them, frequently using extreme discipline as a way to control and dominate them. Children in these families often are living in a shock state, continually fearful about when the next traumatic, abusive and shaming event will occur. The unpredictability of abuse-disguised-as-discipline is often a factor in the depth of the shock states that this young bully-in-training experiences. Bullying is a learned behavior and typically is perpetrated on someone younger and less powerful. Bullying becomes embedded in the shock state of each member of the family when an abusive event occurs in the family, such as when the raging father, dissatisfied with a meal, overturns the kitchen table. This behavior becomes an ingrained pattern in the suggestive minds of young children, only to be repeated on others younger or more vulnerable than they are.

SUICIDE BY A YOUNG, DISGRUNTLED EMPLOYEE

A large electronics store had recently fired a young man who they felt was not doing his job properly. This young man had falsified his employment record and his supervisor had reported that they were receiving customer complaints about him giving poor service and not having the knowledge to recommend the correct products for them.

On Friday, at the end of work, the supervisor handed the man a pink slip and told him to pick up his check and that there was no need to return on Monday. The young man was distraught and terrified to tell his poverty-stricken family that he had been fired. He went home, found his father's gun and shot himself in the head. The family came home and went into shock to discover him laying in a pool of blood in the garage with the gun by his side. The shock of this completely unexpected suicide resounded throughout the neighborhood and ultimately traveled back to his former place of employment.

This firing and resulting suicide triggered rage and anger by other employees toward the lady who fired the young man and toward the company. A band of employees began to leave threatening notes on her desk, writing ugly messages on the mirrors in the bathrooms and ultimately leading to a knife fight one evening in the parking lot.

Shock is, as we have mentioned, contagious. The shock of his unexpected firing and, even more devastating, this young man's suicide, fanned the flames of previous grievances for some employees. Many of the employees took the firing as if it had been done to them. Shock causes people to become numb to their real emotions and subject to the contagion of fear and panic, and losing access to their rational minds.

MEDICAL FIRST RESPONDERS

It is important to remember about first responders that the stressors which they report as the most stressful happen relatively often. A large-scale study of emergency medical service (EMS) personnel in 2013 revealed that rather than large-scale, dramatic events, responders report the most stress from seeing someone die or someone who was recently deceased, encountering an individual who had been badly beaten, responding to a traumatic event where they discover someone personally known to the responder or making a death notification to a family. What we, the public, would consider a relatively commonplace occurrence actually has a more shocking impact on responders than some dramatic or unusual event. There is a danger in the cumulative nature of what most people consider "routine" stresses as much as the overly dramatic large-scale events such as a tornado or terrorist attack.[2]

An example of this is an oncologist (cancer doctor) who sees and has to tell women on a daily basis that they have some type of breast, ovarian or other cancer that is threatening their lives. Physicians have to be the bearers of this horrifying news so often that many become numb to what the patient may be feeling. We recently had as our client a physician who went into full-blown depression, couldn't work and began using narcotics that he had stolen from the patient supply.

As he was being interviewed, he finally broke down to say that his wife had recently been diagnosed with incurable ovarian cancer that had metastasized to her lungs. Having watched so many people deteriorate and die painful deaths from cancer, he knew what was awaiting her and their own family, who would have to go through it with her. The years and years of accumulated stress of having to diagnose deadly diseases on a daily basis and then be the bearer of this horrifying news suddenly took him over and his undiagnosed, untreated PTSD became C-PTSD.

A YOUNG NURSE DISCOVERS A SUICIDE ON HER WATCH

Fran, a young nurse, was working in a hospital. She was recently out of school and very idealistic about how her degree in nursing would give her the skills to help so many. She walked into a patient's room and discovered her female patient hanging from a sheet she had tied around her neck and flung over a door in an obvious suicide. The patient was foaming from the mouth, turning purple, eyes bulging. Fran immediately went into parasympathetic shock, at first just standing there in disbelief, frozen and unable to call for help.

After a few moments, panic hit her and the numbness of parasympathetic shock quickly turned to the frantic activity of sympathetic shock. She ran out of the room and down the hall screaming, in search of help. This shock caused panic and others began running down to the room to view the deceased patient. Remember that shock, often turning into panic in its sympathetic form, is contagious and debilitating. She was in a complete state of cycling back and forth between being frozen, unable to think and not knowing what to do, and then turning to the frantic, non-productive behavior of rushing around screaming for help, like the proverbial chicken. In this state of shock, young Fran was useless and was experiencing complete confusion and internal chaos.

Her next experience was probably the most debilitating and shocking to her. The police were called to the scene and they began to interview young Fran. This seemed to go on forever and Fran found herself going deeper and deeper into shock. Then, when she finally felt she was finished, officials from the human resources department of the hospital arrived and continued questioning her for over an hour. The way she was being interrogated, she began to feel like they were going to somehow try to pin the blame on her! The hospital officials were so afraid of a lawsuit by the family that Fran feared she would be blamed and fired. This is what we call *secondary trauma* and it certainly makes it more difficult to heal.

After Fran and the other hospital workers were allowed to take the client down (they had to leave her body hanging there for hours so that the police and HR could review all the evidence), Fran helped clean up the room and tried to get things back in order. They were told to make it look as if nothing had happened and were silenced as far as talking to anyone about the incident.

At that point, all the attention turned to the suicide and how hospital officials were going to handle the situation. The really shocking part of this tragedy is that, as in most cases like this, there was little or no treatment given to the first responders, the young nurse or all the other staff who had to view the shocking scene of the hanged woman for hours as they were all being investigated. Fran finished out her day and was never asked how she was feeling or what she may have needed.

As our young nurse left the hospital for the day, she continued to be in a deep state of shock and dissociation. She attempted to complete her normal routine of going to the grocery store to pick up some things for dinner. As she entered the grocery store, everything felt surreal to her. She even wondered for a moment if she was in the right store. She wandered through the aisles, unable to choose anything or make a decision about even the simplest items to purchase. She found herself confused and numb and finally just got in her car and drove home.

Once she was there, she did not know how she got there and wasn't sure what to do next. She turned on the television, sat down in a chair and just stared at it for several hours. Suddenly she began to cry and remembered the scene of her patient's horrible suicide. Fran got up the next morning with a terrible headache after having a fitful night's sleep, tossing and turning, interspersed with horrible images akin to nightmares. In general, caretakers do not think of themselves as the ones who need treatment and so they don't tell anyone and certainly don't think to ask for help for themselves. They have gone to school and gained employment to be the helpers and to learn how to care for others in need.

BANK ROBBERY

Our critical incident workers were recently called out by a large bank that was robbed by a masked gang wielding AK-47s. Several of them held the tellers at gunpoint, demanding their money, while other gang members forced the remaining employees to the floor with guns to their heads. Some of the bank employees were crying frantically and begging for their lives, clearly in sympathetic shock. The tellers seemed to be numb, in parasympathetic shock, robotically following directions, barely breathing, with shock-eyed stares.

When the whole event was over, several of the employees became hysterical, shaking and crying. Others were walking around like zombies, frozen in terror. When something so traumatic occurs in a workplace, just as in families, there typically are very few resources after the shocking events occur.

And just as in many of our dysfunctional families, many workplace traumas go unrecognized and untreated. People may just be sent home, expected to come back the next day and continue as if nothing had happened. Or they may be expected to participate in a "cover-up story" to prevent the company from being sued. However, this bank was wise enough to bring in a critical incident trauma team to help heal the shock, break through the terror and begin the healing process.

FIRST RESPONDERS

Some of the most difficult groups to work with are police and firefighters. These first responders are called into the most dangerous and threatening situations on a daily basis. These men and women are trained to be tough and to literally walk through fire. They are trained rescuers and they have been taught to ignore their own feelings and focus on the victims, the *other* victims. Usually they do not see themselves as victims needing treatment: they are frozen with shock in the position of saving the lives of others.

Statistics show that first responders have an extremely high rate of domestic violence, divorce, drug and alcohol abuse and depression. These workers often live with their C-PTSD symptoms for years, which can lead to any of these emotional problems. And yet, because of their professional pride, they often do not accept treatment, let alone seek it of their own accord. They expect of themselves just what their fire and police department supervisors expect of them, that is, to "just suck it up and continue on." They have been trained to be stoic and tough. They do not realize the amount of shock that they are in on a daily basis, since the shock actually serves to protect them from experiencing the horror of what they see.

FIREFIGHTERS

Our critical incident workers often report that it is the police and fire department first responders who refuse their services after severely traumatic and shocking experiences. Just as in the armed services, these people experience highly traumatic events on a daily basis. They see this as their job, their responsibility and what they have been trained to do. Take, for example, the highly-trained firefighters.

One team that we recently worked with was called to a burning school building with hundreds of terrified children and teachers. The children were screaming and crying and the firemen had to carry them out from dangerously hot corners of the building. While doing that, several burning rafters fell right in front of one firefighter, blocking his access to the nearest door. Another rafter fell directly onto one of his co-workers attempting to carry another child out of the building. The first firefighter described being stuck with having to make a terrible decision in this state of shock. "Do I continue down these stairs and rescue this boy in my arms or do I stop, risk his and my life and try to remove the burning rafter which is trapping a co-worker and another child?" He chose to continue down the stairs to bring the child directly to a waiting ambulance.

The firefighter accepted the help of our critical incident workers. He reported that he got the child in his arms into the ambulance and then ran back to try to save his co-worker and the other child, trapped under the fallen rafter. By that time it was too late: that part of the building was engulfed in flames. He has continued to be in a state of shock, reporting anxiety, depression and terrible guilt about not being able to save the others. He told his therapist that after the burning school and the loss of over twenty-five children, many of his friends are experiencing extreme symptoms such as nightmares, inability to sleep and severe anxiety. Many of them talk about the fact that their marriages are falling apart, since his friends refuse to talk about the horrors they witnessed that day and they tend to treat their own shock and pain by spending more and more time at a bar.

During an event such as this, a young, inexperienced firefighter may go into a state of sympathetic shock, frantically running in and out of a building, attempting to rescue more people than is humanly possible. A more experienced firefighter may go into parasympathetic shock, numb, unfeeling and robotically carrying out the children he can realistically reach. The shock in both cases serves an important purpose, which is to get the job done without falling to pieces emotionally. The problem again is that the firefighter then either goes out to a bar, using drinking as a way to deal with his internalized stress, or perhaps goes home and takes out his feelings on his family through aggression (sympathetic shock) or withdrawal (parasympathetic shock).

911 OPERATORS

There was a recent, horrifying case of a young mother calling 911 to report that her husband had taken some drug that put him into a hysterical, psychotic state. He was pointing a gun at her, shouting that he was going to kill her and the children. This was happening as she was speaking to the 911 operator who could hear the manic threats of the disturbed husband through the telephone. Many of us have listened to 911 calls where the caller is frantically reporting a critical incident such as a heart attack, a murder or a natural disaster. The caller is usually screaming, "Hurry, hurry!" and the 911 operator is often methodically asking questions such as what is your address, where is the victim now, etc. This question-asking is actually a calming technique, used to attempt to keep the caller engaged in simple conversation while help is on the way. It is an attempt to provide first aid for the caller's shock so that the caller doesn't also become a victim of whatever is happening on the other end of the line.

In this Colorado case, however, the 911 operator was particularly inexperienced in handling domestic violence and sank into shock herself as she heard the frantic voice of the woman with a gun held to her head by the ranting, crazy husband. The operator went into parasympathetic shock and froze. She could hardly speak and couldn't remember what she was supposed to do in this type of emergency. Due to her inability to get help on the way immediately, it took twenty-three minutes for the police to arrive. The young wife was already dead but it was the 911 operator who needed treatment. Instead, she was under investigation and ended up having a total nervous breakdown.

What is a nervous breakdown? It is the body rapidly cycling between sympathetic and parasympathetic shock and ultimately becoming trapped in the shock state. They usually are unable to remember what happened during the traumatic event. This shock becomes locked in the body and may often create physical symptoms such as backaches, headaches, nausea or myriad other symptoms. We call these *body memories* and we use these body memories in our process of releasing shock from the body.

SERIOUS ACCIDENT

Shock is the body's natural response to trauma, threat or any sudden and unexpected event. Most of us have had the experience of being in a car accident. The almost universal reaction is that time slows down—one experiences the action as if one step removed from it, from the point of view of witnessing the crash, almost emotionless. That response is highly adaptive because it allows one to make rational choices rather than automatically react out of emotion (such as panic, terror, guilt or regret). The "normal" experience is for the shock response to dissipate within a few minutes once the immediate event has played itself out and the person has survived. The problem develops when that shock response flows into an already existing shock pool and then higher levels of shock become an individual's "new normal."

An instance of how shock protects the individual in a traumatic accident occurred recently to a forty-three-year-old woman whose car crashed and was launched over an embankment with her in it. Her head hit the windshield, rendering her unconscious, and the car tumbled down into a ravine, eighty feet below. Hidden from the road and without witnesses, she was trapped in her mangled car.

At first she remembered trying to find her cellphone but then she went into shock and couldn't remember anything after that. She was found five days later and rushed to the hospital. When she came back to consciousness, she described remembering the crash and her car tumbling down the embankment. She says she was in and out of consciousness over those five days but really had no memory of what happened during that time period. After examining her, the doctors said she had had only about eight more hours to live in the car before she would have died from exposure. As it is she will need to have both feet amputated as a result of her injuries. The shock state probably saved her from complete panic until she was discovered by a Colorado highway patrol officer.[3]

VICTIMS OF CRIME

We see this pattern, for example, after an act of unspeakable violence, such as a random public shooting or a terrorist attack. Almost always, the perpetrator of such an act is in a shock state: eyes fixed and vacant, emotionless to the point of appearing calm, acting robot-like as if on autopilot. Many of the people affected by the incident go into a state of shock, which would be expected. But we know that many of these individuals will need post-incident counseling to cope with the lingering effects of the trauma, experienced both emotionally and physiologically. The shock response has become that individual's "new normal." If this new level of autonomic activation is short-lived, if these or other mental disruptions continue for a minimum of two days to up to four weeks within a month of the trauma, we diagnose the condition as *Acute Stress Response (ASR)*. If it lingers on for over a month and seems to get more intense and more debilitating, we diagnose the condition as Post-Traumatic Stress Disorder (PTSD). Some recognizable symptoms of PTSD are sleeping disorders and/or continued nightmares, constant flashbacks or intrusive thoughts.

The individual suffering from PTSD often experiences an increasing amount of tension which doesn't dissipate but actually increases daily. They begin to develop fears that perhaps they didn't have before and increased anxiety on a daily basis. Often, because of the numbing effect of shock, the individuals themselves do not recognize that the symptoms are increasing. Family members, co-workers and friends will often report that a person seems unusually irritable and has extreme outbursts of anger. These friends may even become scared or intimidated to the point that they will no longer want to say anything about the noticeable increase of PTSD symptoms.

Close family members notice the lack of responsiveness or lack of involvement in activities that were previously fulfilling to their family member. They can feel him or her pulling away emotionally from the external world as well as from the people who were previously part of his or her support system. Partners notice decreased sexual desire and a turning away from any type of intimate contact. These prolonged feelings of detachment tend to push the very people that the PTSD victim needs further and further away. It is as if they are developing a cocoon around themselves, with the walls getting thicker on a daily basis. Another disturbance is that, in this state of chronic stress, the individual tends to experience increased loss of memory.

If the under or over-activation of the nervous system continues and becomes habitual, we then diagnose the condition as shock or Complex Post-Traumatic Stress Disorder (C-PTSD).

The National Center for Victims of Crime discusses how crime victims may react to trauma: either physical and/or emotional.[4] One form that the victim's reaction to trauma can take is *shock or numbness*: Victims may feel "frozen" and cut off from their own emotions, disoriented. Some victims say they feel as if they are "watching a movie" rather than having their own experiences. This sense of unreality is a double-edged sword. On one hand, it protects the victim from fully realizing the horrific thing that has happened to him or her. A family that was recently invaded by attackers was made to watch the other family members being tortured and killed, one by one. This experience was so horrific that the numbness of the shock provided a much-needed protection from the horror of the event. However, years later, if this goes untreated, the protection turns into deeply embedded depression and may even lead to suicide attempts on the part of remaining family members.

When shock goes untreated, the victims lose control, feel vulnerable, lonely and confused; the sense of self becomes invalidated, and they may not be able to make decisions or conduct their lives with any semblance of normalcy.

As the shock penetrates deeper into the energetic field of these survivors, they often turn to another form of protection which is *denial, disbelief and anger*: Victims may experience denial, which is an unconscious defense against painful or unbearable memories and feelings about the crime. Or they may experience disbelief, telling themselves, "This just could not have happened to me!" They may feel intense anger and a desire to get even with the offender. The first form (shock or numbness) we identify as parasympathetic shock and the second (denial, disbelief and anger) as sympathetic shock.

Victims of crime typically have some or all of these responses:

- fear that they are losing control over their lives
- trouble concentrating, as though they cannot keep their minds on what they are doing
- negative self-image, fueled by self-doubt, guilt and shame
- depression, a sense of sadness, feeling "down," hopelessness and despair
- disrupted relationships, due in part to the withdrawn behavior that frequently accompanies sadness and depression
- trying to control or avoid the fear response itself, going to great lengths to avoid people, places, things or situations which remind them of the event[5]

These reactions are normal and natural. They may serve a healthy purpose as long as they remain temporary: to protect the person from an overwhelming or unbearable reaction to what has happened to them. However, if these reactions continue on for months or years, the toll on one's physical health, productivity, self-image and relationships is enormous. The key is the last item on the list just presented: the individual is unconsciously trying to avoid the pain of the source trauma. And his or her body, the nervous system itself, has been recruited to enforce the avoidance.

Toni, a young woman with whom we worked, was home alone one night, studying for her college exam in art history. She was a gifted artist, poet and a creative writer working on her Master's degree. Toni heard a rumbling in the kitchen and went to investigate. She suddenly found herself in the middle of a home invasion where four masked gunmen were rifling through the family possessions and pointing their guns at her. She began screaming, at which point one of them grabbed her, shoved a dishtowel into her mouth and blindfolded her. Then he tied her hands behind her back, kicked her and forced her to the floor.

Toni went into an extreme state of shock, became numb and didn't remember anything after that. After they left, she finally made her way to the phone to call 911 and then she collapsed again into nothingness. Later on she realized that she had also been raped but had no recollection of it. Again, this is the benefit of the shock state that protected her from the terror of the experience of being raped and the horror of being completely powerless to stop these thieves from stealing some precious and valuable family possessions.

For many months afterwards, she continued to have nightmares regularly and was unable to sleep without sleeping pills. Toni experienced all the symptoms just described and labeled as C-PTSD. She was referred to traditional victim counseling but soon discovered that talking about it seemed to have little value for her. This talk therapy could not even begin to touch the serious symptoms that continued to increase on a daily basis. The only answer anyone seemed to have for her was more medication. She did not want medication, which she realized was only serving to increase her numbness and completely destroying the access she always had to her creativity. She found that she could no longer write, which just increased her depression and her anger.

It wasn't until she was referred to hypnotherapy and diagnosed correctly that she began the road to recovery. She was educated about shock resulting from the home invasion and given direct therapy to release that shock from her body. This therapy, because it works on the unconscious level, can reach down into the actual place where these traumatic memories are stored and slowly release the shock patterns from her physiology—always accompanied by protective resources. She now has been able to reclaim her sense of inner safety as well as her creative gifts and talents without any medication.

VICTIMS OF SEXUAL ASSAULT

Rape victims provide another clear example of how the body has a mind of its own in dealing with trauma. Rape Trauma Syndrome (RTS) is the psychological trauma experienced by a rape victim, including disruptions to normal physical, emotional, cognitive and interpersonal behavior.[6] Physiological reactions include tension headaches, depression, fatigue, general feelings of soreness and specific symptoms that relate to the area of the body assaulted. Survivors of oral rape may have a variety of mouth and throat complaints, while survivors of vaginal or anal rape have physical reactions related to these areas.

RTS identifies three stages of psychological trauma a rape survivor goes through: the acute stage, the outer adjustment stage and the renormalization stage. The acute stage symptoms may last a few days to a few weeks and may overlap with the outward adjustment stage. The U.S. Rape Abuse and Incest National Network asserts that, in most cases, a rape victim's acute stage can be classified as one of three responses: *expressed* (He or she may appear agitated or hysterical, and may suffer from crying spells or anxiety attacks.), *controlled* (The survivor appears to be without emotion and acts as if "nothing happened" and "everything is fine.") or *shock/disbelief* (The survivor reacts with a strong sense of disorientation. They may have difficulty concentrating, making decisions or doing everyday tasks. They may also have poor recall of the assault.). Not all rape survivors show their emotions outwardly. Some may appear calm and unaffected by the assault, which is the result of the parasympathetic shock that has set in. When this happens, friends, family members and even many uninformed treatment specialists deduce that the victim has handled it and is over it. This is certainly not the case.

Survivors in the outer adjustment stage, which may last from several months to many years after a rape, seem to have resumed their normal lifestyle. However, they simultaneously suffer profound internal turmoil, which may manifest in a variety of ways:

- Minimization (pretends "everything is fine"): They may say things like, "I'm over that" or "Don't worry, I've got a handle on it." This is parasympathetic shock.
- Dramatization (cannot stop talking about the assault): This form of sympathetic shock causes the victim to endlessly cycle through the Victim Drama Triangle.[7]
- Suppression (refuses to discuss the rape): This is also a form of shock.
- Explanation (analyzes what happened): This is consistent with parasympathetic shock, where they are numb and maintain that numbness by remaining in their heads.
- Flight (moves to a new home or city, alters appearance): This is complete denial, which locks these memories in the body and often results in prolonged and chronic physical illnesses, often cancer in the area of the body that was assaulted.

Victims who attempt to return to their lives as if nothing happened are pushing the experience and their response to it underground. The underground stage may last for years with the victim seemingly "over it," despite the fact that the emotional issues are not resolved. This is an outer adjustment, indeed.

During renormalization, the survivor integrates the sexual assault into his or her life so that the rape is no longer the central focus of the person's existence, negative feelings such as guilt and shame are resolved and the survivor no longer blames him/herself for the attack. This so-called renormalization, however, does not occur on its own but, in our experience, is only the result of first treating the shock and then treating the trauma on the deep, unconscious level where all these memories are stored.

COMBAT VETERANS

There are over 2.8 million American veterans of the Iraq and Afghanistan wars (compared to 2.6 million Vietnam veterans). PTSD reportedly occurs in about 20 percent of Iraq and Afghanistan veterans, in as many as 10 percent of Gulf War (Desert Storm) veterans and in about 30 percent of Vietnam veterans. However, these symptoms are highly underreported because of the severe stigma associated in the military with any type of emotional disorder or so-called weakness. It is believed that the number of veterans with PTSD is closer to 50 percent, especially among those who have lost limbs, have brain injuries or have directly witnessed the violent death of a combat buddy.[8]

Before these PTSD patterns develop, people experience common stress reactions after a trauma. When these reactions persist for months without dissipating, they enter the realm of seriously interfering with one's ability to live one's life. According to the Veterans Administration, the common stress reactions for veterans are:

FEAR, ANXIETY OR PANIC

In moments of danger, our bodies prepare to fight our enemy, flee the situation or freeze in the hope that the danger will move past us. But those feelings of hyper-alertness often remain long after the danger has passed. Veterans often feel tense or afraid, becoming agitated and jumpy and feeling on high alert. This often becomes a dangerous situation when a veteran, having returned home, is facing a situation that triggers a war memory. For example, the CBS News program *48 Hours* related a story titled, "War Damaged Vet Kills Girlfriend; Is PTSD to Blame?" in July 2012. An Iraq War veteran named John Needham, after serving more than a year in Iraq, came home shattered physically and emotionally. He'd been diagnosed with PTSD: he was edgy, had mood swings and flashbacks. To make matters worse, he had severe back pain from combat injuries and was prescribed a fistful of drugs which he often downed with alcohol. One night he beat his girlfriend to death in a jealous rage. When the police arrived at the scene, John was naked, crying and smeared in blood. He said, "Unfortunately, with the way I was trained, you know, to react to threats is to neutralize threats. Even with someone I love. I was trained to kill. I came home. I can't adjust to (a) regular civilian lifestyle." Needham continued, "I spun out of control. I needed help."[9]

SADNESS, DEEP GRIEF OR DEPRESSION

Sadness after a trauma may come from a sense of loss—of a loved one, of trust in the world, of spiritual faith or loss of a previous way of life. Veterans often experience having crying spells, losing interest in things they used to enjoy and just wanting to withdraw from most social activities. This is difficult on their families who, having looked forward to their homecoming for several years, now have high expectations of their return to family life. When returning veterans come home with their heads filled with scenes of fighting, friends dying in their arms and gunshots ringing in their ears, it is difficult to go to a family or social function and make small talk. They experience that others have no idea what they have gone through, which contributes to their feeling alone and isolated. These common PTSD symptoms continue to drain them, causing them also to experience feeling exhausted, empty and numb. These symptoms, when left untreated, plunge the returning veteran into shock, which then results in further family disconnection, often leading to divorce.

SURVIVOR'S GUILT AND SHAME

Returning war veterans often feel survivor's guilt that they did not do more to prevent the loss of a buddy. In reality, they most probably did all they could do in the moment. Others may feel ashamed, because during the trauma they acted in ways that they would not otherwise have done. Reports of veterans returning from Vietnam document severe guilt due to remem-bering burning down a village that they thought was filled with the enemy only to discover later that it was occupied by women and children. These veterans are plagued with such deep shame and guilt that their PTSD symptoms often have led to homelessness, social isolation and suicide.

ANGER, IRRITABILITY AND RAGE

Anger often results from feeling that you have been unfairly treated. Anger begins to fester within the mind, typically turns into rage and then, if not released in a healthy manner, is stored in the body, which very often can turn into disease. Veterans may lash out at their partners or spouses, have less patience with their children or overreact to minor misunderstandings.

We were treating a middle-aged man named Mack, who had been in Vietnam when he was younger. This man was having difficulty in his relation-ships with others, because he had a very bad temper and a very short fuse. He had been fired from several jobs. Even though his work skills were great, his inability to get along with others, especially those in authority, was haunting him. He would often get into conflicts with his superiors and was especially vindictive about following instructions, especially if he didn't agree about how a project should be completed. He would mostly undermine projects that were not his idea.

He was working as a carpenter where he was asked to build steps with a banister for the elderly people to hold on to. He did not feel that that particular staircase needed a banister but did not say that directly. He pretended that he was going to add it on at the completion of the staircase. When that didn't happen, he gave another excuse and another promised date of completion. Finally, after several obviously rebellious attempts to undermine what his superior was asking him to do, his employer fired him and asked him to go get psychological treatment. Since he had lost several jobs due to similar conflicts with authority, Mack acquiesced to getting some counseling to deal with his simmering anger, always just below the surface and about to boil over.

Since Mack was a Vietnam veteran, he finally yielded to the idea of going to Veterans Affairs (VA) for his treatment. He walked into the VA building where he was asked to fill out pages and pages of questionnaires, put through a myriad of interviews, waited in endless lines and got little response about when he might actually speak to someone.

As he was sitting there waiting and fuming, he suddenly burst into tears, began shaking and hid under a chair. He was screaming, "No, no, don't let him touch me again."

While this reaction was completely spontaneous, it certainly did move him up in the priority line to be seen by a psychiatrist. It turned out that Mack was having a flashback of being raped by his sergeant when he was only seventeen years of age. He had been from a very rural county in the Old South and was drawn to enlist in order to get out of there, to get an education and to see the world. This sergeant, as it turned out, had raped and sexually assaulted over forty-five young enlisted men during that time period. He told them that if they told, he would kill them and they would never see their families again.

After this experience, Mack went into a deep depression and suffered intense periods of raging outbursts and then deep, grief-filled periods, crying for days on end. He felt this would never end until he met a therapist who, by using hypnotherapy to release Mack's rage, helped to treat his shock and release the memories that had been trapped inside of him for over forty years. Finally the loving man who he truly was began to emerge after years of being plagued by all of this heavy trauma, shock and rage that had been held inside of him for so long.

BEHAVIOR CHANGES, ACTING IN UNHEALTHY WAYS

The returning veteran may drink, use drugs, smoke too much, drive aggressively, neglect his/her health or avoid certain people or situations.

The VA defines four types of PTSD symptoms for combat veterans. One is reliving or re-experiencing the event. Memories of the trauma can come back at any time and in different ways. You may feel the same fear and horror as when the event took place. You may have nightmares or feel like you're going through it again. All these symptoms are called flashbacks. Often there is a trigger—a sight or sound that causes you to relive the event, like seeing someone who reminds you of the abuser or of trauma experienced during combat. In the example above, going into the VA hospital and experiencing the overwhelming demands of authorities triggered a flashback for this man. It is important to recognize what triggers flashbacks since they are locked in the body and are often not controlled by the conscious mind. Deep states of shock act like an iceberg to encapsulate the devastating experiences so they don't destroy us. The icebergs are floating around in our unconscious mind in a desperate attempt to protect us from the memories within, until we are in the presence of someone who has healed their own shock and so is fully prepared to sit with us as we release our shock and shame.

A flashback is most common for a vet when he hears an explosion or a car backfiring. Suddenly that vet may be catapulted right back onto the battlefield and he may drop for cover or search for his weapon even though he may just be sitting at a fast food restaurant in the middle of the city. Thankfully, the shock serves to freeze these triggers until we are mature enough to face them and heal them, until we are with someone who can recognize the shock states and help us to heal them at our own pace.

Another type of PTSD symptom is avoiding situations that remind you of the event. You may try to avoid situations or people that trigger memories of the trauma. You may even avoid talking or thinking about the event. For example, you may avoid crowds because they feel dangerous; if you were in a car accident or if your military convoy was bombed, you may avoid driving; some people may keep very busy or avoid seeking help to keep them from having to think or talk about the event.

Another symptom is called a *body memory*. This sometimes amazing phenomenon is again best treated where it is stored and that is in the depths of the unconscious mind. The body can hold experiences the mind is unable to remember. Often the memory may be too traumatic to remember, especially if one is young or in danger of being re-abused. The shock has a way of storing the memories directly in our cells, bypassing the conscious thought process.

An example of this is a young veteran named Carl who had a nervous breakdown after returning home from service in Iraq. Since his return, when he was under stress, his mother would tell him she noticed a red ring around his neck. He was able to notice it in the mirror and then it would fade away. He recognized other symptoms which revolved around his neck which had plagued him in stressful situations in Iraq. He had sore throats, coughing spells, and one time even painful sores on the inside of his throat. Now he was attending PTSD therapy and reported this to his therapist. She was familiar with the concept of body memories, so she chose to use hypnotherapy with him to get to the source of these symptoms. After inducing trance, she asked him to go back to the memories connected with this throat discomfort.

He returned to a memory of being a young child who was left with baby-sitters quite often when his parents worked. There was a particular teenage babysitter who often bought her boyfriend over. The memory that emerged was a night when the babysitter's boyfriend acted like they were playing a game of hide and seek. He told Carl they had to tie him to a tree so he couldn't look for them until they were ready. He tied young Carl with rope around his neck and body and said he should count up to one hundred so they had time to hide. They said that when he reached one hundred he could untie the rope to come look for them. He would be given an ice cream cone when he found them.

When poor young Carl finally counted to 100, he discovered he could not untie the rope and he was left there, tied to the tree, for several hours while the teenage babysitters went out to a party. He reported having blanked out and doesn't remember them ever coming back or what happened after that.

He had almost completely forgotten about this until the red rings, the body memories, returned during times of stress. It was only during the hyp-notherapy process that he could reduce his shock level down to where he was able to allow these painful memories to come back to him.

Once these memories were recovered and his shock was treated, he recalled scene by scene what happened after that. In the trance state and through the "magic" of imagination, this young child was able to take back his power by mentally releasing the ropes, expressing his feelings to these teens and bringing healing energy to his throat. The symptoms have not returned.

The way you think about yourself and others changes because of trauma. This symptom has many aspects, including staying away from relationships, forgetting about parts of the traumatic event or not being able to talk about them, thinking the world is completely dangerous and that no one can be trusted.

The fourth type of PTSD symptom is feeling keyed up (called *hyperarousal*), being jittery or always on the alert and on the lookout for danger. You might suddenly become angry or irritable. You may want to have your back to a wall in a restaurant or waiting room. A loud noise can startle you easily. If someone bumps into you, you might fly into a rage.

The good news is that all of these symptoms can be treated effectively. A fascinating study (Yarvis, 2008) showed good results in treating PTSD in American soldiers at a combat support hospital in Baghdad, Iraq. Treatment with Heart-Centered Hypnotherapy, compared to cognitive behavioral therapy and critical incidence stress debriefings, showed hypnotherapy to be a most effective means of treating PTSD.[10]

TRAUMATIC LOSS AND GRIEF

Regardless of the nature of the loss itself, the loss of someone we love is usually experienced as a trauma. A shock grief response is more common in those experiencing the loss of a child or loved ones lost in natural disasters, through violence, suicide or homicide. In these situations, grief may become *complicated grief disorder* (included in the new DSM-5). Prominent among the symptoms of complicated grief disorder is a persistent feeling of shock, feeling stunned, dazed or emotionally numb since the death.

One of the greatest traumas imaginable is for parents to have to deal with the death of a child. A child's death is especially traumatic, because it is in violation of the usual order of things in which the child is expected to outlive the parents. The emotional blow associated with child loss can lead to depression, anxiety, marital problems, pain and guilt. All of these issues may lead to complicated grief disorder which can include many symptoms similar to posttraumatic stress disorder.[11]

The other side of complicated grief disorder is just as traumatic and that is a young child or children losing a parent, especially a mother. One of our clients recently came in for hypnotherapy with her presenting issue being general pain in her body. She had gone to doctors who just kept prescribing more medication with no real relief. Because of this, she finally contacted a therapist. She described the pain as often moving from one area to another with no specific illness or disorder found by the medical community. She also described feeling numb, losing her interest in most things she previously enjoyed and generally wanting to withdraw from social interactions. When people have physical discomfort, they usually go to a doctor rather than a therapist. Many doctors have historically described this type of pain as psychosomatic and labeled the patient as a "hypochondriac" which colloquially has come to mean, "it's all in her head." Doctors often give these patients sugar pills, telling them it will cure their symptoms, or they prescribe all sorts of antidepressants, selective serotonin reuptake inhibitors (SSRIs) and pain pills. There are two main problems with this form of so-called "treatment." Not only do these drugs not treat the shock, but they actually serve to lock down the shock symptoms and insure that sufferers remain numb with no access to their feelings, their creativity, or their sexual expression (antidepressant drugs tend to inhibit sexual function). Secondly, many people become addicted to these drugs, especially the pain pills, and then physicians want to refuse to prescribe them. Antidepressants, once prescribed, tend to be used long-term with little re-evaluation. The worst aspect of this common practice of prescribing drugs to treat shock symptoms is that the shock does not get addressed or treated so that patients can reclaim their feelings, creativity and healthy sexuality.

Our client is desperate to heal her pain but, because it keeps moving from one area to another, it is like a moving target. She is beginning to believe her doctors, who say that she is making it up, but then it intensifies again and she becomes more frantic about what to do. She finally sought the help of one of our Heart-Centered Hypnotherapists.

This client and her pain are both very difficult to pin down. She is described by her hypnotherapist as someone who stays in her mind and remains in control of herself and the therapy in this way. We advised her therapist to bypass the conscious mind by just beginning to ask to speak directly to the little child that may have all this pain.

As she regressed to a six-year-old girl in a room with her mother, she began crying uncontrollably. When her crying seemed overwhelming, we brought her into an imaginary safe room for a few moments and invited her to bring in her favorite doll from that period of time. The doll became her resource state, her safety net, and was there to comfort her when no one else was. When she felt calmed down and safe enough, we asked her to return to the room where her mother was. She later clarified that it was not her mother's bedroom, but actually was the cold hard floor of a bathroom, next to the toilet. There was an awful smell of vomit engulfing her memory, which tells us that she was actually regressed and physically experiencing what the child did that day.

In frequent returns to this scene of her extreme discomfort, it became obvious that the little girl's mother had died by committing suicide right in front of her. The mother, seemingly distraught by her own suffering, overdosed on sleeping pills combined with alcohol and other drugs. The little girl attempted to wake her mother for hours until she saw this "horrible stuff" coming out of her mother's nose and mouth. She then ran outside screaming to the neighbors' house to get some help. The neighbor herself went into shock and began to scream uncontrollably when she saw the dead mother on the bathroom floor. Chaos ensued as the police and ambulance were finally called and other neighbors began to appear. At that point, attention was directed to the deceased mother. The small girl was not only terrified, confused and grief-stricken, but also horribly abandoned in her greatest time of need.

She quietly disappeared into her bedroom, grabbed her doll and hid under her bed. She remained there, numb and in shock, for many hours until someone finally came looking for her. This last memory of her mother looking grey with horrible stuff coming out of her mouth and nose and the pervasive smell of vomit was indelibly imprinted onto her unconscious memory bank. She spent most of her life shifting back and forth between parasympathetic shock, completely numb and totally in her head, and sympathetic shock, frantically searching for some professional person to heal her physical pain.

Complicated grief disorder designates those who are significantly and functionally impaired by prolonged grief symptoms for at least one month after six months of bereavement. Studies show that most people are able to integrate bereavement into their lives within six months of the loss.[12] Factors in the survivor's life that may contribute to a more complicated grief response that continues longer are: how sudden the death was, with no time to prepare for it emotionally; how preventable the survivor believes the death to have been, whether they feel that they could have or should have prevented the death, a very common experience; how rigid and restricted the social roles of the bereaved are, that is, when mom identified herself as mother to the exclusion of other roles in life, the more intense the grief of losing her child.

We must be cautious, however, in prescribing a time period that is "normal" or "healthy" to complete one's grieving. In some ways it is never-ending.

The important question is whether the complications of the grief response are interfering with the survivor's ability to continue living a full, rich life. We don't want to add to the stress of someone who is grieving a traumatic loss by fueling their guilt or shame in not "moving on" fast enough. Most workplaces give people a three-day leave for grieving a loss and expect them to return and be over it.

A deep grief response that is one of the most complicated and least addressed in our society is loss through divorce. One of our hypnotherapy students described finally realizing that she needed to leave her husband after twenty-five years of marriage. She was surprised by the deep levels of grief that she was experiencing. She woke up crying for hours and hours, feeling like she was going to die. On one level she loved her husband, probably more as a brother than as a mate. He had a serious emotional diagnosis which caused him to be very loving, predictable and normal for several weeks and then suddenly fall into a crevasse of deep depression and overwhelming rage. When that happened she and the children ran for cover.

She lived with those mood swings for twenty-five years but the unpredictability of them destroyed her sense of safety, her peace of mind and her heartfelt longing for a consistent partnership. They may have also had detrimental and long-lasting effects on her children, who both suffer from anxiety disorders and ADHD (Attention Deficit Hyperactivity Disorder). She finally decided that she couldn't put up with her husband anymore and wanted to start her life anew. In the past, each time she contemplated leaving, her grief and guilt overtook her and she froze in a state of shock, unable to make her move. That longstanding grief actually lived in the underlying shock pool of grief in which she was drowning nearly her whole life.

Her alcoholic and philandering father left her young mother and abandoned his small children (she and her two brothers) when they were just toddlers. Her mother had no financial support and had to go out immediately and find work. Without an education, her mother could only find menial jobs. This meant that she could not afford sufficient food, rent and childcare for her three small children. They were left alone on a daily basis with our client, the only girl, relegated to the task of becoming the little mother at age six with the daily responsibility to raise her brothers, take care of the house and prepare the meals until her mother returned home. It was always her job to keep the family together and to take full responsibility for their care and feeding so her mother could work. And then she took care of her exhausted mother when she returned home from a hard day of physical labor.

So as our client was making the decision to leave her husband since her children were just about grown, she couldn't understand the deep, deep grief that she was feeling, especially since she had made this decision from a very clear place. She finally realized that it was her little girl who was carrying all of this grief that had been frozen in her shock pool from the time that her own father abandoned her family and they were not allowed to cry. Then more grief filled her shock pool that had been stored there from the loss of her normal, carefree childhood. She finally remembered one occasion of cooking dinner, as she did daily during her youth, looking out the window at the other kids riding bicycles, roller skating and laughing.

Our client finally decided to leave her husband as she unconsciously dove into the depths of her own shock pool and unknowingly retrieved the long-stored emotions she was never allowed to feel. She was grieving the loss of her current family but also the loss of her mother as well as the loss of her childhood and innocence. She invited the little girl within her to cry along with her. Together they both began to cry and to express her anger, disappointment and deep grief. She began to understand the depth of her grief and how expressing it drained the longstanding pool of shock.

NATURAL DISASTERS

Susanne Babbel wrote in *Psychology Today*: "Like many causes of trauma, natural disasters can be sudden and overwhelming. The most immediate and typical reaction to a calamity is shock, which at first manifests as numbness or denial. Quickly—or eventually—shock can give way to an overemotional state that often includes high levels of anxiety, guilt or depression."[13]

Because natural disasters are not circumscribed events with a defined endpoint, they produce two sets of psychological consequences: the actual threat effects and disruption effects. The effects—including ongoing exposure to devastation, property loss, displacement, fragmentation of families and financial stress—often last for years, having the potential to keep survivors in high states of arousal and hopelessness. Studies have shown that PTSD symptoms naturally drop by 50 percent in the first eighteen months after the disaster, even without intervention. However, between eighteen and twenty-four months post-disaster, little further decrease occurs.[14]

Chapter 12

SHOCK AND SPIRITUALITY

Up to this point, we have been focusing on the physiology of shock and how that plays out in day-to-day matters. We've also talked about the true self as well, which we're calling the soul. Now we want to speak about spirit. We feel that you can share your love with others, revealing that true self, but that the spirit is something much deeper and more personal. It is not of this world and cannot be shared here, revealed or known.

We believe that shock—the result of trauma embedded in the nervous system—affects every aspect of an individual's life, including his or her spiritual experience and practice. After all, a splintered or devastated soul leaves the individual disconnected from his or her spirit and therefore stranded in life without a "lifeline" to the Divine. Spiritual shock manifests as *spiritual numbness* (parasympathetic)—an inability to fully experience awe, reverence, ecstasy or surrender, or as *spiritual distraction* (sympathetic)—a redirection of one's spiritual energy out into the mundane world. In each case, the individual's chronic shock state serves to maintain a barrier to real, felt spiritual experiences. This forms a "spiritual nourishment barrier."

Spiritual Distraction (sympathetic shock) may take the form of:

- **"Spiritual busyness"** or filling up one's time set aside for spiritual practice with activity, pursuit, efforts to achieve *some particular* *experience*, e.g., to become the "best" meditator, yoga teacher, Christian, Buddhist, etc. ever. This distraction is one of attending to what seems to be most *urgent* spiritually but not necessarily to what is in reality most *important*.

- **"Spiritual crusades"** or fighting for a dogmatic principle or against a perceived external evil. It is often easier to identify, judge and condemn an external threat than it is to honestly face an internal one.
- **"Spiritual materialism,"** in which "we can deceive ourselves into thinking we are developing spiritually when instead we are strengthening our egocentricity through spiritual techniques."[1] This is a case of the ego driving the spiritual bus.

Spiritual Numbness (parasympathetic shock) may take the form of:

- **"Spiritual suicide,"** in which one chooses to fall asleep spiritually, to hide from the challenging existential questions of a relationship with the Divine through mindlessness and monotony.
- **"Spiritual depression,"** in which one denies anger and resentment toward God and redirects it inwardly, feeling disappointed in oneself and despondent in life. One may be confusing spirituality with dogma and religion, and one's anger is in actuality directed at religious authority.
- **"Spiritual bypass,"** in which one confuses dissociation, visions from the astral plane and the efforts of spiritual practices with a true awakening. These experiences are used instead to avoid intimacy in relationships and engaged participation in society.

AN EXAMPLE: SPIRITUAL CRUSADES

There are those people who have extremely strong opinions about spiritual matters. They seem to be on a crusade about certain areas of their own beliefs. Fred was a student who grew up attending a particular church and spent much of his time railing against it. In fact, his extreme judgments and emotional reactions have ruined several of his relationships with women whom he loved. Fred was often attracted to women who were members of his church and, when dating one, eventually ended up judging and berating her for her religious convictions. He was angry about what he felt was the hypocrisy of the church, most specifically regarding the hierarchy of its authority.

To understand this better, let's take a look at Fred's background. As a young boy, he was harshly abused by his older brother who shamed, teased, judged and severely tickled him to the point of throwing up. Fred's brother was ten years older and had been an only child until Fred came along. At first Fred tried to fight back during these abusive teasing sessions, but was certainly too little to have any effect on his older brother. He kicked and screamed (sympathetic shock) and then went into parasympathetic shock and just froze. When this happened, the older brother tickled Fred even more violently and even pulled down Fred's underpants to shame him and laugh at his genitals. The more Fred went into shock, the more this behavior escalated to the point that the brother began doing this at school in front of other kids.

Fred never felt safe in his home, especially considering the fact that his parents seemed to be completely oblivious to how his brother was physically and emotionally abusing Fred. It was as if they were complicit with the emotional torture by their silence.

Fred was also expected to attend church regularly with his older brother, who told the nuns lies in order to get them to punish Fred. Fred often went into severe states of anxiety at the thought of having to go to church, since he never knew what lies his brother was going to tell the nuns or what punishment they would then impose on him.

This pattern was the foundation of Fred's growing hatred of authority and rebellion against his church. As a child, his magical thinking was that if the ministers and nuns were God, how could they let this happen to him and not see the lies his brother was making up about him?

As an adult, Fred denounced the church of his upbringing and struggled for years with his own spirituality. He longed for a spiritual connection but couldn't find it in the old-fashioned religion with which he had grown up. So he went to India and searched for many years to find spiritual fulfillment. There he finally developed a relationship with an Indian guru but he still railed against his old church.

The meditation he learned in India gave him some peace for a time. However, later on in his life, it turned into spiritual bypass, where he spent hours meditating to avoid relationships, work and participation in society. He was living in a state of shock that protected him from the abuse he suffered as a child, but now it was separating him from his life. Inside, even though he looked peaceful when he meditated, he was still furious with his brother, the clergy and his other family members for not seeing what was happening to him as a child. In jobs, he often got into conflict with authority and soon was fired, usually feeling as if he was being victimized all over again. He was unable to quiet his mind as battles were still raging inside of him.

When he began coming to us for hypnotherapy, Fred started to put the puzzle pieces of his life together—to see how what he thought was his spiritual practice of meditation was actually a dissociative shock state that he used to avoid dealing with his internal battles. He could see that whenever his sympathetic shock was triggered, he would begin the authority conflict conversations within his mind. In an attempt to get rid of those, he would switch over to the parasympathetic shock state and try to meditate. Thus he was following the same pattern that he developed in reaction to his brother's abuse.

After resolving many of his traumatic memories and releasing his shock, Fred was much more present in his life and was able to form a fulfilling relationship with a woman and get married. He was able to reclaim his true spirituality and to truly feel peaceful. Now his meditations are filled with spirit rather than avoidance or conflict.

ANGRY AT GOD

Kathryn, a young woman with whom we have been working, has what we have discussed previously as a nourishment barrier. Kathryn came to therapy stating that whenever she felt other people (like her clients, her students, even her children) being extremely needy and demanding of her, she started eating compulsively. She stuffed herself unconsciously with whatever she could find, even though she may have just eaten a big meal. She knew enough to realize that this was emotional eating. When asked how she felt in these situations, she said "overwhelmed and numb." This is definitely a sign that shock may be involved.

When we used hypnotherapy to return to the most recent time she experienced this, she felt suffocated by the neediness of other people making demands on her time and energy. Then when we did an age regression for this feeling, she went back to her mother's womb. Her experience in the womb was that of being starved by her anorexic mother. This young mother had a terror of getting fat, as well as the shame of having others know she was pregnant since she was unmarried. So the fetus—our client Kathryn—was struggling to survive in a womb filled with cigarette toxins, alcohol and very few actual nutrients. The mother often wore tight girdles to disguise the pregnancy and to hide that she was "getting fat."

So the mother's needs were suffocating the baby. This baby in the womb felt she had to struggle to survive. The nourishment coming in through the umbilical cord was extremely toxic, filled with her mother's shame, fear and self-hatred. It was also toxic due to the cigarette smoke and the diet pills her mother was using. In the end, our client Kathryn was born two months premature, weighing only four pounds. She struggled just to stay alive for the first few months of her life. Her experience in the womb was that she was in a toxic environment and that her mother, instead of feeding her, was stealing any nutrition that was available. She was born into a state of shock where her only way to survive was to stay numb in order not to feel the pain.

Kathryn was not nursed, since her mother felt she did not have any milk. Kathryn experienced a battle to survive. During her session, she expressed to her mother, "You're starving me and you're trying to kill me. You want me to disappear so you can get rid of your shame."

Most people, as we've discussed, draw many unconscious conclusions about themselves during these early experiences that actually become the blueprints for their lives. Kathryn's conclusion from this was that she was worthless. Kathryn felt her mother would be better off if Kathryn was dead. Her unconscious decisions about how to behave in her life as a consequence of this conclusion were deadly. For instance, she decided, based on her conclusion that she was worthless, to kill herself. She attempted this in many different ways such as getting into fights and using drugs and alcohol. She began smoking around age eight and then drinking around age eleven. Kathryn then got into heavier drugs such as cocaine and heroin. She has literally been trying to kill herself since early childhood. All of the drug use is another example of the shock states that Kathryn was in. Later on in her life, it became apparent that she had developed Multiple Personality Disorder or Dissociative Identity Disorder (DID) as another way to split off and remain in the shock/dissociation states.

Toward the end of our session, we asked about her spiritual connection and she realized that her life experiences had made her angry at God. We needed to do a lot of spiritual repair work: after all, how could a child trust a God who would bring her a mother that was so abusive and unable to care for her? The spiritual repair work required that the child ego state have many conversations with God, ultimately leading to release of the anger and blame.

As a major part of her healing, we encouraged Kathryn to change her conclusion that she was worthless and that her needs didn't matter. She was finally able to come to a new and healthy conclusion: "I am a child of God and a Divine gift." By releasing the layers of shock through hypnotherapy, Kathryn finally had a spiritual breakthrough in her relationship with God and with herself. This is essential in order to repair the spiritual as well as the physical suicide.

SOUL MURDER

Life can traumatize us in many ways; it's not always a matter of intentional abuse from another person. Any form of trauma can send us into sympathetic or parasympathetic shock and disconnect us from our souls and spirits in the ways shown above. But we would argue that the most disturbing form of spiritual shock is when trauma comes from intentional abuse by those we are supposed to trust and rely on, especially when we are children, because children are so naïve, so innocent and so unconditionally loving. They haven't learned discernment yet and may never do so if they are abused by the ones who are supposed to be protecting them.

Here we are speaking about the father who sexually molests his sons or daughters. Or the mother who verbally shames, yells at or otherwise intimidates her children. Or the older sibling who unmercifully teases, tickles, frightens or sexually abuses his or her younger siblings. Or abuse by teachers, coaches, babysitters or anyone entrusted to care for a child. All of these are forms of spiritual abuse, because they are done intentionally and cause a disconnect from the most important connection of all: that of our ego with our spirit.

In fact, the more a child *should* be able to trust someone and the more repeated or violent the abuse, the more we call this *soul murder*, because this person is driving the child's essence, or soul, into hiding. Soul murder describes "the deliberate attempt to eradicate or compromise the separate identity of another person. The victims of soul murder remain in large part possessed by another, their souls in bondage."[2] The playwright Johan August Strindberg used the term soul murder to mean taking away a person's reason for living.

Henrik Ibsen used the term referring to a mysterious sin for which there is no forgiveness, that of killing the instinct for love of life in a human soul.

Leonard Shengold, referring to soul murder patients as "people who have suffered so in the concentration camps of childhood," says they tend to a destructive compulsion to repeat their traumatic past, to experience murderous rage and to face a terrible double bind between feeling dependent for rescue on abusive yet indispensable parents and wanting to kill them.[3]

Given that the trust factor plays such a role in soul murder, and that the deepest problem is a true disconnect from our spirit and God, you can understand why we think the most heinous form of spiritual abuse may be that committed by a so-called representative of God. When a person takes a vow to become a minister, a priest, a nun or a rabbi, we trust that they have taken up the chalice of protection of our most innocent, vulnerable souls. When that emissary of God takes their sanctified vows following years of study and prayer, this supposedly sets them above others in our society for morality, faith, protection and wisdom. They are set up in our culture to bring God's message to us. So their betrayal, in the instance of abuse, is all the more devastating, especially in the mind of a child, because that child cannot handle the dissonance of God or His messenger harming them. Therefore this kind of abuse is one of the easiest ways to kill the soul, separating an individual from his spirit.

Frieda, a recent client of ours, has had severe problems all of her life and developed splits, causing the psychologists to label her DID (Dissociative Identity Disorder). She has also been given many other diagnoses such as Borderline Personality Disorder, Bipolar Disorder and Dysthemia (depression). She has been prescribed drugs, all types of therapy and even electroshock treatments.

As we began to do hypnotherapy with her, Frieda regressed to remembering sexual abuse by her father when she was a small child only three years old. Her father lured her into his bedroom with sweets during a time when her mother was hospitalized with cancer and wasn't expected to live. Frieda was already in shock learning that her mother might "never come home from the hospital." She lived in terror every day, which caused her to cry, tremble and have nightmares. The father, dealing with his own fear, began inviting Frieda into his bed at night to "keep him company." He violated her in every way imaginable, and all she could do was dissolve into shock and to split off like a mirror smashed with a hammer, falling into a thousand pieces.

This in and of itself was severe spiritual abuse, especially because it was perpetrated by her only trusted parent once her mother had died.

Frieda's father did not know how to handle his own grief, loss, fear and emptiness, especially once his wife was gone. Being a Christian, he turned to the church and brought his daughter with him. She began attending Sunday school on a regular basis. When we continued our hypnotherapy work with Frieda, we did as we always do with clients: ask if she had a spiritual connection. We asked if Frieda wanted to bring in God, a goddess or whatever she believed in for protection, guidance and spiritual connection. When we asked this question, Frieda got hysterical, crying and going into sympathetic shock. This spiritual area was clearly a "trigger" for her.

So we regressed Frieda back to the source of this reaction and she instantly became that small child frantically yelling that the Sunday school teacher was telling the children that they were all sinners and were going to be punished. It was traumatic shock and she was frantic. We began treating her shock by having her sit up, take a sip of water, and look into our eyes. We put a cold pack around her neck. She soon was able to calm down and we asked her to bring in her adult Frieda to tell us what happened to the child. Frieda was finally able to explain that this teacher had repeatedly warned the children that they were born sinners and that they had to atone or face eternal punishment.

As we explored further with Frieda, she had a major breakthrough about why she could never connect with Jesus and could not believe in God. She realized that she had so much shame and confusion about spirituality, because she had never been able to admit that she hated God before.

Frieda began to cry deep tears of pain, regret and relief. She finally understood why she had split off, and why she could never get spiritually connected in a way that felt fulfilling to her. It took many sessions to repair all the devastation to Frieda's psyche. We included soul retrievals in her sessions to bring back the splintered, fragmented parts of her, psychologically as well as spiritually.

This was intense and difficult work for Frieda. We knew, however, that going into the unconscious mind was the only way that healing could happen on a deep spiritual level for Frieda. The conscious mind is only about

10 percent of the mind and just did not have access to all of the information we were seeking.[4] It is by having access to these deeper channels of information that the shock can be healed, the soul connection repaired and the spirit reactivated.

Another client of ours, Carole, began her work with us in an extreme state of shock. She was numb to her feelings, confused and terrified to reveal anything about herself. She did not trust anyone in authority and projected/expected that her roommates might be trying to kill her. One example is that she often came to morning class agitated, reporting that she could not sleep during the night. One night, when she finally did fall asleep, she was awakened by her roommate making sounds that to her sounded like "pounding on wood." She was in a severe shock state, first trembling and crying uncontrollably (sympathetic shock) and then becoming numb and not feeling anything (parasympathetic shock).

Once she had been induced into a hypnotic trance, we began the age regression. Carole went back to age five, when her insane, raging, alcoholic father was making her get into his truck with him so they could go horseback riding together. She was terrified, because she knew sexual and physical abuse would follow. She was screaming, trying to pull away from him. Her mother and grandmother were there telling her to just be a "good girl" and go along with whatever he wanted. They said everyone would be better off if she would just go and make him happy. The young girl got into the front seat with her drunken father, who began driving and then proceeded to unzip his pants, expose himself and force her to perform oral sex. He kept her head held down forcefully for a very long time and she could barely breathe. He had an orgasm and would not let her up. The sticky stuff all over her face was suffocating her and she went completely into shock. She felt like she was dying and, in fact, she felt like she wanted to die!

He finally pulled up to the horse barn and let her out of the truck. She started to run but he grabbed her, threw her up against the horse stall and repeatedly raped her, vaginally as well as anally. At first she was screaming and crying and then she was quiet and limp. He took her parasympathetic shock state as acquiescence. The main memory she had was the horse pawing against the wooden horse stall.

During that horrible memory, Carole felt pieces of her splitting off like glass shattering into shards. She felt like her soul had left and that was what needed to happen in order to protect the vulnerable parts of her. She felt like her soul had been murdered, like her essence was gone and that there was just a shell left.

The conclusion she drew about herself was that she was poisonous or toxic to her family. The decisions she made about how to behave were: 1) I have to disappear, to become invisible in order to be safe. 2) Don't breathe because when he hears me breathe he thinks I'm sexually responding. 3) Never look pretty because that makes men do this to you.

Her father kept telling her how pretty she was as he raped her. These conclusions and decisions explained many things in her life, including the asthmatic reactions she had whenever her husband intiated sex with her as well as the complete numbness and lack of ability to have orgasms or enjoy sex in her marriage. But more importantly, it explained her many suicide attempts and her contempt for God.

As she began to explore this contempt for God, she referred to him as "God the Father." Then suddenly, she got it! As a child, whenever she heard the term, "God the Father," she immediately was overcome with terror, shame and shock. She dreaded having to go to church, since she assumed that God the Father was going to rape her the way that *her* father did. In her session, we had Carole question her old conclusions and decisions. And importantly, she began to separate the image of her alcoholic, insane father from God. The adult part of her informed the child and helped to bring in the healing. We told the child within that God does love her and actually saved her life in these dangerous situations where she could have choked to death or died from the horrible abuse of her father.

We asked Carole to find her soul pieces and bring them back into the parts of her body where they had split off. Her father had committed soul murder and these parts needed to be revived. Carole has now written a play about her childhood and how she has survived. Her play has brought healing to her as well as to many others who have been traumatized by family members.

Samantha's Psychodrama: Umbilical Shock

Samantha is a middle-aged woman who goes by the nickname Sam. Prior to her work with us, she had been playing out a "victim drama triangle" of addictions, sexual confusion and extreme rage. At the time, she had been married for ten years to another woman named Ronnie, but they were now in a long, drawn-out process of getting divorced.

In her professional career, Sam was a successful psychotherapist despite all the dysfunction in her own life. Privately, she lived in constant fear of being abandoned, which is typical of people who have Adult Reactive Attachment Disorder. Her most recent drama was that she had been rescuing a young (twenty-one-year-old) woman named Allie for the last five years. Allie was a client of hers, and Sam knew she had violated ethical boundaries by allowing Allie into her private life. Sam took Allie to an Alcoholics Anonymous meeting and introduced her to her partner, Ronnie. Before long, Ronnie and Allie were having sex and fell in love. Allie moved in with Sam and Ronnie, which served to escalate this victim drama. They each moved around the drama triangle, from playing the roles of persecutor to victim to rescuer.

When we started working with Sam, we began her psychodrama right there, with her deep feelings about being abandoned by both Allie and Ronnie, who were having this passionate affair in her own home. Her deep, underlying emotions of rage took over and erupted as she screamed and cried with fury. We learned that her partner Ronnie had told Sam that if she would have had sex with her, she wouldn't have had to have sex with this young woman. It appeared that Sam was what we call sexually anorexic. Just as in food addictions, anorexia refers to starving oneself of something—in this case, sex. But to us, Sam also appeared to be food anorexic, as she was very tall and extremely thin.

In both food and sexual anorexia, a person is totally obsessed with what they withhold from themselves. This is an example of the nourishment barrier. Sam's basic needs for nourishment from food and intimacy felt contaminated to her and, ironically, she was poisoning herself with tobacco and other toxic substances.

As we regressed Sam in a psychodrama to the source of this nourishment barrier, she found herself back in a childhood scene in the front yard of her home. Her mother had been drinking heavily and was leaving the family. Sam's father was trying to pull Sam back into the house as she desperately clung to her mother, who was getting into a taxi, saying, "I'll never leave you. I love you. I love you. I'll be back, Sammy. I'll be back!"

Sam's father dragged her and the other children back inside as they screamed and cried for their mother to come back. The scene was firmly imprinted in Sam's unconscious mind, connecting the words "I love you" and "I will be back" with love and relationships. Her mother never did come back, which became a blueprint for relationships in Sam's life.

When regressed even further, she found herself in her mother's toxic womb. She began frantically moving around, making faces and coughing. Her mother was smoking and drinking alcohol. As this fetus frantically tried to avoid the toxins, she went into sympathetic shock (frantic movement) in the womb. Later, as Sam was being born, the umbilical cord was wrapped around her body and throat. However, any attempt to move back into the womb would have meant going back into a toxic shock pool. So she was caught between the proverbial rock and a hard place—one option was to suffer from the toxins, the other was to get strangled by the cord. So she went into parasympathetic shock. She couldn't move at all and felt that she was going to die. At this point, the conclusion she drew about herself was, "My mother is killing me. Something is terribly wrong with me. I'm a burden and I don't deserve to live." Her first existential decision here was: "I'll stop trying." Then, as many souls do, she began rebelling, resisting and fighting back. Her next decision was, "I'll fight to the death."

Next, Sam felt herself being pulled out of the womb by forceps and she quickly experienced a rage at the "authority" of the doctors pulling her out by her head with cold metal prongs. She felt violated and resisted coming into this unwelcoming world of cold metal objects, bright lights and no warm, welcoming mother to hold her. Yet she knew on a soul level that she did not want to remain in the toxic shock pool of her mother's womb. She embraced the "lesser of two evils" and accepted rescue by the doctor, reluctantly and resentfully. A lifelong pattern was etched deeply into her psyche: to expect inadequate and even toxic nourishment from loved ones in her life, abandonment and ultimately annihilation. And then to resentfully accept whatever help was available.

Sam has since learned to recognize that there are people in the world who are fully capable of loving her in a healthy, nurturing way and even to expect that she can attract such people into a relationship with her. She knows now that her desperate attempts to rescue Allie were actually disguised attempts to rescue herself, the young Sam—following the template established by the doctor with his forceps—and she now is committed to consciously providing for her own healthy self-care.

COMING APART

Just as the human being comes apart at death, with the body dying and decaying while the *breath of life* (the "soul") persists, we've talked throughout this book about how people come apart in a similar way from traumatic moments in life. But we should point out that this coming apart also occurs in moments of ecstatic spiritual experience and delirious orgasmic transcendence. There is a vital difference, however, between these two paths of coming apart. Trauma is filled with dread, despair and terror; what comes apart under these traumatic circumstances tends to stay apart, because the precipitating threat continues to menace the individual with further harm. Spiritual experience or transcendence, on the other hand, is filled with buoyancy, trust and passion, and here a soothing, graceful transition usually brings us back to wholeness after we have come apart. However, sometimes an individual may experience the spiritual coming apart as disorienting or even traumatic, leading to a "dark night of the soul." But the distinction is that this individual's essence, or soul, has not been stolen or murdered but rather allowed to loosen the tether that binds it to the person's ego. This is indeed an important part of spiritual development.

SPIRITUALITY, RELIGION AND SHOCK

It is common for spiritual conflicts, resentments and fears to be generalized to all authority figures. Many of the people we have worked with have spiritual issues, because in our cultures some confuse God with "father," too often with an all-too-fallible earthly father. If your earthly father was cruel or shaming or absent, you are likely to see God through that same contaminated lens. And if a person's reaction to the father was to enter a protective cocoon of shock, the individual is likely to recreate a similar response in spiritual encounters.

This anger with God or spiritual authority figures is not on a conscious level and is transferred to other authority figures in our lives. Also, most religions teach that it is a sin to be angry at God, so from a very early age we cannot express our negative feelings toward God and this makes it more difficult for people to have an intimate, honest spiritual connection.

We have encountered many people who feel spiritually empty inside. They don't often realize this until they begin doing Heart-Centered work. In fact, many of our new students say that it was the term *Heart-Centered* that initially attracted them to our trainings. They believed that religion should fulfill their inner longing for spiritual connection. And for many people it does. But there is a growing number of people who either consider themselves religious because they attend church, synagogue or a mosque and yet still experience spiritual emptiness or have had negative experiences in traditional religious institutions and so they cut off all connections to God. In fact, these folks have confused religion with God. In general, religion is a set of beliefs and tenets by which to live life. For many people these work well. However, God is not one specific religion or any religion, for that matter. God is God.

When people begin to do Heart-Centered work, they often have a very powerful spiritual experience near the completion of their sessions. By this we mean they often feel their heart center sopening up with an outpouring of love. They may see a beautiful, bright light or encounter a spiritual being such as Jesus, Mary or an angel. While in the trance state, this is a physical experience that one does not forget. They feel warm all over, more love than ever before and complete forgiveness of self and others. Suddenly all the people they were angry at are forgiven and a strong feeling of oneness with all of humanity encompasses them. It is what Eastern philosophy considers an enlightenment experience. This is what our work is really designed to accomplish. Our students tell us that as they begin to release their resentments, fears, anger, blame, judgments and shock, the spiritual energy now has a place to inhabit. It is almost as if when we are so filled up with our emotional baggage, there is no room for real joy to fill us up. Certainly when we are in parasympathetic shock, frozen and numb, or frantic in sympathetic shock, there is no space for spirit to come in. When we are in shock, we may not feel our pain but we also don't feel the joy of life. We're not feeling, not alive. We're not truly *in* our lives at all.

Once we begin to release our shock and feel alive, it is like thawing out. Then enlightenment can become more and more a part of our daily lives. We can stop and really smell the roses, receive joy from simple acts of kindness or read a biblical passage from a place of love rather than guilt and shame. So, to sum up, this is the goal of our work and certainly one of the many benefits of releasing shock.

Chapter 13

FIRST AID VS. LASTING TREATMENT— TIPS ON MANAGING SHOCK

Self-help with shock is challenging, because it is at its heart a dissociated state. When you are in shock, you are not aware of your experience in your body or in your emotions. You are "checked out" in a very basic way. So self-help or any help with treating shock begins with awareness. Only when you bring your attention to the current balance (or imbalance) of your nervous system can you hope to make an intentional change in it.

Most people need a little help from their friends. We recommend that you have a partner/friend who places the same value you do on being as conscious and present in your life as you can be. Here are some steps you can take to provide first aid for your shock symptoms for each other:

1. Read this book and fill out the questionnaires. Then share them with each other.

2. Determine specifically who/what triggers your parasympathetic shock. In other words, notice when you go numb and feel sleepy when you're not really tired. Who are you with when you feel your eyelids shutting down and you just can't seem to keep them open?

3. Determine what people and situations seem to trigger your sympathetic shock. These would be people with whom you notice

yourself speaking rapidly to keep up or interrupting them just to get a word in edgewise.

4. Which people quickly increase your stress levels, because you are trying to please them or you fear their judgments about you?

5. Which situations do you engage in where you notice that you are just not fully present, either by being too busy or by racing around frantically?

Explain to your close and trusted friend that you now recognize that your tendency to be super-productive and always busy is actually a shock state that has caused you stress and failure rather than success, because of the imbalance it requires. This life pattern is actually "burning the candle at both ends," a constant state of sympathetic shock that is unhealthy for your physical health, your emotional well-being and your intimate relationships. If your friend understands how important it is for you to change these patterns, to bring balance back into your life, then he or she will be eager to gently and lovingly remind you when you start falling into that old pattern again. You may be able to provide similar support to that friend to change an unhealthy pattern of shock in his or her life—providing mutual awareness and support to bring balance back into your lives.

Once you have become aware of the shock in your body, you can provide first aid for it. You can do something to bring yourself back into connection with your body, which is to reverse the dissociation and to intervene in the habitual pattern. Here are some of the first aid techniques we teach people to use for themselves once they've gained awareness of their shock:

- Sip some cool, refreshing water. That is different, importantly, from drinking hot coffee, a sugary soda or an alcoholic drink. Any of these actually reinforce the shock state, be it sympathetic or parasympathetic. Coffee is a stimulant, sugar can activate both sympathetic or parasympathetic systems and alcohol activates the parasympathetic.

- Place an ice pack (the soft blue ones sold in pharmacies to reduce inflammation) on your neck, chest or forehead, or a hot pack on your neck or stomach. Think about how soothing it is to have something cold on your forehead when you have a headache or a fever.

Sympathetic shock is a lot like having a fever; the internal engine is running too hot. When you are tired or discouraged, it often feels nurturing to have something warm to cuddle up with, like a warm puppy. Parasympathetic shock is a lot like that: the internal engine needing to be warmed up on a frosty winter's morning.

You will want to be selective and conscious of how you introduce heat or cold into your body's experience. Drinking an ice cold, sugary drink may provide the needed coolness but it also delivers a lot of sugar and empty calories. The sugar in it is also addictive and so is not a good choice.

Pure, ice cold water is the best choice; drink a lot, slowly. Keep a nice tall refrigerated cup with you to have cold water available all day.

Drinking hot coffee may be a habit you have developed, but remember that caffeine, milk/dairy and sugar can actually reinforce the shock cycle and certainly are not included in the first aid treatment of shock. Caffeine also stimulates epinephrine (adrenaline) release, has psychotropic (mood altering) properties and is an addictive stimulant. Instead, drink hot peppermint tea or other pure herbal teas without caffeine; they are very soothing and the perfect first aid treatment for shock.

• Change your posture. Posture conveys information about interpersonal relations, personality traits such as confidence, submissiveness and openness, social standing and current emotional states. These lifelong behavior patterns are carried in the autonomic nervous system and in the body's habitual musculature and posture. People who have an aggressive nature tend to lean forward, use gestures of pointing and speak loudly and quickly. Disappointment is tied to slumping posture. When people do not want to cry, they can tighten their jaws, which suppresses tears. Stress and anger tighten the muscles along the spine and thighs, which can manifest in pain in those body parts if the stress is prolonged.

Many studies have shown that certain patterns of body movements or postures are indicative of specific emotions, that is, posture has a significant effect on one's emotions. We call these *shock postures*. Take a few moments to notice if you feel frozen in a certain position. Move gently out of the shock state, taking some sips of a beverage that soothes you, and notice how you move out of the shock posture.

Use one or two simple yoga poses to help move you out of any shock position you may be in.

Conversely, one's emotional state largely determines one's posture. Therefore, deliberately changing that posture or presentation, e.g., by doing a yoga pose, actually begins changing the habitual nervous system pattern.

- Take a few deep breaths. A person under stress will often have greater muscle tension and shallow breathing, a classic way of dissociating. Deep breathing relaxes the muscles and dissipates the tension. When you breathe deeply, you fully fill your lungs and you will notice that your lower belly rises. For this reason, deep, relaxing breathing is often called diaphragmatic breathing, abdominal breathing or belly breathing. Deep breathing encourages full oxygen exchange—that is, the beneficial trade of incoming oxygen for outgoing carbon dioxide. Not surprisingly, this type of breathing slows the heartbeat and can lower or stabilize blood pressure.

- If you are not good at remembering to breathe, walk up and down a flight of stairs a few times to naturally increase your breathing rate, which moves you out of your current shock posture.[1]

- Look into another's eyes or into your own eyes in the mirror to calm anxieties and focus your awareness on the present moment. Eye contact often brings us back to reality if we have left for a few moments.

FIRST AID VS. TREATMENT

We have been suggesting immediate first aid tactics to deal with an acute shock response. This can happen automatically in reaction to an event that triggers a habitual shock state. For example, an individual may have developed a fear of being punished by authority, perhaps from a childhood filled with incidents of an abusive, punishing father berating him for everything he does. Many years later, when that individual is called into his supervisor's office, his body initiates the same old habitual trauma response. His mind is filled with catastrophic images of being fired and shamed, his breathing becomes shallow, his posture collapses inward and he experiences mental confusion and emotional numbness. If this person can somehow recognize his shock pattern *in the moment*, he can stop the progression into full-blown dissociation by sipping some water, breathing deeply and holding a cold bottle of water in both hands. This intervention could take less than a minute and so it is very doable. This is the application of first aid.

The individual has not actually changed the deep-seated habitual nervous system response of fear in the face of authorities, however. For that real, lasting change to occur, he will need to *treat* his shock. And treatment involves utilizing depth psychotherapy with the ability to regress to the age of onset of the pattern. By returning to those moments of terror and shame with his abusive father, he can create a corrective experience: perhaps he can yell at his father to stop hurting him, perhaps he can jump up and allow his body to immerse in the liberating somatic feeling of running away to escape the abuse, or perhaps he can imagine bringing into the scene a safe and loving grandfather to protect him from the abuse.

Treating shock means resolving the underlying residual tension of a natural response that could not be completed. The boy's body initially reacted to his abusive father with a surge of sympathetic activation—his body prepared to fight or flee. But he quickly learned not to resist his raging father, because that meant worse abuse, and so that sympathetic surge was squelched. The sympathetic activation of the nervous system was interrupted mid-stream. It was not allowed to follow through to completion, and instead remains stuck, unfinished and tense as a coiled spring. In treatment, the spring is allowed to free itself from its habitual constriction, to complete the interrupted cycle and thus release the tension that has enforced his fear of authority for decades.

Hopefully, the information in this book will point out to you ways that you have been in shock without being aware of it. That is a big step in healing the body's underlying trauma response. However, it can be difficult to "pull yourself up by your own bootstraps." If you are dissociated, numb to your feelings and not in your body, how do you wake yourself up enough to know that you're in that condition? When you have gotten used to functioning with some of your faculties dulled or dimmed, how do you turn on the light of awareness?

CONCLUSION

By introducing the concept of *shock* and then adding the word to our vocabulary, this intrinsically begins to awaken our consciousness. The general public cannot seek treatment for something about which it is completely blind. Each year new words or terms are added to our language, and we anticipate that our context for the word *shock* will become more and more a part of the vernacular.

For example, the term Post-Traumatic Stress Disorder was first coined in the mid-1970s, in part through the efforts of anti-Vietnam War activists. The condition was formally recognized in 1980, when it was added to the DSM-III (the Diagnostic and Statistical Manual of Mental Disorders published by the American Psychiatric Association). Over the years, this term has been accepted into our general vocabulary, referred to in the media and become the basis for medical and psychological treatment. In reviewing much of the current literature on treating trauma, most authors do not use the term *shock* but instead are beginning to refer to complex trauma and complex post-traumatic stress disorder. Shock refers to the psychological as well as physiological symptoms people experience and yet it has not been previously addressed to the general public or, sadly too often, to the professionals who treat them.

Hopefully, readers are now aware just how pervasive this shock state of being is and how it affects massive numbers of people among the general public as well as combat veterans, abuse survivors and trauma victims.

Through our thirty years of training professionals internationally in trauma treatment, we have come to recognize how pervasive trauma (and the resulting state of shock) is in all cultures and how it often goes unrecognized and thus regrettably untreated. Our first awareness was the vast number of treatment professionals themselves who grew up in abusive, addiction-ridden and dysfunctional families or environments. These tens of thousands of professionals from all over the world have been our students, and have taught us, through seeing into their inner worlds, that dysfunction is not just limited to those we have defined as patients or clients. In fact, we have observed and concluded that a majority of people are unconsciously attracted to joining the helping professions in an attempt to understand and heal their own personal dysfunction as well as that of their families.

Further, psychotherapists, health care providers and clergy are subjected to "vicarious traumatization" or "secondary traumatic stress" (sometimes called *compassion fatigue*) just by virtue of their constant proximity to those who are suffering from PTSD. Many of those in the helping professions, however, do not recognize that they are in any way debilitated by traumatic stress, whether primary or secondary, and do not seek treatment.

Self-awareness regarding shock among therapists and healthcare providers is growing, however. We have been called to train an increasing number of professionals entering the field of Integrative Medicine. The Dr. Tanya Edwards Center for Integrative Medicine at The Cleveland Clinic holds trainings in Heart-Centered Hypnotherapy twice each year and offers our advanced internship training for interested staff members and for new therapists they seek to employ.

There has been a huge increase in the number of alternative therapists, healers, Reiki masters, energy and body workers, coaches and spiritual advisors. Obviously the general public is seeking and paying for any type of help it can receive. There is also a vast increase over the last twenty years in the acceptance of hypnotherapy and the resulting research indicating people's search for healing and for more rapid therapies. This public search for healing reflects the profound hurt, physical pain, emotional suffering and deep dissatisfaction that people all over the world are experiencing. Americans spent $33.9 billion out-of-pocket on complementary and alternative medicine (CAM) over the previous year, according to a 2007 government survey. CAM is a group of diverse medical and healthcare systems, practices and products such as herbal supplements, meditation, chiropractic and acupuncture that are not generally considered to be part of conventional medicine. CAM accounts for approximately 11 percent of total out-of-pocket expenditures on health care in the United States.[1]

In our book, *Breaking Free from the Victim Trap*, we attempted to modernize Eric Berne's universal and profound concept of the victim triangle.[2] The principal concepts here are that people who are helpers/rescuers often attempt to "fix" those who they see as victims or less fortunate. However, in trying to fix others, we actually are robbing them of their personal power and thus they become resentful. This pattern becomes more clearly focused when the victim or so-called "person in need" then releases his or her anger and begins to persecute the rescuer/helper. The rescuer/helper reacts by feeling unappreciated and misunderstood, which causes him or her to switch to the victim position of, "Poor me, look at all I've done for you; how could you treat me this way?"

Breaking Free has been popular for twenty-five years because it is so universal in families, workplaces of all types, schools and universities, addiction treatment facilities, domestic violence shelters and mental health agencies. The material pertinent here is that people who enter the helping professions usually do so wanting to help others but may slide down the slippery slope into rescuing. Because of the pervasive amount of shock that most people carry in their bodies, these well-intentioned therapists/healers do not realize that they are actually seeking their own personal healing. We are now realizing, twenty-five years after writing *Breaking Free*, that the entire Victim/Persecutor/Rescuer pattern exists on a deep, unconscious level in a majority of humans and is driven and maintained by a variety of shock states.

We have learned that shock states often begin in the womb, which is a concept very difficult for most people to understand or believe. The developing research on pre- and perinatal psychology is beginning to be noticed by many awakening treatment professionals. We would have also been among the doubting Thomases if we had not been trained in hypnotherapy over thirty years ago. We ourselves, perhaps just like you, the reader, were *amazed* during our first experiences with hypnotherapy when our clients regressed to the womb! It was difficult to believe or trust; however, we could not deny what was right in front of us.

When Sigmund Freud and Carl Jung began to experiment with hypnosis one hundred years ago, they had experiences of the power of hypnosis. Each of them eventually discarded the tool of hypnosis because of its power and their lack of understanding of how to use it most effectively. Freud wrote in 1891, "There is no doubt that the field of hypnotic treatment is far more extensive than that of other methods of treating nervous illnesses."[3] Carl Jung did incorporate hypnosis into his clinical work when he opened his private practice in psychiatry. In fact, one of his first patients was a woman who presented with a painful paralysis of the leg, and he "cured" her using hypnosis. She then spread the word of Jung's remarkable hypnotic abilities. Her recommendation was responsible for his "local fame as a wizard," and for the first private patients who came to him.[4]

Thankfully, we had training which allowed us not to discard hypnosis, but to transform it into a profound and useful tool in trauma treatment and healing. After our initial experiences of clients regressing to the beginning of their lives and describing how it felt in their mother's wombs, what they needed and the conclusions they drew about themselves, we were very careful not to make any suggestions that could lead them there. As more and more clients regressed to the womb, we discovered all the material we have put together in this book and our book *Longing for Belonging* regarding universal human experiences upon entering into this world through the womb. We have observed virtually the same regressions to pre- and perinatal events in China, South Africa, Kuwait, South America and with other international students.

When we studied with Dr. William Emerson, he brought together the concepts of early shock states and birth. His work with pre- and perinatal psychology, combined with our methods of hypnotherapy, has helped us to advance the ideas of just how, where and when early shock begins.[5] We have become aware of how much educational work needs to be done from the beginning of a woman's pregnancy in order to prevent shock from taking hold. This will also prevent much of the violence in our culture, since there are devastating statistics regarding this connection. When traumas occur prior to or during birth, the quality of bonding is radically reduced. This reduction occurs because of the dulling of mind and body, a natural defense against pain.[6] K. Magid and C. McKelvey reported that children with severe bonding difficulties do not develop a conscience and perform asocial or antisocial acts without remorse.[7]

HOW MANY PEOPLE HAVE BEEN TREATED SUCCESSFULLY FOR SHOCK—WHAT CAN THE READER HOPE FOR?

Over the past thirty years, we have trained thousands of professionals internationally, who themselves have healed from shock and then returned to their communities to treat tens of thousands of their own clients, individually and in groups. This is an ongoing process. You can heal from shock; however, people can become re-traumatized by natural disasters, family deaths, divorces and a myriad other traumatic experiences that occur unpredictably merely by being in a human body.

Our students consist of a diverse group of professional psychologists, social workers, marriage and family therapists, addiction specialists, trauma treatment specialists, nurses, doctors and counselors as well as alternative healers and coaches. This means that Heart-Centered Hypnotherapy, considered one of the foremost techniques in the healing of trauma and shock, is becoming more widely available to the general public.

We have discovered that the quickest way to educate, heal and release shock in the general public is through active participation in our transpersonal healing groups called *Personal Transformation Intensives*®, referred to as PTI groups. The popularity of these groups is increasing and thus the numbers offered around the country are growing by leaps and bounds. Clients who participate experience deep and profound healing, which they are then excited to share with their families and communities. Some PTI graduates are so inspired by awareness of their own levels of shock and the resulting healing they receive that they go back to school to get degrees and then join our classes so they can provide the same healing to others.

Clients usually begin their treatment in individual sessions in the offices of their therapists, who recognize the depth of the shock they may be experiencing and thus begin the treatment. The clients may then be referred to a PTI group.

WHY IS TREATMENT OF SHOCK MORE EFFECTIVE WHEN DONE IN A GROUP?

Personal Transformation Intensive usually consists of eight to sixteen people, most of whom have been clients of one of the therapists. Or they may be friends or family members of previous clients who have been encouraged to attend. The group begins on Friday evening and completes on Sunday afternoon. These weekend groups meet once per month for five months and are held in a retreat environment, sharing meals and sleeping quarters.

Men and women are separated for lodging except in the case of couples attending. The same group is required to commit to attend all five meetings and no new members are added once the group forms. This structure provides safety and continuity, which stimulates the fastest healing for all members.

Within the larger PTI group, members are taught to form Master Mind groups consisting of three or four people who support each other to share and reach their goals. They are taught processes to achieve the highest potential and to follow through on their commitments, especially to themselves. These Master Mind groups usually meet over the phone between sessions so that members of the group can stay connected.

In this book, we have explained the many symptoms of shock and the wide variety of ways that it manifests: the way that sympathetic shock can emerge in busyness, fast talking and multi-tasking, and the way that parasympathetic shock often results in quietness, withdrawal or sleepiness. We have discussed the many ways people treat their own shock with the behaviors of overeating—especially carbohydrates, sugary foods and unconsciously stuffing food down—and with drinking lots of coffee, colas and stimulants such as chocolate and energy drinks.

When therapists only see clients in their own offices, they only see a tiny sliver of who the clients are. They only see what clients are willing to present or share and they mainly have the clients' perspectives on their lives. Also, most office visits only consist of fifty minutes of talk therapy or ninety minutes of hypnotherapy. Hypnotherapy is naturally much more revealing, because the client's defenses are minimized for that ninety minutes. In a group, the therapists (always at least two in our PTIs) can observe each client over an entire weekend, observe and interact with them in the group as well as at mealtime and during recreation. We can see how they handle authority, how they withdraw or participate in group interactions and how others perceive them. All of these social interactions give us valuable information about the depth of the shock states they may be in and their traditional social interactions with others. This is invaluable first-hand information that could never be gotten just from the client self-reporting in individual sessions.

Within this group setting, we can easily observe who is in shock, whether they are in sympathetic or parasympathetic shock and how their shock states affect their most intimate relationships as well as their social interactions. Thus our information gathering about each client in the group is ongoing and greatly enhanced by our first-hand experience and witnessing by our team of therapists in the group. Also, we observe through the Master Mind process how they interact with others or what shock states are triggered when they are asked to participate in the smaller groups.

We have created a profound tool we call the *Clearing Process* which is especially valuable in observing states of shock. This process is used when one member becomes triggered or has a reaction to an interaction involving another student or a teacher. In many previous personal growth or addiction treatment groups, there was no clear way to handle reactions to other participants or teachers. The use of the Clearing Process provides the whole group with an enhanced feeling of safety. It also provides the therapists with much more information about when and how the individual students go into shock states. When a student reacts to another and requests a Clearing, this is provided in the center of the group with one therapist facilitating. The process is well defined, completely structured and designed to help the students clear judgments, projections and shock from their bodies. One of the reasons we always have two teachers to facilitate PTI groups is that when the Clearing is with one of the teachers, the other teacher can facilitate the Clearing and keep the participants safe. They can also observe and treat the shock of the participant who is doing the Clearing.

Every process in the group is an opportunity to observe what puts each person into shock, how he or she handles it, and to help participants recognize their own physiological signs of shock. One clear example of this is merely when we open each morning with group sharing. Each person gets a couple of minutes to share what they are feeling today and what they would like to address in their process. The entire group observes each person's sharing and this is a great teaching time for all to witness their own shock states as well as that of others. An example is when a person goes on and on without taking a breath in between words. We call this "shock talk," meaning that they have dissociated, are not actually aware of feeling anything (even though they may even be in tears) and often have a blank stare in their eyes. This shock stare is what William Emerson refers to as a low "blink rate," which is greatly reduced when people are in shock.

In the group, we ask the person to stop and take some deep breaths, as shallow breathing is another indication of shock. They often try to keep going so we may have to actually go over to them and gently offer them a few sips of water. We also ask them if they would like a cold pack or a hot pack. These are well-accepted and rapid treatment methods for shock. The cold or heat helps them come back into their bodies and thus into their feelings. We have also used some natural oils rubbed into their palms and inhaled. Oils such as lavender are very calming and much more healing than the old-fashioned way of treating someone who has fainted with "smelling salts." We now realize that someone fainting from a shocking experience is certainly the same type of shock state to which we are referring.

THE TOOLS THAT WORK MOST EFFECTIVELY IN HEALING SHOCK

1. Heart-Centered Hypnotherapy performed by a trained and well-qualified professional therapist.
2. Group work in the Personal Transformation Intensive.®
3. Group work in our Wellness Institute therapist trainings. All of our certification and advanced training programs are done in group settings so that the therapists can heal their own shock and personal issues. This prevents counter-transference or projecting their unfinished business onto their clients.
4. Learning to quickly recognize your own personal symptoms of shock and treating them as quickly as possible.
5. Belonging to an ongoing training program or a Wellness Institute community of supportive people who can give you honest feedback if your shock has taken over and you are not actually in your body (not experiencing your true feelings).

RECLAIMING THE LOST CHILD FROM
ITS FASCINATION WITH THE CIRCUS

When children respond to trauma by splitting and sending a part of themselves to the circus to recruit a powerful ally, they enhance their chances of survival. God bless each one of us who found a way to survive the intolerable by forming an alliance with the tightrope walker, the fat lady or the lion tamer. We were, after all, seeking refuge. That fateful choice, however, has become so ingrained, habitual and unconscious that today's rational, healthy adult is too often overpowered when dealing with stress.

When trouble begins to brew for the "tightrope walker man," he becomes focused to the exclusion of everything else. He has developed an unnatural ease with the tension of imminent disaster, acting as if it's a walk in the park. In fact, because this has become his dominant social skill, he actually attracts high stress and danger into his life, although unconsciously. The small child who formed an alliance with the tightrope walker so many years ago as a survival strategy is still carried by this man today. The tightrope walker is still a part of him that can step in and take over at the first sign of a situation reminiscent of the trauma that prompted developing the strategy in the first place.

Now it is not in the man's best interest to banish the tightrope walker, even if he could. The skill of maintaining precarious balance in the face of conflict and danger is too valuable when it is used in the service of his highest good, determined by his healthy adult, rather than in service of supposedly protecting the vulnerable child within from now-nonexistent threats. So what will serve this man's healing and growth best is to find a way to separate the frightened, powerless child from the powerful defense represented by the tightrope walker, so that the skill and power of the defense is available to the man's healthy adult. That is not easy, because it feels to the vulnerable child within like life-or-death: If I do not successfully finesse maintaining balance in the face of stressful challenges, I will fall one way or the other to my death. Relying on the tightrope walker strategy is death-defying, indeed, and necessary to survive. And it is enforced and reinforced by a nervous system recalibrated so that the precarious has become the new normal. Sympathetic shock is needed to maintain hypervigilance and concentrated attention to the constant threats that surround him.

Our task here is to assist the vulnerable child within to feel more support and safety, less threat and powerlessness. As this child part (some call it a subpersonality) begins to feel more secure and protected, the original need for the powerful defense is reduced. The motivation to cling to this strategy subsides from life-or-death and the nature of this lifetime pattern is brought to conscious awareness. As the deeply embedded sympathetic shock begins to relax, this man begins to realistically develop the capacity to make conscious choice about how to react to stress and especially to a situation reminiscent of the original trauma. The nervous system is no longer set to sympathetic shock autopilot.

What specifically helps this man to deal more effectively with stress and conflict? Experiences that add to the man's ability to relax in the face of stress. Experiences that recalibrate his nervous system back to its natural state and away from the hyperalert tension of sympathetic shock. Experiences that reinforce trust in intimate relationships and safety in all relationships. Experiences that encourage him to speak up and advocate for his needs and his point of view. Experiences that increase his mindfulness and appreciation for the beauty and harmony of the world around him.

A student of ours who identified with the tightrope walker as a defense came to us after having been fired from his third position in law enforcement. He has a background as a state policeman and has worked for law enforcement in urban areas with gangs for many years. He was extremely stressed and burned out. As he began to understand the concept of shock, he realized that not only was he operating in a state of shock, but so were most of his colleagues. The tightrope he walked for most of his life was to balance between being hyperalert to threat or danger when someone steps out of their car when stopped or arrested by him, yet remaining polite and professional in order not to escalate a potentially explosive situation. He was written up many times for being overly aggressive and eventually was fired due to having fallen off the tightrope he constantly attempted to maintain. One day he was being threatened by a gang member he was questioning about a gang murder and his partner, who was numb and in parasympathetic shock, was not able to protect him. Our tightrope walker fell off the wire and began to pistol whip the gang member. Suddenly other gang members appeared and the two police officers, in a state of panic and sympathetic shock, began shooting randomly.

They called for help but ended up killing one gang member and wounding several others.

This incident caused great conflict in the community and the two officers were put on extended leave without pay. Our tightrope walker came to us for treatment and began to recognize not only his current stress levels but the deep states of shock that he would go into as a defense in these high-intensity situations. He was in a constant pattern of fight or flight. As we used hypnosis, he regressed to his childhood, where he became aware of using the tightrope walker defense within his family. His father was also a stressed-out inner city policeman who came home at night drunk and raging at the family. Our client would balance between protecting his mother and siblings and trying to calm down his father. His strategy didn't always work and he often got beaten himself, falling off the tightrope with no net underneath to catch him.

Through hypnotherapy work, he began to reclaim this small child from the circus to which he had run away. He developed confidence and skills to help him survive without having to feel responsible to protect victims from their abusers. In reducing his own level of shock, he realized that he didn't have to respond to every call for help and that he could now develop a safety net of support for himself. This work succeeded in reducing his shock levels and in educating the child within to feel safer. Not only has he built a strong safety net of family and community support for himself, but he has actually de-constructed his need to walk that tightrope wire.

Now let's look at another example of reclaiming the lost child from its fascination with the circus. The child who established an alliance with the Contortionist is able to tie herself in knots. She can fit into tiny spaces. She will bend over backwards to accommodate others' requests or demands. She bends in ways that most people won't or can't. Her strength is the agility to compromise like a chameleon. Her nervous system's new normal has become parasympathetic shock. She surrenders, retreats and complies.

This was an effective strategy as a small child, no doubt, in navigating through a home environment in which any assertion on her part was rebuffed, ignored or punished. The tragedy is that now, decades later, she is still accommodating everyone else's needs at great personal cost. When she can't say "No," she ends up overbooked, exhausted and resentful. When she deliberately holds herself back in order to allow someone else to take the prize or the credit, she denies herself promotions, relationships and opportunities that are legitimately hers.

The grown woman's inner little girl, so intimidated by the threat of rejection, is actually yearning for a healthy adult to step in and set things right, to protect her legitimate interests, and to relieve her of the unreasonable responsibility for others that she has always taken on. Ideally, she wants that healthy adult to be her mother or her father, but it is too late for that now. The only one who can step in and provide this precious, vulnerable little one the protection she craves and unburden her of the incessant responsibilities is the grown woman. That can happen when the woman begins to recognize who is "driving the bus" every time she contorts herself to accommodate someone else. It has become such an automatic, unconscious pattern in her life that there can be no change in behavior until that recognition is brought into conscious awareness. She must treat the paralyzing parasympathetic shock that stifles her creativity and her energy like a heavy shroud.

What specifically helps this woman to deal more effectively with stress and conflict, to stand up for herself? Experiences that reinforce autonomy and safety in all relationships. Experiences that encourage her to speak up and advocate for her needs and her point of view. Experiences that increase her excitement about her place in the world around her. Experiences that allow her to give back to others whatever responsibility she has taken on for them. Experiences that add to this woman's ability to become energized in the face of stress. Experiences that recalibrate her nervous system back to its natural state and away from the suffocating oppression of parasympathetic shock.

It is through therapy and these positive experiences that people can shed the shroud of their shock states, finally leave their circus shadows behind them and move on with their lives, clear-headed and shock-free.

THERAPIST ADVICE ON TREATMENT
OF SHOCK AND TRAUMA

Most clients do not enter treatment saying that they want to work on their trauma. The nature of trauma and the many defenses we humans have become so adept at using, such as denial, projection, confusion and repression, means that the presenting problem can be anything from anxiety and depression to physical illness, such as Crohn's disease or chronic back problems. Clients often come in with something like relationship issues or substance and behavioral addictions. As we use hypnotherapy or other regressive techniques, we immediately become aware that the presenting issue is just that, the tip of the iceberg. If we only work on the presenting issue with cognitive therapies, we may be helping the client to understand it better, but certainly not to heal it on the deepest psychological and physiological levels. Therein lies the difference between regressive techniques and cognitive methods of treatment.

As we've discussed throughout this book, the physiology that allows for shock is really something of a miracle and an irony. It has served to protect us from experiencing the deepest and most intolerable experiences of pain as children and yet, as adults, it has caused us to be emotionally unavailable to those who love us the most. While protecting us from memories we may not have wanted to face, shock has caused those experiences to be pushed further and further into the recesses of our body, mind and spirit. This deep repression most often manifests as physical illness that causes folks to seek out doctors, surgeries, naturopaths, restrictive diets, all types of pills and procedures. Many of these procedures are necessary in order to cure the body of the disease which has finally gotten our attention. We are often only treating the *manifestation* of the illness or discomfort rather than its source. The use of anti-anxiety medications or anti-depressants has increased now to the point where massive amounts of drugs are being prescribed for millions of school-age children rather than attempting to treat the cause of their anxiety, Attention Deficit Hyperactivity Disorder or depression. We have seen how mental illness, unaddressed, has manifested in school children bringing guns to school, shooting classmates, teachers and ultimately themselves.

Shock is a complex system that allows us to handle everyday stresses and to move back and forth between sympathetic and parasympathetic reactions. In nature, we see animals dealing with life-threatening stresses and then being able to shake off the excess energy if they've survived the event. So we can be grateful for this design of things. However, when stress leads to shock and we are permanently hampered by a nervous system that can't let go and emotional reactions that control how we live our lives, it's important that we undo the damage and reprogram the body. For healing to occur, we must bring ourselves back from the splitting off, from the retreat to the circus, then mend the broken parts and make them whole again.

Even our ability to align the personality with a "bigger than life" energy or entity (as we do when we run away to the circus) has its place in our development. All primitive societies and tribes have their rites of initiation, often highly developed, which play an important part in their social and religious lives. Through these ceremonies, boys are made into men and girls into women. The noted psychologist Carl Jung cites the example of the Kavirondos people, who stigmatize those who do not submit to circumcision and excision as "animals." For them, the initiation ceremonies are a magical means of leading man from the animal state to the human state.[1]

These rites could be labeled a kind of "controlled trauma." In the process, the individual aligns with an archetype, god or spirit. For this to be a moment of spiritual development or growth, this kind of encounter must be accomplished without:

- Identifying with the archetype, inflating one's ego or
- Projecting the archetype onto another, opening oneself to hero worship and "the good fight" against demons; or
- Replacing archetypes with stereotypes. Jung speaks of the gods as having "become diseases" through literal interpretations.[2]

Trauma and shock that happen outside an intentional initiation rite also align us with these archetypes, as we've discussed. In this case, however, we are taken over or possessed by the archetype, which steps in to respond to any situation that we perceive as a threat similar to the shock that first caused the possession. The archetype becomes our ego in these times, and as Jung once said, this possession turns the person into a "flat collective figure." However, we have the opportunity for healing if we can experience the original, traumatic event(s) in a new way, accepting the encounter(s) as an initiation like the Kavirondos, transforming from the animal state to the human state.

Earlier in this book, we discussed that trauma (psychological) and shock (physiological) are distinct issues and need to be treated differently as a result. You cannot use the same tools to undo them. In fact, if you use the tools meant to treat trauma when dealing with a person in shock, it can be counterproductive. It can end up reinforcing dysfunctional patterns.

Now we'll speak to the therapist, in terms of how to distinguish between trauma and shock, and then we'll discuss how they need to be treated as separate matters at first and then how the treatment is integrated. If you're in therapy or looking for a therapist, this should also help you to understand the techniques we believe are needed for a true recovery.

DISTINGUISHING BETWEEN TRAUMA AND SHOCK

The most important thing as you begin working with a client is to understand whether you're dealing with trauma only or whether shock is also involved. One of the easiest ways to recognize it in your office with a client is by seeing 1) how connected or dissociated they are with their emotions and 2) whether a cathartic release occurs when expressing one's emotions during a regression. In our work, we might follow an adult who is doing reparative therapy back to a traumatic experience as a child, and then take him or her through a corrective experience. For instance, we regress a man who is now re-experiencing a time when he was being abused as a six-year-old, so we want to find a way, in the context of that age-regressed ego state, for him to experience fight or flight.

So in this case, we might employ his internal defenders to push the abuser away, to yell out, to tell what happened, to put it into words, verbalize it and express his emotions which may include anger. We might encourage him to yell out, "I hate you for what you are doing to me!" When a person can experience that energetic release cathartically—the level of wounding we're working on—then we know we're helping him to release the trauma from his mind as well as his body.

Sometimes, however, we find that someone in this process, being abused in that child's ego state, can't find the power within himself for fight or flight. He's terrified and frozen, having gone into the witness protection program that we spoke about in chapter 4. As you know by now, this is a clear sign of parasympathetic nervous system dominance, and therefore you're dealing with shock and have to treat it accordingly. In this instance it's shock because he physically can't respond, but in the first instance it was only trauma because he could physically respond and release it.

It is very important, in both instances, that the therapist:

1. Has done *his or her own trauma resolution work* so that he or she can remain present for whatever emerges for the client.
2. Knows how to facilitate the *energetic release* of strong emotions such as anger, grief, shame and fear.
3. Knows and recognizes the difference between shock and trauma.

Shock can manifest with dominance in the sympathetic nervous system as well. Sometimes, as in the last example, you might give that client a tennis racquet and say, "Hit the punching bag and release those feelings of resentment within you." Perhaps your client will take the tennis racquet and start hitting and yelling, "I hate you! I want you to stop! You have no right!" And so on. But they keep on hitting and yelling and, no matter how long the person engages in that behavior, *it doesn't deplete the energy underneath.* Or the client may just keep hitting the air with the tennis racquet without using any words, without releasing any emotions.

If you're dealing with a client's trauma, where the person is still physically connected to his or her emotions, this kind of action will reduce and eventually deplete the angry energy because behavior and inner experience are still tied together. In the case of shock, they are no longer physically connected to their emotions because they've gone into the witness protection program. Instead, someone else—another identity—is associated with the emotions. So the energy never depletes. This is how you know that you're dealing with shock, and at that time, it's important that you step in as the therapist to treat the shock first by redirecting the therapy.

You might think of it like having your foot holding down the gas pedal in your car, while the brake is also on. The car is in gear, it's trying to move, but it can't and you're burning up the engine. That's what happens when we encourage cathartic release when someone is deeply in shock and unable to dissipate the underlying emotions.

So when the therapist is trained to recognize that shock is present, another approach to treatment is necessary. That's why it is so essential that over the past few years, this concept has become well accepted among therapeutic professionals who have been privileged to be introduced to it. In truth, there are still millions of therapists and drug treatment specialists who still have not learned how to recognize or treat shock. Once the concept of shock is introduced to professionals, the light bulb goes on as they realize that their most difficult clients are the ones who are suffering from untreated shock. One of the many reasons talk or cognitive therapies can be ineffective with some people is that shock affects the memory. Clients most often report that their cognitive memory is clouded; however, with regressive therapies, it is easier to treat the shock and thus recover a good portion of the memory that has been in a frozen shock state. This will also improve the day-to-day cognitive memory.

If we allow an action to continue that never unwinds the energy, then we're actually re-enforcing dysfunctional patterns. We want to first address the shock and reconnect someone to their emotions before we can use cathartic therapies for releasing the trauma. For those whose shock has activated the sympathetic nervous system, we want to help them activate the parasympathetic nervous system as the antidote, and vice versa. In addressing sympathetic shock, the "time out" or "cool down" provided by a few quieting breaths, a sip of cool water and an ice pack on the neck or forehead allow the client to access an inner calm, systematically reducing the levels of shock. In addressing parasympathetic shock, the inner resource is an awareness of an activation of energy somewhere in the body which, by focusing on it, can be expanded into the remainder of the body, thus systematically reducing the parasympathetic shock.

We often ask clients which they would prefer, heat or cold. Some prefer the cold experience of an ice pack around their necks, over their eyes or just to hold. Others prefer a warm heating pad to be placed upon their navel or other areas. There are even some clients who go into deep shock and want both, each to be placed on different areas of their bodies. Some clients also like the smell of essential oils as a method for treating shock. The feeling of the warmth and/or cold, the essential oils, along with sips of water, bring clients back into their bodies so that they can proceed to process and thus release the traumatic memories.

Imagine that you are treating a female client who is having difficulty sleeping and has been diagnosed with a sleep disorder. Perhaps she remembers being deeply afraid of ghosts or the dark as a child and hiding under her bed for protection. When you've regressed this woman and she's in the ego state of that little girl, hiding terrified under her bed, clearly in a parasympathetic state of shock, it doesn't work to go to that three-year-old child and say, "Just yell at that ghost and tell it to go away. Tell the ghost it has no right to be here." At this moment she's in parasympathetic shock, numb, frozen with fear and therefore doesn't have the ability to fight off the ghost.

Instead, we have to meet her in a place to which she can relate, so we slow our client down. We quiet ourselves and our client so that we can both become centered and connected. Then we get down to her level and offer eye contact or a hand to hold. We create a sense of security as we, ourselves, are becoming less active. And at that time, we begin to ask, "What would help you to feel even safer? Would you like a blanket around you? Would you like me to sit a little further away or a little closer? What would help you feel safer right now?" Slowly, we coax her into speaking and expressing her feelings and coming out of her terrified state of shock.

As the client begins to take action, which brings her into a more active state of the nervous system, we can slowly move her forward. Perhaps we invite her to imagine having a flashlight, so to speak, and inspecting her closet for the ghost. As we help the young child to feel supported, she may begin to feel safer so that she can face the *real* fears which have caused her to take refuge under her bed or in the closet. We may encourage the client to bring in someone as a resource, like a grandmother who can hold her hand and protect her. The therapist provides her with resources that she may not have realized were present for her then as that small, terrified child. The therapist provides her with some new tools to take action on her own and to truly come out of the parasympathetic shock state. Only then, when you've brought the client out of the shock, will you be able to work with the trauma level so that she can face her actual traumatizing demons and experience a true cathartic release.

LAYERS OF HEALING

In our work, we recognize three layers of healing: ego (personal), existential (social/ cultural) and transpersonal (archetypal). This is true whether you're talking about ego development or spiritual growth.

The **ego level** is organized around the self-image of "I" as separate and unique from all that is "not I"—the physical dimension of being with nature and the social dimension of being with others. Here psychotherapy is focused on "What I am not, what you are." In other words, the client discovers long-held erroneous beliefs about herself (such as "I am shameful" or "I am bad" or "I deserve everything bad that happens to me") and discards them, declaring her innocence. At the same time, she must attribute responsibility or guilt onto the perpetrators of neglect or abuse in childhood. The individual here is limited to black-or-white thinking—"you and I are nothing alike." Work at the ego level builds boundaries, integrates polarizations, replaces nonfunctional concepts of self and others and modifies character structure for more fulfillment. According to B. Wittine, "Once individuals have developed a more cohesive egoic identity, they can embark on a process that takes them further on the journey of self-discovery, that of unfolding their existential self, or their true inner individuality."[3]

The **existential level** is organized around the "I" living the "human condition;" that is, life on earth itself and the social, cultural and spiritual ramifications of it—the personal dimension of being with oneself. Here psychotherapy is focused on "What you are not, what I am." In other words, the client explores a deeper layer of unconscious experience including his own culpability, his secondary gains for maintaining a dysfunctional *status quo* and his shadow side. At the same time, he begins to have compassion for those who victimized him, recognizing that they are not the entirely bad people he railed against in the first layer of healing work. He is beginning to see many more gray areas—"You and I are not so different." People's existential issues are related to their mortality and impermanence, their experience of freedom of choice (or lack of it), their sense of worthiness and their sense of separation from or connection with others. Work at this level is to loosen the rigidity of the self-image, to expand relationships to incorporate the sacred and to integrate the profound influences of prenatal and perinatal experiences and one's relationship with death.

The **transpersonal level** is organized around the parts experienced as "not I," including rejected and repressed parts, introjected and attached energies and unrealized potentials—the spiritual dimension of being a human with meaningful and conscious choice. Here psychotherapy is focused on "What 'I' am when I witness myself in the same way as I witness the world." One is opening to the subtleties of paradox, to the reality of the invisible, to the possibilities of peaceful coexistence through embracing the tension of opposites. The work at this level includes identifying and healing repressed shadow parts and unconscious anima/animus (these are two primary anthropomorphic archetypes of the collective unconscious in Carl Jung's analytical psychology) constellations through re-collecting one's projections, identifying and reclaiming the transcendent parts previously beyond reach (such as archetypal, karmic/past life, pre-conception) and establishing collaborative relationships with archetypes from the collective unconscious (such as spirit guides, angels, gods, "the muse," and energies in the natural world like the forest, wind or fire).

As you can imagine, people do not work on these layers strictly sequentially, so that for someone who is primarily at the biographical/ego layer there may be occasional forays into both of the others, and for someone who has progressed to working primarily at the archetypal/transpersonal layer, it may be useful to occasionally address the other two.

The perspective of the subject shifts emphasis as we progress through these layers. First the 'I' is separate and unique (what I am not); it moves to an 'I' connected to the human condition (what I am) and then to an 'I' that incorporates both without being limited by either (what I *really* am). Clarifying who 'I' am involves discovering early introjections and dis-identifying with them, discovering all the many projections and re-collecting them and dis-covering the other psychical subjects who populate the unconscious...then forming alliances with them.

Someone can discover shame or fear or rage or grief, all of which were early introjects from a shame-filled, fearful, raging or broken-hearted parent; indeed, "I am not that." Continuing to a deeper layer, though, that individual will find that she does, in fact, belong; that she is, in fact, smart and capable and worthy. She has seen these qualities in others and felt jealous that they had what she did not, but now she is ready to claim them for herself; indeed, "I am that." Yet she also has seen pettiness, jealousy and lack of integrity in others and felt relief that she wasn't like that; now she is ready to re-collect those projections and claim those qualities for herself as well; indeed, "I am that, too." Continuing to a still deeper layer, she finds that the reclaimed shadows have turned out to be guides of introduction and initiation to rela-tionship with the archetypes that inhabit the unconscious.

NAVIGATING CLINICALLY BETWEEN LAYERS

The metaphor we've used in this book is that when someone experiences shock, they have "run away to the circus" and therefore we have the existence of a complex. The more deeply embedded the shock state, the more autono-mous is the complex. Working with shock, we have found it's very helpful to regress a client back to the source trauma to discover and differentiate the two aspects of any complex: (1) the original, essential part of the client's child that split (ran away to the circus) and (2) the archetypal energy (the bodyguard circus character) with whom he became identified. The first is the core of the complex and the second provides the "bigger than life" quality to it. When we facilitate healing a complex, we are liberating the split-off essence to return and flourish and we are also liberating the archetypal energy to return to its imagined realm. Each one is freed from its bondage to the "unholy bargain" made so many years earlier. The Perfectly Nurturing Mother or Trapeze Artist archetype is now liberated from the contamination of personal projection and is available once again as a powerful resource.

Because of this, therapeutic facilitation requires us to navigate between these two layers of wounding and their respective sources. However, when dealing with individuals deeply wounded by early trauma, you'll want to understand and prepare for the client's resistance to treatment. The therapy relationship may actually remind them of the original abuse, betrayal or other trauma, and now you're asking them to undo and relinquish the survival defenses that have made life possible up until this point. Indeed, we're not just asking them to remember, but to re-experience the unbearable trauma that they've spent a lifetime trying to avoid. The part of the client's personality that is resistant is the most powerful part—the bodyguard hired so long ago. The wise therapist welcomes the challenge from this inner authority (the archetypal bodyguard), although it may well feel like an obstacle. The appearance of resistance provides the clearest map of the inner landscape on both the personal layer (ego and shadows) and the archetypal layer (complexes).

Working with adults to heal early trauma calls on both the therapist and the client to navigate what we call the *borderland*, a concept developed by Jerome Bernstein.[4] The borderland is that space in the mind where the rational, the "trans-rational" and nature meet and are integrated. The borderland personality is one who may have experienced the same trauma and anxiety as the borderline personality but doesn't split as a result of his/her "trans-rational" experience(s); or it's someone who has healed the split that occurred. The borderland personality is able to tolerate ambiguity, is at home with the natural world and the archetypal realm and has expanded her identity beyond the ego and personality.

At some point during almost any session—even one focused on the transpersonal layer—it becomes clear that residual emotional content from the past is "bleeding through" into the current work in the form of projections. The client may be dialoguing with a symbolic image or dream figure or may be expressing the perspective of that figure in role reversal, and as a result experiences abreactive emotion (fear, hate, jealousy, grief, etc.). It's often helpful to age regress the client at this point for further clarification on the source of that reaction. You can do the age regression *either* from the ego state of the client *or* of the archetypal figure, whichever the client is in when the need for regression surfaces. This is because regression from either one will go back to the source trauma and therefore the source of the shock state. We can regress to the source by following either of the two aspects of the complex (the essential part of the client's child that split or the archetypal energy—the bodyguard). Either route will take you back to the same originating traumatic event(s).

A significant difference between working with shock on the *personal* and the *archetypal* layers is the nature of the resources that we use when we introduce them to the client. In both cases the resource is external to the client. In work that is predominantly personal, we bring in a healthy, nurturing adult (e.g., a grandmother, teacher or parent from the client's childhood or perhaps the client's own adult ego state). The age-regressed child ego state needs to have the *corrective experience* of safety and nurturing provided by an appropriate caregiver. In work that is predominantly archetypal, we bring in a powerful symbolic resource instead: it may be a figure or image from a dream, a Tarot card or an active imagination.

We want to make sure that we use the appropriate resource, depending on the layer with which we're working. Using archetypal resources for a client working at the personal level ends up collaborating in spiritual bypass, suppressing emotional distress rather than healing it. Using personal resources for a client working at the archetypal level simply facilitates psychological bypass, reinforcing old patterns of self-limitation rather than moving beyond them.

Ultimately, our goal for corrective experiences needs to address all layers. In doing so, for example, the client needs to experience liberation from a suffocating birth canal *and* needs a transcendent pathway opening up to grand new horizons. The client needs to reclaim and nurture her own traumatized six-year-old *and* recognize kinship with the "I'm in control here" Drill Sergeant archetype that stepped into her life at six. Thus, we contribute to healing in the personal unconscious *and* in the collective unconscious.

USING DREAM SYMBOLS

In our work, we often use symbols such as those that come to us in dreams to access the archetypal layer of our psyches. These symbols are often easier for us to accept so that we can ease into the deeper meaning of what our unconscious minds are communicating to us. Dr. Carl Jung taught us how valuable these symbols are in order to understand and communicate with the deepest parts of ourselves. From the Gestalt therapy model, developed by Dr. Fritz Perls, we learn a clear method for having our clients play the role of their dream symbols in order to receive the deepest teaching from them.

One of our clients, Jerry, has had a very problematic relationship with women his whole life. He has a beautiful, devoted wife who has stood by him through many difficult times. Often, these times have been exacerbated by Jerry's sexual and romantic fantasy addiction with other women. He has had trouble accepting the true love of his wife and has continually looked to other women to meet these unmet childhood needs. His relationships with women have actually been conducted by the insecure young boy within him.

His psychodrama session began by having him remember a deep fear that came over him during a dream with a powerful symbol representing the Divine Feminine. He was strongly drawn to this Divine Feminine, yet something about her was causing him great fear. He was terribly confused by the irrational fear he experienced in his dream and every time afterwards when he recalled this beautiful symbol of femininity.

In his first age regression, Jerry visited an incident at age eight when he was taking a nap with his brother and mother in her bed. He was innocently stroking his mother's hair, feeling love for her, but when she awoke she suddenly slapped him across the face, accusing him of something inappropriate and sexual in nature. He began to feel fear and confusion about mother's love and the safety of bonding with her and with women in general.

Next, we regressed Jerry to his birth experience, when the umbilical cord was wrapped around his neck and he was choking, believing that he was going to die. He felt suffocated by the source of his nourishment, the umbilical cord attached to his mother. So his first attachment with Mother, with the Feminine, with the essence of Motherhood, was experienced as deadly and suffocating on the deepest level. This put him into sympathetic shock where he was frantically kicking, trying to get untangled and attempting to take his first breath of life. The more he attempted to untangle the cord, the tighter the cord wrapped around him and the more suffocated he became.

In his psychodrama session, Jerry's first reaction was to want to cut the cord around his neck to stop the suffocation. But it was vital that Jerry recognize that he needed his connection to his mother through the umbilical cord in order to live through the birth process. We had to help him detoxify that experience by releasing the shock that was keeping the experience locked in his psyche. He re-enacted his birth, gently and slowly untangling the cord that was wrapped around his throat. We did this by asking him to bring back the beautiful dream of the Feminine Deity and asking her to unwrap the cord.

As she began disentangling the cord in the psychodrama, he began to feel the most amazing, devotional love for her. He relaxed, sensing the inherent protection of the Divine Mother's presence. As she (the representation of the Divine Feminine) continued to assist him in gently disentangling the cord, he felt completely freed and was able to proceed joyously through the birth canal.

We helped Jerry to bring the safety of the Divine Feminine, represented by the dream symbol of the Divine Mother, together with his relationship with the earthly feminine, represented by his mother. He began feeling tender appreciation for his mother, no longer defined by the two threatening incidents he experienced during birth and at age eight. He also began opening up to wanting closeness with his wife. He could see clearly how the embedded shock from those two early traumas had been contaminating his relationships with women and with his dear wife. It had caused him a lifetime of searching for feminine connection in relationships that were toxic and deadly, compulsively repeating the primal, terrifying birth experience.

TREATMENT IMPLICATIONS

Stephen Porges's therapies for healing trauma, based on his Polyvagal Theory, confirm the principle that less stimulation is more effective for a challenged nervous system. A second principle is that the intervention must take place in a safe environment and a third principle is that brainstem regulation is the foundation of the self-regulation process.[5]

Because we know that sympathetic and parasympathetic responses differ and yet interact, we also know why it's so important to have differential approaches to treatment. While accessing the hyperarousal or hypoarousal response, we need to help clients stay present, feel safe, communicate their experience and feel empowered. Following are some suggested guidelines for treatment of trauma, complex trauma, Disorders of Extreme Stress Not Otherwise Specified (DESNOS), which "refers to a condition resulting from exposure to multiple traumas or from exposure to high levels of chronic stress"[6] and Complex Post-Traumatic Stress Disorder (C-PTSD), which we are calling *shock*. These guidelines assume that the clinician is able to differentiate between trauma and shock levels of pathological damage and that they employ the three principles just stated.

1. **Approach traumatic material gradually** to avoid intensification of the affects and physiological states related to the trauma. The pace and intensity of any cathartic intervention needs to be "calibrated so as not to overwhelm. It must match the client's capacity."[7] Be watchful for the client's overwhelm and "retreat" above (sympathetic shock) or below (parasympathetic shock) the optimal arousal zone. When that occurs, immediately stop working with the content of the trauma memories and treat the shock by addressing the need for safety, containment, body awareness and connection to support. "Containment of out-of-control emotions and thinking processes will help restore a feeling of control over the psychological self. Positive body-awareness will help restore a sense of the body and its sensations as friend, not foe. Dual time awareness will help to separate that the trauma occurred in the past even though it feels as if it is occurring now."[8]

2. **Cultivate an acute awareness of inner body sensations** (bodily feelings of a distinctly physical character, such as trembling lips, heaviness in the chest, twitching in the hands, clamminess in the feet, tightness in the throat, tension in the buttocks, pounding heart, numbness in the extremities, tingling in the right arm, shallow breathing or vibrating sensations in the solar plexus area, etc.). According to Pat Ogden and Kekuni Minton of the Hakomi Somatics Institute and Naropa University in Boulder, Colorado, "Through cultivating such awareness and ability for verbal description, clients learn to distinguish and describe the various and often subtle qualities of sensation. Developing a precise sensation vocabulary helps clients expand their perception and processing of physical feelings in much the same way that familiarity with a variety of words that describe emotion aids in the perception and processing of emotions."[9]

   You can do this, for instance, by pointing out subtle sensory motor changes and gross muscular movements through a simple awareness statement such as, "Seems like your neck is tensing," "Your hand is clenching into a fist" or "There's a slight trembling in your left leg." Here we use the Gestalt techniques of asking the body to describe itself. "Give your neck a voice. If your tight neck could speak, what would it say? I..." This ingenious technique actually allows the body to give us clear messages of what is happening in the deeper levels of the unconscious mind. This encourages the client to drop way down, below the limits of conscious thoughts, to the emotions that are stored in the somatic levels of the body. It gives the repressed emotions a method for surfacing into the conscious awareness of the client, as well as to the awareness of the therapist.

In our work, we try to stay away from asking mental questions that bring the person out of the unconscious mind and back into the thinking mind. The main questions we might ask would be ones that direct the clients' awareness out of their thoughts and into their somatic awareness: "What are you aware of in your body?" The client may say, "I have a tightness in my heart." Okay, Give that tightness a voice and let it express to us. Or give your heart a voice, let it speak; "I'm tight..."

3. **Access enough traumatic material to process, but not so much as to dissociate**. You'll want to "hold" the client's arousal within the optimal limits while encouraging access to, exploration of and expression of the traumatic memory. When arousal reaches the upper levels, we give the client methods for releasing the energy from the body. When these emotions are released, we help them to increase the energy of the emotions again and then use that to have their unconscious mind, using the emotional bridge, take that thread which leads to the underlying traumatic event. These emotions, which have been stored in the body for years as stress or even disease, can now be expressed and released.

4. **Work toward cathartic release** or other physical forms of release such as "unwinding" the paralyzed energy in limbs or organs of the body. The concept of "exchanging...an active response for one of helplessness" is coaxing the person to use willpower and the support of the therapist or group members to initiate a sympathetic response (fight/flight) to replace the deeply embedded parasympathetic

response (freeze).[10] For the person to experience the active defense sequence (pushing with legs or arms, moving out of paralysis into proactive movement, yelling "No!") brings her out of dissociation into her body and begins a *kinesthetic reframing* process. The client may begin to experience the somatic pleasure of physical resistance and defense, and the emotional delight of a new experience of personal power. The sequence, produced through encouragement and trust, becomes a template for the same new response to occur spontaneously in the future.

5. **Give the experience of having personal needs acknowledged and responded to** by a caring and safe support person. You may offer a drink of water (which also flushes toxins from the system), offer heat or cold if it would be soothing, offer additional means of protection (such as something to cover the vulnerable umbilicus, the hand to hold of a supportive group member or bringing into an age-regressed scene someone from the person's life at that time to stem the terror) or establish direct contact nurturing (touch, open eye contact). We also include the value of your expressions of acceptance of the person's feelings, outrage at the abuser, empathy for the hopeless predicament of the child or the affirmation that any child would react the same way in order to normalize the child's behavior.

6. **Speak the experience of victimization** in order to integrate the memory functions and lessen the immobilizing emotional/sensory reflex. The client is literally reconnecting the experience (implicit or body memory) with the cognitive context for it (explicit memory) and in the process is repairing the physical damage done to her hippocampus.

7. **Reframe basic assumptions** about the self as secure and intrinsically worthy, and about the world as orderly and just. Your client's most deeply embedded beliefs are accessible for review and reframing because through age regression you've arrived at the very scene of their inception.

8. **Ask clients what conclusions they drew about themselves.** We are always amazed that, regardless of the age of the baby, they can always get in touch with self-deprecating conclusions they made

about themselves. Then we ask what decisions they have made about their future behaviors. An example may be, from a child who was unwanted, "I'm worthless." And then the decision might be, "I'll just die." These conclusions and decisions are like the programming that is stored in our computers. They remain in operation until the computer is reprogrammed. So a big part of the treatment process must include discovering what these early conclusions and decisions were and how to change (reprogram) them.

9. **Release the anger and blame directed against the self** for the inability to defend against the abuse. A common response among trauma survivors is to interpret their dissociation and freezing as a personal weakness.[11] This is a golden opportunity for re-establishing a loving, accepting relationship with the inner child, who until now has likely been reviled and rejected. Releasing the self-blame, internal shame and self-hatred that most trauma survivors experience is the key to a healing path. This is essential for true long-term recovery.

10. **Locate the traumatic experiences in time and place** to start making distinctions between current life stresses and past traumas. It has been shown that, during a traumatic threat, the hippocampus becomes suppressed. Its usual function of placing a memory into the past is not active. The traumatic event is prevented from becoming a memory in the past, causing it to seem to float in time, often invading the present.[12] In the words of an incest survivor in treatment, "I'm stuck in my past. It is like a never-ending past life."[13] We need to recognize, too, that traumatic memories are stored as emotions and senses (implicit memory), and are therefore often hazy, impressionistic or kinesthetic. So, understandably, survivors become haunted by feelings and senses they suspect are related to the trauma, but cannot clearly identify as explicit memories. The more the client can tolerate facing the trauma that they experienced, the stronger they become as they peel away the layers of shock and reclaim their own personal power. As a defense, some people will say, "Oh, I don't want to live in the past, I just want to be in the future." However, if they become strong enough to uncover what someone else has done to them, this strength allows them to release the shock

that has kept the past trapped in their bodies. Just as the old saying goes, if we don't learn from history, we are doomed to repeat it. Shock will insure that repetition if we don't release it energetically from our bodies.

11. **Help the client to trust and surrender to a healthy interpersonal relationship** with you as a therapist as you demonstrate an ability to understand the client's distress and tolerate the description and re-experience of her trauma without withdrawing, becoming hyperaroused or hypoaroused. When you, as therapist, have resolved your own reservoir of trauma, you will be nonreactive yet empathetic to your client's trauma. By dissipating your own shock pool you will likewise be inoculated against the contagion of your client's shock. Thus the client will have a direct corrective experience of her overwhelmed state being contained and her deep pain being soothed.

    Be aware, you cannot help someone to heal something that you cannot face in your own life. Many therapists collude with the denial of their clients because it matches their own denial and inability to see their own truth. The therapist's healing is always our first priority in this work. And the concept of the wounded healer seems to be nearly universal in our over thirty years of experience in training and working with therapists. It appears that people are attracted to the field of therapy because they are desperately searching for their own healing. Therapists have just as much, if not more sexual abuse, family dysfunction, addictive behaviors and depression and anxiety as the clients they serve. If this goes untreated, then this does the therapists as well as their clients a great disservice.

12. **Help the client recognize that current life stresses tend to be experienced as somatic states**, and accept physical symptoms as allies rather than enemies. Physical symptoms are the body's way of communicating an unmet need to the person; they are not a statement of defiance, mutiny, hostility or weakness. Developing an awareness of inner body sensations and a precise sensation vocabulary is helpful for restoring a sense of the body and its sensations as friend, not foe and helps dissipate the accumulated shock in the body's nervous system. An illness or disease is the arrow

that points the way into the body and where the somatic healing is needed. The mind, body and emotions are intricately connected and must be treated as one organism, not as separate entities. They all contribute to self-discovery and thus, when integrated, contribute not just to healing but to personal transformation.

13. **Develop new outlets for discharging stress** and for creating a sense of well-being. The individual may have relied on re-enactment of stress and trauma—through endorphin release and dissociation—to achieve relief, numbing of the pain and what has passed for a sense of well-being. The pattern is to seek re-exposure to stress for the same effect as taking pain-killing opiates, providing a similar relief from stress. Expression rather than repression of feelings now becomes a new, healthier option for the person.

14. **Increase self-regulation and thereby prevent the escalation of arousal** to the point of discharge through aggression or other undesirable behavior. Hyperactive defenses can take the form of uncontrollable rage or frantic frenzy and become very destructive in interpersonal relationships. When the shock has been treated and dissipated, the client now is much more able to express his feelings in a safe and healthy manner. When people are operating from shock states, they only have two responses: usually numbness without any expression or frantic and often abusive overreaction. This is very common in domestic violence situations where one person goes into a sympathetic outburst of pent-up emotions and the other goes into parasympathetic shock and thus continually believes the aggressor that it will never happen again.

This numbness with underlying anger can be witnessed by observing various mass shooters. They go into the school or movie theater with weapons and begin to fire. Witnesses have often described these shooters as being completely calm as they blasted rounds of bullets into the audience or group of school students. The perpetrators often then calmly turn their weapons on themselves. This is a severe parasympathetic shock state. The shooters are not wild or frantic, which takes people by surprise. But understanding shock makes this completely logical.

Perhaps some of these devastating acts of violence can be prevented by recognizing and treating the underlying shock and trauma of these young people. By learning to sense the physical precursors to full-blown aggressive outbursts and by treating the underlying shock, this will increase the aggressor's own feelings of safety and prevent some of these attacks from occurring.

15. **Increase the sense of personal safety** by helping the client experience all of the above. Whenever a person's shock pool is activated, he is subject to taking a deep dive into that pool and repeating the abuse or perceived abuse that has happened to him. Fear of being attacked physically or emotionally often elicits deep feelings of shame and thus is an intense trigger for abusive behavior.

RESISTING LIFE—HOW WE CAN SEE SHOCK

With shock, we often see what we would call a resistance to life. Many people might think that's a difficult concept to understand at first and may ask us, "What do you mean, I'm resisting my life?" Maybe they're hard workers. Maybe they feel engaged. They don't consciously understand.

In most of the cultural traditions we're aware of, the optimum life experience really involves being present in the here and now. However, most of us don't live that way at all. So when we talk about resistance to life, we're talking about not being fully present. John Lennon said it well in his lyrics to *Beautiful Boy (Darling Boy)*: "Life is what happens while you are busy making other plans."

There are three primary ways of creating that pattern of resistance to life. One is concerned with **avoidance and engulfment**. Avoidance is the strategy of compulsive self-reliance, denial and inhibition. For instance, you take the time to talk with someone and they never look at you or acknowledge that you're talking with them. Maybe they're great at multitasking and can honestly give you attention like this, but it's likely that they're not fully present with you.

That classic picture of a dysfunctional marriage occurs, where the wife complains that the husband is preoccupied with his big toys or his work and he never pays attention to her. He is avoiding her. And meanwhile, those who have participated in marriage counseling may know how often the man's return complaint is that his wife is too controlling. This is the opposite of avoidance, when someone is intrusive, over-involved or engulfing. Someone at either of these extremes is failing to be in the present moment, embracing life. Meanwhile, the synthesis between these two extremes is connectedness. So for those who exhibit shock through avoidance or engulfment, the antidote or cure to these is finding the ability to connect intimately yet with healthy boundaries, to be open and receptive to life experiences.

Ambivalence and rigid intolerance are the second strategies for resistance. Ambivalence is a strategy of preoccupation with both what is wanted and what is not wanted. The problem here isn't about knowing what you want and taking action toward that goal, while at the same time knowing what you don't want and taking steps to avoid it; the problem is the preoccupation with both to the point that you're never in the moment taking action. This person is trapped in a never-ending shock state of internal debate. This can happen, for instance, if you grew up in a family where any choice you made was ultimately judged to be the wrong choice, so you learned it was better not to make a choice at all. You would be stuck knowing what you wanted and didn't want while feeling sure that action toward either would make things worse and deprive you of the other. This leads to perfectionism and procrastination, other forms of resistance to life.

The opposite of ambivalence is intolerance or rigidity. We all know someone who always knows the "right way" to do everything, and who becomes anxious when others do it differently. This individual is attempting to create safety by imposing his own obsessive lifestyle on those around him. He may have grown up with parents who demanded that he adhere to their habitual ways, and enforced that demand rigidly. When this individual can't force others to comply with his demands, he is likely to grudgingly go along or to simply refuse to participate. The synthesis of these two extremes is the ability to make passionate commitments, and this is the antidote to the shock that manifests in either extreme.

The third strategy for resisting life is **having control or giving up control**. Control is about regulating internal distress by controlling the environment or the outside world. "If I can just control my spouse and my boss and the neighbors and the police and the Congress and God…" The individual is certain to be frustrated and therefore feel unsafe, because in anyone's life there are many more things that are beyond our control than those that we actually do control. Unfortunately, his solution is to try harder to maintain even tighter control.

The opposite of control can take a couple of forms: either uncontrolled (undisciplined and wild) or helpless and noncommittal. Some people regulate their internal distress by throwing caution to the wind and, in the process, abandoning any semblance of controlling their lives. They profess to be prepared to let anything come their way, and they often even seem to tempt fate with impulsive choices that carry real risks. Another way of giving up control is to become impotent in life, unable or unwilling to make decisions or to take a stand. This strategy lends itself well to a "victim consciousness" because one can always take refuge in the comfort of knowing "I didn't choose this," no matter how badly anything turns out. The synthesis between these extremes, the antidote for either symptom of shock, is ego-resilience—the ability to adjust relatively easily to the unexpected, even if it is unwanted.

ENERGY MANAGEMENT TECHNIQUES

Most people would say, "Sure, I want connectedness, passionate commitments and the ability to adjust easily to the unexpected. But how do I maintain these in the midst of all the craziness in my life?" Because of life's fast pace, the question is understandable, which is why we teach some simple methods for staying connected, passionate and flexible anytime—maybe especially amidst craziness. We refer to these as energy management techniques.

The first technique uses central nervous system management via the vagus nerve. Even through this one energy management option, there are several methods of doing this, and we're listing just a few here.

One of the points we like to make in working with clients experiencing shock is this: everything below the heart and lungs is regulated by the parasympathetic nervous system, so their processes relax you. When you have an orgasm, you relax. When you digest, you relax. When you eliminate waste, you relax. This system responds to traumatic threats with precipitous relaxation: the freeze response or "death feigning." Everything above the heart and lungs is about activation, fight or flight. It includes the extremities. So you are looking, smelling, speaking or even yelling, running and fighting—these are all controlled by the sympathetic nervous system. Where is the big connection? In the heart and lungs, because these regulate what is below and what is above. This is why regulation of the heartbeat and breathing are so useful in therapy, because they provide a window of access to both parts of the nervous system at once, allowing an opportunity to balance and harmonize the two systems.

We discussed heart rate variability (HRV) in our chapter on physiology. Today a lot of work is being done in that field. You may be familiar with software by both HeartMath and Wild Divine. These measure and give friendly feedback about the user, helping him or her to bring the heart into more optimal rhythms. The primary method of affecting HRV is through the breath; in general, breathing slowly at a rate of six breaths per minute (five seconds on each inhale and five seconds on each exhale) is optimal.

In our chapter on physiology we talked about accelerated breathing as a symptom of hyperarousal and we gave the example of walking down a dark street and hearing a sound that scares you. Then you find it's just a nearby cat knocking something over. You could continue to carry the unused and unwanted stress hormones that were just produced in the body, or you could consciously choose to release them; you can do this with a good shake, an involuntary shudder. But you can also do so by breathing. Breathing is perhaps the single most effective and accessible mechanism in our bodies at our beck and call to affect the state that we're in.

Many ancient wisdom traditions and yogic practices teach the use of breath to affect the physiology. In our Heart-Centered therapies, we train participants to use Conscious Connected Breathing, often referred to as "breathwork." This produces a divine return to the body, mind and spirit of the person. Properly taught and supervised breathwork releases layers and layers of shock stored in the body as well as in the energetic field of the client. Basically, if you learn to breathe consciously, you can immediately change the state you're in. By using these methods, you can help to bring yourself into the present moment, to pull yourself out of preoccupations with the past and future. We have already discussed how this is very much a matter of resolving shock.

Our second technique for energy management is reclaiming inner resources and soul retrieval. What we're doing in soul retrieval and age regression work is retrieving resources that have been taken from us as children or that were otherwise contaminated. We are bringing these resources back to where they belong, into the present moment. It is courage and innocence combined with healthy femininity, masculinity and integrity. By eliminating the shock stupor, we are able to reclaim those inner resources we know we once had, but that seemed to have been lost along the way. They belong to us, and they're what make us powerful when we have them here with us in the moment. By eliminating the shock stupor, we are reclaiming our memory for even the everyday things in our lives that seem to have previously slipped away. So in an experience of self-doubt or when feeling overwhelmed, along with a few calming breaths allow yourself to remember that you *do* have your courage, your competence, your innocence and all the other resources that seem to have slipped away.

Our third technique for energy management is discernment of what within me is "mine" and what within me is "other than me." We need a method of separating and releasing that which is other than us. We've all probably had the experience of walking into a room where someone is fuming mad and being affected by the other person's emotions in a negative way. If I can remain neutral and not take on the other person's negativity, I can stay with my own inner state and remain true to myself. In hypnotherapy, we have an opportunity to accomplish the same thing on a lifelong time frame.

Let's focus on the conception experience. When we entered the earth realm, we did it the way all human beings have and all mammals do through the genetic material of the father and the mother. We jumped right into whatever mom and dad consisted of at that point in time. So in that moment, a big part of our existence was defined by everything carried in the sperm and egg. If there was fear in that moment, we could not help but absorb some of that fear. If there was anxiety or guilt or shame, or if there was exuberance for life, we could not help but absorb some of that. All through our childhood, right up to this moment, we have been influenced by so many other people and forces that we have introjected. Especially in our early years, in our time of magical thinking, we did this: "Father was angry with me and so, magically, I know he is right and that I'm messed up. I'm wrong. I'm bad."

An example of this was a recent psychodrama with a woman who is very accomplished in her field and yet has to fight negative thoughts about herself, especially when she's about to make a professional presentation to her peers. The words "Something is wrong with me" scream at her constantly. In the psychodrama, she regressed back to being a small baby where her mother did not really want another baby and definitely did not want a girl. When she was asked to play her mother, she kept saying, "Do you want me to play the mother who is screaming that something is wrong with me or the loving mother that I wanted her to be and that she has become?" She actually had internalized this *rejecting mother* to such an extent that this mother was in a frozen shock state within her mind, constantly having the power to criticize her. Once she released this introject of the young, fearful mother who had lived within her mind and body all of her life, she experienced a joyful freedom and acceptance of the loving mother whom her own mother had actually matured into being later on in life.

The important thing for us to know as therapists, and for us to help our clients grasp, is that it was manufactured by someone else, even if we took it in and identified ourselves *as that*. If we took it in, through clarity and consciousness we can give it back. That's one of the powerful things we do in this healing work and it's especially powerful in the age-regressed ego state. In age regression, the earlier we go in our history the more possible it is to discern what is ours and what is not and to give back what we've mistakenly believed to be ourselves.

Our fourth energy management technique involves ascending toward spirit and descending toward the soul in order to establish balance. It's not an accident that we've incorporated Kundalini meditation (meditating to awaken inner spiritual energy in order to purify the system) in all of the work we do. We're working with vertical conduits of energy, taught to us through the Vedic scriptures (the oldest scriptures of Hinduism) and located along the spine: the Ida carries yin parasympathetic energy; the Pingala carries yang sympathetic energy and the central channel, the Sushumna, carries the Kundalini spiritual energy itself. These are the elevators that we use to communicate between our bodies and the energetic field where our souls reside and the penthouse where the spirit abides. We need a way to keep energy and communication flowing in both directions. If the flow of energy through these channels is blocked or at least constricted by shock in the system, which impedes growth and development spiritually as well as emotionally, it is urgently imperative to unblock these channels. Kundalini meditation, pranayamaic breathwork (yogic science of breathing) techniques and Kundalini yoga are important ways for that natural flow to occur, and for that reason these practices are very helpful in repairing the damage caused by chronic shock patterns in the body.

Finally, our fifth technique for energy management uses additional methods of neuropsychological integration to resolve patterns of structural dissociation. Chronic shock in the nervous system is an example of structural dissociation and we can repair that damage, revitalizing the part of the body's structure (nervous system) that has become dysfunctional through blockage and atrophy. That return to integration is vertical, involving the parasympathetic and sympathetic nervous systems, the heart, the brain and the chakras (energy points) from the root chakra of survival to the crown chakra of transcendence.

All of the things that we do in our protocols are important contributions to that vertical integration. Another important form of integration is horizontal—for example, left brain and right brain. We know how different these two hemispheres are: the right brain is intuitive, synthesizing, creative, holistic and more agile in novel situations while the left brain is rational, analytical, sequential, objective and more active in routine processing. To function optimally, we need them both to be balanced and integrated so that we can call on the part of the brain best suited to any particular task. The work we do catalyzes integration of left and right brain in a number of ways. Language functions such as grammar, vocabulary and literal meaning are typically processed by the left brain and language prosody functions such as rhythm, intonation and emotional state of the speaker by the right brain. We encourage the client to verbalize her experience from the age-regressed ego state during an age regression, which places demands on both hemispheres. The hypnotic trance itself exercises both sides of the brain, using the ability to focus on specific objects of awareness (such as a discreet set of body experiences or memories), and simultaneously calling on the ability to observe the "big picture" and recognize overarching, lifelong patterns.

There is also integration horizontally from front to rear in the brain, from the newest part of the brain and cortex to the oldest part of the brain— the reptilian brain, the brain stem and the limbic system. PTSD and chronic PTSD symptoms reflect that traumatic memories were laid down directly by the amygdala in the limbic system, with the emotional threat alarm blaring its warning. Years or decades later, whenever the memory is triggered, the alarm sounds just as if the threat were still present. Having a client re-experience the traumatic source event(s) in age regression allows the therapist to assist the client in modifying the actual memory by incorporating a context for it. The threat occurred on *that* night, with *that* perpetrator, when I was *that* age. "That was then and this is now" context helps to turn off the ever-present alarm bell by expanding the brain's processing of the experience to include the frontal cortex so that it is no longer only held by the reptilian brain's fear response. This is how the damage done to the brain by abuse can be repaired.

In essence, we are discussing the re-empowerment of right hemisphere functions, tyrannized in the trauma survivor by archetypal energies and primitive affects. Donald Kalsched summarizes the parameters of treatment for such persistent states of shock.[14] Repair, he says,

---

...depends less on insight (left) than on experience-in-the-body (right); less on technical vocabulary and more on metaphor; less on abstractions and more on immersion in the particularity of experience; less on the past and more on the present moment; less on analysis of the patient's explicit memories and more on his/her implicit experience in dreams and other imaginal products; less on the patient's separate psyche and more on the paradoxical "potential space" that emerges "between" the psychoanalytic partners.

SHOCK IS CONTAGIOUS

One more interesting point about shock is that it's highly contagious. One person's shock can trigger another person's. It is the right brain that is more connected to the primitive emotional centers in the brain stem and limbic system, and to the autonomic nervous system which regulates sympathetic or parasympathetic regulation. Allan Schore's research has shown clearly the importance of right-brain-to-right-brain communication.[15] It is in this intimate and unconscious exchange that shock states are contagiously passed. And when the therapist begins to use right-brain-to-right-brain communication consciously and intentionally, repair is possible. It follows the description provided above by Kalsched.

First, we must become aware of the contagion that can affect us; only then can we protect ourselves against being unconsciously infected and then go the next heroic step to conscious utilization of the phenomenon for the healing of the client. So we like to caution therapists about this and remind them that we are all humans and all susceptible to shock, regardless of whether we are the client or the therapist. This doesn't take away from our power to help them, and we shouldn't be ashamed of working on our own shock patterns even while we're helping others. In fact, it is essential! We, as professionals, cannot help to heal others if we ourselves are unhealed. We cannot see or even stay present for the deeper emotional release required if we fear the deepest emotions within ourselves. And we will most certainly collude with the defenses of denial within our clients if we continue to deny our own unhealthy behavioral patterns. A model for all of us could be the accepted strategy in the field of addiction treatment of hiring recovering addicts. The emphasis is on the treatment personnel themselves being in their own recovery process.

One example of how shock is contagious occurs when you feel yourself getting sleepy and your eyes closing while working with a certain client. It may often be the case that your client is in parasympathetic shock and your shock is being triggered. You may just be deprived of sleep, but if you don't have another reason for falling suddenly into a stupor, take this as a clue. Alternatively, if you begin to become agitated and restless and you are desperately searching for a solution to your client's problem, it may be that she is dissociating into sympathetic shock and that you have been infected by her shock contagion. This is most apparent when you continue to offer solutions for the client and she plays the "Yes, but..." game. She continues to shoot down all the wonderful suggestions you are making for her to solve her problems. Besides the fact that you have fallen into the Victim, Rescuer, Persecutor triangle trap with her, you'll need to do something to bring yourself out of this shock state if she is ever going to find healing through your facilitation.

One weekend we were doing a psychodrama where a client, Janet, was working through a heavy abuse situation. As Janet described her feelings to her therapist, Susan, we wondered, at first, why the therapist wasn't guiding the psychodrama. Suddenly we realized that the therapist had gone into shock herself and was distracted and dissociated. So we gave the therapist an ice pack: The cold temperature helped to bring Susan out of shock so she could continue the work with Janet. Never hesitate to do something similar for yourself so that you remain fully present and useful to your client.

FINAL THOUGHTS ON HEALING SHOCK

When people suffer from shock, one of the things they lose is their libido or passion for life. The process of splitting away from the true self has shame at its foundation, and therefore a deep sense of loneliness. When the child ego state experiences connection and acceptance from the therapist and from the person's adult ego state, and from this a release of the underlying shame, it brings relief from the loneliness. But there is also another level of disconnect, and that is the loss of libido. As famed British psychoanalyst Donald Winnicott put it, "The state prior to that of aloneness is one of unaliveness, and the wish to be dead is commonly a disguised wish to be not yet alive."[16] We have also spoken of it as *resistance to life*.

Sometimes this resistance is a defense against some unwelcome intrusion in our life: a parent's judgments or abandonment, a public failure or a private obsession. James Hollis is clear that "we are also haunted by absences... absences are still presences and that death, divorce, or distance do not end relationships."[17] For example, a looming influence in one's life could be the absence of a parent who died in childhood, or the disheartening loneliness of unrequited love. And, as Hollis quotes Kierkegaard, "The most painful state of being is remembering the future, particularly the one you'll never have." Both unresolved past and unattempted future are huge obstacles in our ability to be present for our life experience.

This resistance to life can lead many people to be actively suicidal, but many more are passively suicidal. This includes people with eating disorders such as anorexia where the person is quietly and secretly starving herself to death. Or the compulsive over-eaters quietly creating heart conditions, pre-cancer patterns or diabetes. The bulimics who refuse to absorb the nutrition along with the calories of the food they ingest and are on a path of slow suicide. This includes all the active alcoholics and drug addicts possibly creating heart disease, cirrhosis of the liver and the ever-present possibility of overdosing. We are most aware of the life-threatening dangers of smokers actively creating cancer or heart disease for themselves and the families who reside in the smoke-filled house along with them. This also includes all the sex addicts who don't use protection and may be setting themselves and their unknowing partners up for STDs and AIDS.

These are all shock states and, if left untreated, will certainly create early, very preventable, death for the participant and possibly for their unwitting family members.

Releasing the abandoned child ego state from its purgatory of perpetual limbo between life and not-life brings spontaneity, playfulness and creativity into the daily life of the now-unified client. And that is the importance of the work you're doing as a therapist, especially when you've understood the difference between trauma and shock and can more successfully, more confidently, more consistently treat them both.

The results will tell you what a real difference you're making in people's lives. One example from our experience is Judy, one of our clients, who had spent thirty years in an abusive marriage with a husband who had numerous humiliating sexual affairs and on one occasion raped her in a drunken rage. Feeling totally helpless in this relationship, she had retreated emotionally into a pervasive state of shock and dissociation over almost the entire thirty years. She functioned very well in her profession and socially among the many well-to-do acquaintances in her upper-middle class life. So how could this happen? How could an intelligent, educated professional woman live in a state of confusion with an abusive man for so long and not confront the situation? The answer lies in her self-replicating supply of abusive somatic memories and what Freud called repetition compulsion.

In one psychodrama that we did with Judy, she began working on her persistent feeling of choking, which went back to her husband choking her as he was raping her. This is a body memory. This memory carries somatic energy which lives in her system and resonates and attracts whatever is similar in the system. As she regressed on the somatic bridge, Judy went back to other times in her life when she had that same choking feeling. This took her back to many episodes in childhood when her own mother was abusively choking her, and she dissociated from the shock of the betrayal. We began to realize that Judy had a long childhood pattern of going into shock because of the abuse suffered from her mother, who had Borderline Personality Disorder. The energetic somatic memories of what happened in childhood had literally set the stage for Judy's passive acceptance of her abusive husband in adulthood. Judy's unconscious conclusion was that "I am bad and I don't deserve to live" and her behavioral decision based on that absolute unworthiness was that she was just going to have to be quiet and endure. She was not living, she was enduring; rather than thriving, she was merely surviving and possibly not for very long.

Through her healing work, Judy was gradually able to redirect the energy in her throat from that of choking to the energy of assertiveness and freedom. The physical sensation in her throat became a trusted barometer for her of how passive or assertive she was being in life situations. The more passive she was, the more her throat constricted. The more assertive she was, the more her throat relaxed. Soon, she exerted her personal power with her husband by divorcing him and demanding an equitable settlement. Judy got her life back while reclaiming her dignity and her faith in humanity. She released the shock that had kept her confused for so many years and is now vibrantly alive and making healthy choices for herself in her new life.

Katherine, another one of our clients, is a young woman with persistent PTSD symptoms as well as a long history of alcohol and drug abuse. She describes her childhood and adolescence as painful. Even though she is intelligent and a successful professional, she nearly lost her whole career due to her inability to stop using drugs. She was desperately attempting to numb her own pain, although she was totally unaware of where the pain had originated.

During hypnotherapy, Katherine regressed to a time when she was very young and had a severe rash in her vaginal area. Her mother took her to the doctor, who used her as a teaching resource by inviting several other doctors to observe his treatment of her. Her mother did nothing to protect her, even though Katherine violently expressed her wishes not to be treated in this way. She was tied to the table, something was put over her mouth to quiet her and her legs were attached to the stirrups. You can imagine the trauma for this young three-year-old girl. Katherine was not only traumatized, but the experience was so overwhelming that she went into shock. Then she became mute for several years and was unable to speak, an expression of shock stupor. This response to trauma brought her the label of being emotionally withdrawn, possibly catatonic and hysterical. Actually, her dissociative defense against the trauma had become "crystallized in the body,"[18] and she was physically and emotionally unable to penetrate through that blanket of shock.

Katherine's hypnotherapy focused on helping her to release the dissociation that accompanied the trauma of her abusive loss of control over her body and the resulting shame and helplessness. It is a gradual process of supplanting early experiences of helplessness with new corrective experiences of agency and personal power. She has been able to reclaim her voice and express the feelings that went unheard by her mother and the doctors. Katherine is learning to trust again, allowing her therapist and group therapy members to serve as transitional figures in her journey toward re-parenting her inner child. She is now clean and sober from drugs and alcohol. Katherine is committed to continuing her self-exploration and healing.

The path of healing for Katherine will be slow and difficult, because of the degree to which the traumatic imprint of helplessness was crystallized in her body. The depth of her early dissociation segregated mental and emotional associations, disturbing the integrated organization of her identity, memory and consciousness. The result has been varying degrees of depersonalization, amnesia, numbing and shock stupor. Facilitating Katherine's healing, the release of her identification with helplessness, requires creating immense safety for her, insuring that she has many, many corrective experiences of controlling her own body and her life experience. Her healing can be measured in her growing self-identity as a fully developed and fully present young woman with an internal locus of control.

It is precisely those successes that remind us of just how powerful this work is, of just how powerful each of us can be as therapists when we undo the unhealthy contract between ego and archetype, aligning each correctly with their own worlds to play the healthy roles they were meant to play. By bringing clients out of trauma and shock patterns and into the present moment where they have their strength and their purpose, we help to release the power of souls into this world—souls who have work to do and who, unhindered, can do great things full of life and joy and service. We strongly believe that is the work that we, as therapists, are here to do.

Appendix 2

TREATMENT OF THERAPIST SHOCK

The famed psychologist Carl Jung wrote: "The patient, by bringing an activated unconscious content to bear on the doctor, constellates the corresponding unconscious material in him...The doctor by voluntarily and consciously participating in the psychic suffering of the patient, exposes himself to the oppressing contents of the unconscious and hence, also to their inductive effect...Doctor and patient thus find themselves in a relationship founded on unconsciousness."[1] This is, in fact, the contagion of shock states, carried through the mechanism of right-brain-to-right-brain communication.

Since some therapists have not previously been aware of the manifestation of shock in their clients, they are also not aware of how it affects them personally. It is vital for therapists to address their own shock first, in order to treat their clients effectively. It is similar to what the airline crew instructs us to do in case of an emergency: we need to put on our own oxygen masks first so that we're then able to help our children or others. If the therapist is in *parasympathetic shock*, the symptoms may take the form of feeling sleepy or drowsy while listening to a patient's story. The therapist may feel his or her eyelids closing, may need to yawn or may have difficulty staying present with the client. This sleepiness reduces the therapist's effectiveness but it can also alert the therapist that he or she has entered "a place of connection with a part of the patient that languishes in a kind of paralytic slumber."[2]

A therapist in *sympathetic shock* may feel agitated while listening to the client's story. Rustling papers, shifting around in the chair, tapping the foot or fingers, and having racing thoughts to come up with "helpful" suggestions for the client are all symptoms of this form of shock. Many therapists become frustrated when they offer what they believe to be obvious solutions and yet the client returns the next week having followed through on none of them. The reason is clear when you understand the principles of shock. Their helpful suggestions really come from their own seductive shock response of offering unwanted solutions to the client. This is just one example of why the therapist needs to resolve his or her own shock.

Ideally the therapist is fully capable of monitoring his or her own state and reactivity, and is aware of how to self-regulate whenever he or she begins to respond with *sympathetic* or *parasympathetic shock*. Indeed, that may well be a primary goal for the client as well.

DEFINITIONS OF SHOCK TERMINOLOGY

Allostatic load (shock pool): Trauma load of difficult, overwhelming, undigested experiences. Only when it interferes with life does it become a problem.

Abuse: This can be any violation to the mind, body or spirit of a prenate, infant, child, teenager or adult. Abuse does not necessarily look traumatic to an outsider but certainly feels traumatic to the receiver. A common form of abuse is called bullying. This abuse by one child toward another may look to the adults like "kids will be kids." However, the most devastating form of all abuse/bullying contains shaming. In China it is called "losing face," which is an apt description of why it is so destructive to young, vulnerable souls. Bullying is often learned in the home environment, where the father may bully the mother, grandparents, neighbors or children. It certainly can also be a pattern of behavior learned from the mother, who may feel powerless in her life and thus bullies others in an attempt to regain "the face she may have lost." Abuse can also consist of physical, mental, emotional and/or sexual disrespect and trauma. There is a long continuum of behaviors that are prevalent in abusive families, churches and schools. Children are captive to the adults around them and therefore even though the abuse may not seem all that bad to an outsider, if it is done on a consistent basis without escape, then it turns into pervasive trauma which leads to the shock response.

Anesthetic shock: An incredibly numbing dissociation from consciousness that results from a baby or child experiencing the terrifying onset of unconsciousness sweeping over him/her. It originates when a fetus gets an overdose of anesthesia during surgery or the birthing process. The amount of anesthetic given to the mother is based on her body weight and as a result the dosage is massively more than what the body weight of the fetus might require or be able to tolerate. If the child is then given subsequent doses of anesthesia for a medical procedure, this further complicates the anesthetic shock.

Apparently normal personality (from the Theory of Structural Dissociation): The aspect of an individual that, in a traumatic split in childhood, progresses to become adaptive using age-inappropriate behavior, e.g., the substitute spouse or the hypervigilant one who anticipates others' needs and meets them. This personality develops in a split-off shock state so that the child can avoid further abuse and try to keep up the appearance of everything looking normal, when in fact it isn't. The apparently normal personality is resentful toward the other part of the split in personality, the **emotional personality**, judging it to be weak and inadequate.

Archetypes: Primordial, structural elements of the human psyche, common to all humanity. They are systems of readiness for action, the most effective means conceivable of instinctive adaptation. They are often represented by characters in fairy tales and myths or by circus characters. The King and Queen, the Magician, the Clown and the Ringmaster are just a few examples of archetypes that may be used by children to feign power, to create distraction from painful experiences or to maintain a smile when deep pain needs to be covered up.

As If personality: A description named by Helene Deutsch for a type of patient in which the individual's emotional relationship to the outside world and to his own ego appears impoverished or absent. The patient himself appears to be unaware of this absence, though he may complain of feelings of emptiness. Deutsch explains her use of the term *as if*, observing the inescapable impression that the individual's whole response to life has something about it which is lacking in genuineness and yet outwardly runs along "as if" it were complete.

Bi-Phasic Response to Trauma: The body's attempt to avoid hypoarousal and hyperarousal by maintaining itself in the optimal arousal zone.

Body memory: A somatic experience or sensation at a specific location in one's body that is the residue of an earlier trauma experienced in that part of the body. An instance is when young girls who have been sexually abused often have excessive pain later in life with menstruation or intercourse. The tightening of the vaginal muscles called vaginismus has been reported as an example of a body memory for a sexual abuse victim. Children who have been physically abused often develop physical symptoms in the specific area of the body where they were traumatized.

Catatonia: An extreme example of the unresolved freeze response, a deep state of shock/dissociation in which the individual cannot respond in any way.

Catatonic stupor: Symptoms of immobility, rigid and waxen mask-like face, fixed and unfocused gaze or stare and lack of reaction to stimuli, which nevertheless accompany evidence of alertness. Despite their apparent unresponsiveness, they often have a surprising level of mental functioning with awareness of events going on around them. This represents an extreme form of the parasympathetic form of shock—paralyzed.

Catatonic excitement (hyperkinetic catatonia): Appears with symptoms of apparently purposeless agitation not influenced by external stimuli. This is the sympathetic form of shock in which the traumatized person is highly active yet that activity is completely non-productive. It is the physiological response to severe stress usually triggered by something that reminds the person of abuse or re-traumatizes.

Collective unconscious: A structural layer of the human psyche containing inherited elements, distinct from the **personal unconscious**. According to Carl Jung, each person not only has his or her own unique unconscious mind, but also shares some elements of unconsciousness with all other people. He called this the shared unconscious or the collective unconscious. Jung suggested that there are archetypes (images and memories of important human experiences) that are passed down from generation to generation. The collective consciousness refers to the common human experiences that we have all shared in the process of being human; that we as human beings carry the memories of what has happened to any of us. So on an unconscious level we all know what it is like to be the victim and to be the perpetrator. We may know what it is like to be the tortured Jew and the powerful Nazi, the devastated rape victim and the violent rapist and the indigenous people and the self-righteous colonizer, claiming the land. We know what it is like to be the martyred Christ and to be the crowd of angry onlookers, yelling for the hanging.

Complex: An emotionally charged group of ideas or images that becomes a primitively organized alternative self that has its own identity. A complex is a split-off (dissociated) part of the individual which has attached to an archetype at its core. Complexes are relatively autonomous from the known ego-self. For example, we have commonly heard of the Mother complex. It is called a complex because it contains so many of the experiences we have of "the Mother," from both personal experience and the collective. An example of what is contained within the Mother Complex for a particular person might be: 1) the loving, nurturing mother who meets our needs; 2) the distant mother who is too busy meeting the needs of all the children, and is thus emotionally unavailable; 3) the explosive, angry, terrible mother who is unpredictable and unsafe; 4) the Madonna as the perfect spiritual mother, truly altruistic with no needs of her own. Another well-known example is the "inferiority complex" which can step in, push the everyday ego out of the way and impose its own version of reality to sabotage any efforts to excel or master a given challenge: "I can't do it," "Anybody else could do it better than I could," and "I don't even want to try because I know I'll fail." We all have many complexes.

Complex trauma: The level of trauma that has become embedded in the individual's autonomic nervous system, what we're calling "shock." Complex trauma refers to the fact that there is often one traumatic event piled upon another traumatic event. It is like building blocks—each, by itself, may not be that heavy. But when one block is piled upon the next, this is when trauma leads to overwhelm and the nervous system responds with sympathetic or parasympathetic shock.

Depression: Severe despondency and dejection, accompanied by feelings of hopelessness and inadequacy. A condition of mental disturbance, typically with lack of energy and difficulty in maintaining concentration or interest in life.

Discovery shock: The reaction of the fetus when one or both parents feel fear or shame or anger in the moment that they discover that they are expecting a baby. When the parents are unmarried, are very young, are impoverished or uneducated, they may discover that they have an unplanned pregnancy. When the young mother discovers she is pregnant, *her reaction is immediately felt by the fetus*. If her reaction is shock and then anger, fear, shame and/or regret, this can thus become the prototype for how the individual (the baby in the womb) expects to be received by others throughout his or her life.

Dissociation: A pattern of reaction to unpleasant or unexpected experiences which often involves moving our consciousness from our bodies and emotions to somewhere outside of ourselves. We call this "leaving your body" and there are various ways in which people do this. Sometimes the individual will stare at something like the television, the computer screen or out the window. This is called eye fixation and is a common method of inducing an immediate trance state. If the pattern of dissociation is called upon frequently due to living in intolerable situations, it becomes embedded in the nervous system as a shock pattern. Because hypnotherapy directly addresses these dissociative states, it is most effective in their recognition and treatment.

Egg shock: The traumatic experience that can occur at conception when, from the perspective of the egg, it may feel invaded and like it needs protection. The experience is a sense of being threatened and overwhelmed by the surrounding activity.

Emotional personality (from the Theory of Structural Dissociation): The aspect of an individual that, in a traumatic split in childhood, regresses to an infantile state of helplessness. Pre-verbal, this aspect of the personality often expresses through somatic symptoms and intense emotional outbursts. This aspect of the personality is judged as weak and inadequate by the **apparently normal personality**, the progressed part which is coping through adapting as best it can.

Heart rate variability (HRV): Considered a measure of neuro-cardiac function that reflects heart/brain interactions and the dynamic coherence (or lack of it) of the sympathetic and parasympathetic branches of the autonomic nervous system. It is a valuable tool which can help to assess the different shock states a person may be in and can also be used to self-regulate the body's systems toward a more optimal homeostasis.

Hippocampus: A seahorse-shaped structure located in the medial temporal lobe of the limbic area of the brain. It plays a central role in flexible forms of memory, in the recall of facts and autobiographical details. It gives the brain a sense of the self in space and in time, regulates the order of perceptual categorizations and links mental representations to emotional appraisal centers.

Homeostasis: In biology, designates when the body tries to maintain a balance point for optimal health.

Hyperarousal: An excessive fight or flight response to stress or threat—rapid breathing and heart rate, heart palpitations, raised blood pressure, hypervigilance, accelerated pace and amplitude of thoughts and emotions, intrusive memories and difficulties in concentrating. People often experience this as anxiety or stress resulting from a traumatic experience. If these traumatic experiences are frequent and/or prolonged, the individual may be living constantly in this extreme state of hyperarousal and hypervigilance. This eventually develops into disease symptoms and drugs may be used to mitigate the symptoms. However, if the underlying shock is not treated, new symptoms will continue to appear and re-appear, becoming chronic illness.

Hypoarousal: An excessive freeze response with decreased heart rate and respiration, lowered blood pressure, helplessness and hopelessness, sudden and extreme immobility, social isolation and withdrawal. This pattern of responding to traumatic events leads to depression and a quiet state of parasympathetic shock (as opposed to the anxiety resulting from hyperarousal). The hypoaroused individual rarely asks for help and often goes unnoticed until he or she may attempt suicide or begin to have a series of "accidents."

Implantation shock: The traumatic reaction of the conceptus to difficulty implanting into the mother's uterine wall. The mother may be afraid or ashamed of being pregnant, it may just not be a "good time" to be pregnant or she may be a fearful, nervous person. So when the conceptus attempts to implant into the uterine wall, it may receive a tense, cold, unwelcoming reaction. This experience of not being welcomed into the uterus at a very critical and vulnerable time will often create a shock response that results in a potentially lifelong prototype expectation. On the other hand, the uterine wall may reflect the mother's engulfing need to control others or to fill up her own emotional emptiness. In this case, the conceptus may then feel the shock of suffocation and engulfment.

Individuation shock: The traumatic response when the embryo begins to grow back out of the uterine wall, separating from the mother's flesh at two to three weeks after conception. This separation can bring relief and a sense of freedom and accomplishment, but it can also initiate a profound sense of alienation, rejection and loneliness.

Indwelling or **embodiment**: The mutual commitment between body and soul to make a life here on Earth. The terms are taken from Donald Winnicott. If the body is less committed than the soul, there may be medical issues and somatic complications, yet a strong will to survive even "against all odds." If the soul is ambiguously committed, there may be failure to thrive which cannot be explained medically.

Parasympathetic dissociation: A defensive effort to achieve a semblance of homeostasis in the body as a response to unpleasant or traumatic events. The person may often experience "spacing out," being a "couch potato" vacantly watching television or compulsively spending an inordinate amount of time on the internet. The parasympathetic dissociation is most often reinforced by addictive, numbing behaviors such as excessive, unconscious overeating. This category includes people who can sit and eat a whole bag of chips or cookies, an entire carton of ice cream or a whole batch of baked goods. Other drugs of choice for these folks can be tobacco, alcohol or marijuana, which basically exacerbate the numbness and insure that the dissociation lasts for longer and longer periods of time. Children who are in parasympathetic dissociation are reported by teachers to be staring out the window, not paying attention or basically not involved or interested in school.

Parasympathetic nervous system: The branch of the autonomic nervous system that activates to relax, digest, eliminate or allow vulnerability.

Personal unconscious: The personal layer of the unconscious, distinct from the **collective unconscious**. The personal unconscious contains lost memories, painful ideas that are repressed (i.e., forgotten on purpose), subliminal perceptions (sense-perceptions that were not strong enough to reach consciousness) and contents that are not yet ripe for consciousness.

Polyvagal theory: Based on work by Stephen W. Porges, who suggests there is a third branch of the Autonomic Nervous System called a social engagement system, which is characterized by neuroception. Neuroception is the process that suggests we continually evaluate, without awareness, the context of a situation for its inherent threats to survival and match the body's physiological state with social engagement, fight-flight-freeze or shut-down behaviors.

Projection: An automatic process whereby contents of one's own unconscious are perceived to be in others, e.g., rather than acknowledge my own tendency to be judgmental, I see that quality (and judge it) in others. It is certainly self-sabotaging when it is unconscious. When one projects onto others, assumptions are made without being checked out. Then judgments are made and these interpersonal patterns are the basis for most negative human interactions. For example, in marriages, one person (person "A") may be sexually attracted to a third person but then projects that desire onto the spouse (person "B"). Now person "A" assumes person "B" is having an affair, or wants to, and acting on the assumption perhaps becomes abusive or withdraws emotionally. Projection can be the basis for wars when one country or culture basically follows the same pattern. Projection can be positive when used to see the hidden shadow parts of ourselves that we often don't want to see. It is through psychotherapy, especially hypnotherapy and psychodrama, that we can begin to see our projections clearly and thus the personal transformation process begins here.

PTSD (Post-Traumatic Stress Disorder): A debilitating mental health condition that contains the ongoing residue of stress readiness, caused originally by a terrifying, traumatic event. Symptoms may include flashbacks, nightmares and severe anxiety, as well as uncontrollable thoughts about the event. Typically there are certain *triggers* that may jog our memory of a previously repressed traumatic experience. An example is a veteran who hears a car backfire and is suddenly transported back to the war zone. He may instantly feel like he is actually there and that bullets are coming in his direction. It is similar for people who were verbally, physically and/or sexually abused as children. Any trigger, such as the smell of alcohol on the breath of a lover, can transport them back to being a small child being abused by an adult who had been drinking. Because PTSD is a dissociative state, it is best treated through hypnotherapy, which can access the memories which need to be retrieved, resolved and released.

Shadow: A hidden or unconscious aspect of oneself, either good or bad, which the ego has either repressed or never recognized. It can be an aspect judged to be too bad to own ("I'm not *that* kind of person") or too good to accept ("I'm not *that* talented"). Any kind of psychic split from trauma is effectively a loss of some aspect of the individual, which is then replaced with an "other" that fills the void where the loss occurred. This "other" is a shadow. It is often these disowned parts of ourselves, these shadows, that we project onto others, but usually not in ourselves, The shadow is like the blind spot in your rear view mirror; you may just catch a glimpse of what it contains, but then it quickly moves out of sight again into the darkness. Even though our own shadow parts are hidden from us, our friends, family members and co-workers can often help us to identify them.

Shock: The residue of trauma embedded in the nervous system. Shock affects most of our population to different degrees. We can see it in the eyes of those who stare blankly, who talk incessantly and who go through life not present in their bodies. We can identify it in ourselves when we feel disconnected and sleepy, or frantic and stressed out. We can identify the types of shock we may be "medicating" by the "drugs" we use. People in parasympathetic (paralyzed) shock usually seek out stimulants such as excessive caffeine drinks and drugs such as cocaine or stimulants such as methamphetamines. People in sympathetic (frantic behavior) shock usually seek out more calming drugs such as alcohol, pot, antidepressants or sugar.

Shock pool: A reservoir of unassimilated distress carried by every person as a personal energy field, like the cloud of dirt and dust that follows the Peanuts character "Pig-Pen" wherever he goes. The pool stores any shock that a person has had from conception on, as well as the habitual behavior patterns, self-limiting beliefs and disease in the body's organs and nervous system.

Shock posture: An unconscious, habitual, automatic stance of the body that initiates the "auto-pilot" to take over. When a person goes into a shock posture, it may involve rocking, self-soothing or repetitive anger eruption without actually releasing energy. This may happen in a regressed state where an abusive memory is occurring and this shock posture keeps the person from experiencing the extent of the abuse.

Somatic dissociation: Split or altered perceptions (not only of *self* and *reality*) but of parts or regions of the *body*. This is most common when a child is beaten, punched or hit with objects. The pain, both physically and emotionally, may be so unbearable that these parts of the body become numb. It may also occur when children are sexually abused and those parts of their bodies may actually respond, at first with arousal. This makes the child feel too vulnerable and so a process of somatic dissociation takes place in order to protect the child from the unwanted sexual experience of arousal. What at first is a valuable protective defense later on becomes a problem: when this person gets older and now wants to have a loving sexual relationship, they discover that their body is still in the state of dissociative shock. They may be unable to feel any sexual arousal, unable to respond to their partners or have orgasms. They begin to "fake the orgasm" and in doing so ensure that it will probably never happen. Another problem with somatic dissociation is that in order to maintain the dissociation, the energy flow is stopped to this part of the body. This pattern is completely unconscious and opens the door for disease to enter this "deadened" area. All areas of our bodies, in order to maintain healthy tissue, require free energy flow which keeps tissue vibrant. So this is the irony: the pattern that keeps us alive as children can often kill us later in life. This is why all the mind/body healing modalities within integrative medicine play such an important role in achieving one's optimal health.

Soul Loss: The wounding of a child that is so invasive and devastating that some part of his/her essence is forced to "abandon ship" in order to preserve life. In our common language, the term "lost soul" is often used to refer to someone who just does not seem to be present in his or her life or body, someone with debilitating somatic dissociation. Yet, this term has more meaning than most people realize. When pervasive trauma happens from a very early age on, this can cause the soul to fragment and to jettison some parts. This is the good news and the bad news. The good news is that this most delicate part of ourselves can be protected by splitting and leaving! The bad news is that the person goes through life feeling empty, disconnected and without purpose. Again, with energetic work, the soul fragments can be retrieved so that the previously "lost soul" individual can begin to really live again.

Soul Retrieval: An ancient shamanic practice whereby the shaman (native healer) journeys out energetically to find and bring back the missing fragments of soul for an individual who has suffered soul loss. In hypnotherapy, we invite the people themselves to return to the location where the trauma or abuse took place, and where the fragments of their souls may have been left. It is amazing that in the hypnotic trance state, the client can usually begin to see the fragments of the split off or even shattered soul and gather up those pieces. They often have colors, and will return their soul pieces to the proper energetic areas of their bodies (chakras) where they belong.

Soul splitting: A very common occurrence in connection with trauma and shock. An analogy is to think of the soul as a magnificent piece of finely sculpted glass which covers our energy field and protects us. It is magnificent and yet very delicate at the same time. When abuses of the spirit occur, pieces of the soul may disconnect in order to remain pure and unviolated by the abuse. When abuse is prevalent and occurs in the very household where the child or infant is supposed to be safe, the soul may splinter just as if the glass were hit with a hammer and shatter into many little fragments.

Sperm shock: A sympathetic traumatic experience that can occur at conception when, from the perspective of the sperm, it may feel hypercompetitive to reach and claim the egg, or overwhelmed with all the frantic activity. People with this kind of shock are generally anxious and constantly in movement.

Spirit: An archetype and a functional complex, often personified and experienced as enlivening, analogous to what the archaic mind felt to be an invisible breathlike "presence." In Carl Jung's perspective, Spirit is the activating force for the psychic unconscious.

Spiritual busyness: Filling up one's time set aside for spiritual practice with activity, pursuit, efforts to achieve some particular experience, e.g., to become the "best" meditator, yoga teacher or Christian ever. This distraction is one of attending to what seems to be most *urgent* spiritually but not necessarily to what is in reality most *important*. This spiritually busy person looks to the outside world as if they are the most spiritual being alive. In actuality, they are spiritually hungry and yet unaware of how to experience connection with the highest parts of themselves.

Spiritual bypass: Confusing dissociation, visions from the astral plane or the efforts of spiritual practices with a true awakening. These experiences are used instead to avoid intimacy in relationships and engaged participation in society. People who engage in spiritual bypass often believe that they have reached the highest states of consciousness when in fact they have often only reached the highest states of dissociation.

Spiritual crusades: Fighting for a dogmatic principle or against a perceived external evil. It is often easier to identify, judge and condemn an external threat than it is to honestly face an internal one.

Spiritual shock/depression: Denying anger and resentment toward God and redirecting it inwardly, feeling disappointed in oneself and despondent in life. One may be confusing spirituality with dogma and religion, and one's anger is in actuality directed at religious authority. Some children are taught that they are sinners and that they are responsible for the death of Jesus. They learn that God is angry at them and that he is always watching them to see if they are perfect. This puts an inordinate amount of pressure on children and fills them with fear of God rather than love. They grow up longing for the beauty and innocence of the Divine only to realize that their fear and anger gets in the way. They have learned to hold in their feelings because you are never supposed to be angry at God, or the church, or the priests, ministers or rabbis. As we treat this religious/spiritual shock, most people realize that they have been angry at God but could never express it. As they begin to address and release their feelings, it becomes apparent that they must separate God from the church and from the religious dogma they were taught. This is a profound process of self-discovery which is essential in healing spiritual shock. And it is a process in opening up the heart to truly being able to love God and Self.

Spiritual materialism: Deceiving ourselves into thinking that we are developing spiritually when instead we are strengthening our egos through purchasing spiritual techniques and materials. Many feel if they buy and read more books, purchase just the correct statue or replica of God, enlightenment will be theirs. Ironically, it is this practice of spiritual materialism which keeps one from true connection with Self and God.

Spiritual suicide: Choosing to fall asleep spiritually, to hide from the challenging existential questions of a relationship with the Divine through mindlessness and monotony. It is the practice of either pretending that one has achieved enlightenment or pretending that one doesn't really care about it. Many people don't awaken to their spiritual needs until they are facing death. For some this may be too late. For others, hopefully, it is perfect timing.

Splitting: A term used to describe the dissociation of the personality, marked by attitudes and behavior patterns determined by complexes. The very young child who is not safe because of an abusive parent turns to the other parent, a grandparent or older siblings for protection. When these elders are themselves being abused and are in shock, there is nowhere else to go. The child begins to split off the most vulnerable parts of themselves or, as we call it, run away to the circus. They split off into different shock states to become the circus characters who hopefully will protect them from the abuse. A common one is the Clown who keeps the family laughing so that no one will address the shameful behavior that may be happening. It is a protective device; however, for many this splitting continues throughout life and those valuable, tender parts that ran away to the circus are difficult to retrieve without the help of a skilled therapist.

Sympathetic dissociation: A defensive effort to achieve a semblance of homeostasis in the body as a response to unpleasant or traumatic events. The person may often experience mindless busyness, incessant talking, chasing endless lists of "must do's" and constant attentiveness to others' needs. Sympathetic dissociation is most often reinforced by addictive, numbing behaviors such as excessive exercise or other pursuits, gambling or other thrill-seeking activities or high-risk sexual encounters.

Sympathetic nervous system: The branch of the autonomic nervous system that activates to excite, engage with the environment or prevent vulnerability.

Tend and befriend: A uniquely female stress response of tending to dependent children and seeking out social support, prompted by the hormone oxytocin.

Theory of Structural Dissociation (proposed by Ellert Nijenhuis and associates): Each aspect of a split can be thought of as a cluster of mental/emotional states, and that we have both an "Emotional Part" (EP) and an "Apparently Normal Part" (ANP) created by this divide.

Toxic nourishment: Nourishment or nurturing received by an individual that has been contaminated by the one providing it. The toxic contamination could be negative emotions such as anger, fear, jealousy or shame or it could be environmental negativity such as cigarette smoke, alcohol, anesthesia, stress, malnutrition or violence.

Toxic womb: A mother's womb that provides toxic nourishment to the neonate inside.

Trauma: An intense emotional assault, often accompanied by repression and a splitting of the personality. The traumatic experience activates a fight or flight response (sympathetic activation), unless the individual has descended into "learned helplessness" and the response is to freeze (parasympathetic activation).

Twin loss shock: The unconscious feeling of bewildering grief at the inexplicable loss of a twin in the womb.

Umbilical shock: The residual birth shock in the body's nervous system from the umbilical cord being cut prematurely, while blood is still flowing through it.

Unconscious: A state of psychic functioning marked by lack of control over the instincts and identification with complexes.

Victim Drama Triangle: A model of human interaction used in transactional analysis where there are three psychological roles: the victim, the persecutor and the rescuer. Often the victim is not as helpless as he seems to be, the persecutor does not have a valid basis for his coercion, and the rescuer is not really helping. The participants can switch roles, moving around the triangle.

REFERENCES

American Psychiatric Association (1994). *Diagnostic and Statistical Manual of Mental Disorders Fourth Edition – DSM-IV*. Washington DC: American Psychiatric Association.

Benz, D., & Weiss, H. (1989). *To the Core of Your Experience*. Charlottesville, VA: Luminas Press.

Bernstein, Jerome S. (2005). *Living in the Borderland: The Evolution of Consciousness and the Challenge of Healing Trauma*. London & New York: Routledge.

Britton, R. (1998). 'The suspension of belief and the "as if syndrome"'. In *Belief and Imagination*. London: Routledge.

Bustan, M. N., & Coker, A. L. (Mar 1994). Maternal attitude toward pregnancy and the risk of neonatal death. *American Journal of Public Health*, 84(3), 411–414.

Carmen, E. H., Reiker, P. P., & Mills, T. (1984). Victims of violence and psychiatric illness. *American Journal of Psychiatry*, 141, 378–379.

Castellino, R. (1997). *The Caregiver's Role in Birth and Newborn Self-Attachment Needs*. Santa Barbara, CA: Birthing Evolution-Birthing Awareness.

Childs, M. R. (1998). Prenatal language learning. *Journal of Prenatal and Perinatal Psychology and Health*, 13(2), 99–121.

Courtois, C. A. (2004). Complex trauma, complex reactions: Assessment and treatment. *Psychotherapy: Theory, Research, Practice, Training*, 41(4), 412–425.

DeCasper, A., & Spence, M. (1982). Prenatal maternal speech influences human newborn's auditory preferences. *Infant Behavior and Development*, 9, 133–150.

Deutsch, H. (1942). 'Some forms of emotional disturbance and their relationship to schizophrenia'. *Psychoanalytic Quarterly*, 11, 301–21.

DiPietro, J. A., Novak, M. F. S. X., Costigan, K. A., Atella, L. D., & Reusing, S. P. (May 2006). Maternal psychological distress during pregnancy in relation to child development at age two. *Child Development*, 77(3), 573–587.

Dixon, A. K. (1998). Ethological strategies for defence in animals and humans: Their role in some psychiatric disorders. *British Journal of Medical Psychology*, 71, 417–445.

Eigen, M. (1999). *Toxic Nourishment*. London: Karnac Books.

Emde, R. N., Swedburg, J., & Suzuki, B. (1975). Human wakefulness and biological rhythms after birth. *Archives of General Psychiatry*, 32, 780–783.

Emerson, W. R. (1996). The vulnerable prenate. *Pre- & Perinatal Psychology Journal*, 10(3), 125–142.

Emerson, W. R. (2002). Somatotropic therapy. *Journal of Heart-Centered Therapies*, 5(2), 65–90.

Farkas, B. (2004). Etiology and pathogenesis of PTSD in children and adolescents. In R. R. Silva (Ed.), *Posttraumatic Stress Disorders in Children and Adolescents [Handbook]*, 123–140. New York: W. W. Norton.

Feldmar, A. (1979). The embryology of consciousness: What is a normal pregnancy?" In D. Mall & W. Watts (Eds.), *The Psychological Aspects of Abortion*, 15–24. University Publications of America.

Fraiberg, S. (1982). Pathological defenses in infancy. *Psychoanalytic Quarterly*, 51, 612–634.

Freud, S. (1937). "Analysis terminable and interminable". *Standard Edition*, 23.

Freyd, J. J. (1994). Betrayal trauma: Traumatic amnesia as an adaptive response to childhood abuse. *Ethics & Behavior*, 4(4), 307–329.

Giannakoulopoulos, X., Fisk, N., Glover, V., Kourtis, P., & Sepulveda, W. (1994). Fetal plasma cortisol and B-endorphins response to intrauterine needling. *Lancet*, 344, 77–81.

Gilbert, P., & Allan, S. (1998). The role of defeat and entrapment (arrested flight) in depression: An exploration of an evolutionary view. *Psychological Medicine*, 28, 585–598.

Givens, A. M. (1987). The Alice Givens approach to prenatal and birth therapy. *Journal of Prenatal and Perinatal Psychology and Health*, 1(3), 223–229.

Gurrera, R. J. (1999). Sympathoadrenal hyperactivity and the etiology of neuroleptic malignant syndrome. *American Journal of Psychiatry*, 156, 169–180.

Hepper, P. G. (1988). Foetal 'soap' addiction. *Lancet*, ii, 1347–1348.

Hepper, P. G. (1991). An examination of fetal learning before and after birth. *Irish Journal of Psychology*, 12, 95–107.

Huizink, A. C., Mulder, E. J. H., & Buitelaar, J. K. (2004). Prenatal stress and risk for psychopathology: Specific effects or induction of general susceptibility? *Psychological Bulletin*, 130(1), 115–142.

Hull, W. F. (1986). Psychological treatment of birth trauma with age regression and its relationship to chemical dependency. *Pre- and Peri-Natal Psychology Journal*, 1, 111–134.

Jaffe, P., Wolfe, D., Wilson, S. K., et al. (1986). Family violence and child adjustment: A comparative analysis of girls' and boys' behavioral symptoms. *American Journal of Psychiatry*, 143, 74–77.

Jung, C. G. (1946). Psychology of the transference. *The Collected Works of C. G. Jung, Vol. 16, second edition*. Princeton: Bollingen.

Jung, C.G. (1966). The Mana Personality. *The Collected Works of C. G. Jung: Two Essays on Analytical Psychology. Vol. 7, second edition*. Princeton: Bollingen.

Kalsched, D. (1996). *The Inner World of Trauma: Archetypal Defenses of the Personal Spirit*. London and New York: Routledge.

Kalsched, D. (2003). Daemonic elements in early trauma. *Analytic Psychology*, 48, 145–169.

Keleman, S. (1989). *Patterns of Distress: Emotional Insults and Human Form*. Berkeley, CA: Center Press.

Kimbles, S. L., & Singer, T. (2004). *The Cultural Complex: Contemporary Jungian Perspectives on Psyche and Society*. Brunner-Routledge.

Klaus, M. H., Kennell, J. H., & Klaus, P. H. (1995). *Bonding: Building the Foundations of Secure Attachment and Independence*. Reading, MA: Addison-Wesley Publishing Company.

Kosfeld, M., Heinrichs, M., Zak, P. J., Fischbacher, U., & Fehr, E. (June 2005). Oxytocin increases trust in humans. *Nature*, 435(7042), 673–676.

Kosten, T. R., & Krystal, J. (1988). Biological mechanisms in posttraumatic stress disorder: Relevance for substance abuse. In M. Galanter (Ed.), *Recent Developments in Alcoholism*, 49–68. New York: Plenum.

Kurtz, R. (1990). *Body-Centered Psychotherapy: The Hakomi Method*. Mendocino, CA: LifeRhythm Press.

Lake, F. (1982). *With Respect: A Doctor's Response to a Healing Pope*. London: Darton, Longman & Todd, Ltd.

Levine, P. (1997). *Waking the Tiger*, Berkeley, CA: North Atlantic Books.

Lieberman, M. (1963). Early developmental stress and later behavior. *Science*, 141, 824.

Malone, A. (2003). An Interview with Donald Kalsched. Retrieved from http:// www.cgjungpage. org/index.php?option=com_content&task=view&id=187 &Itemid=40.

Mann, S. C., Caroff, S. N., Keck, P. E., & Lazarus, A. (2003). *Neuroleptic Malignant Syndrome and Related Conditions* (2nd ed.). Arlington, VA: American Psychiatric Publishing.

Marquez, A. (2000). Healing through prenatal and perinatal memory recall: A phenomenological investigation. *Journal of Prenatal and Perinatal Psychology and Health*, 15(2), 146–172.

Mehler, J., & Christophe, A. (1995). Maturation and learning of language in the first year of life. In M. S. Gazzaniga (Editor-in-Chief) & S. Pinker (Language Section Ed.), *The Cognitive Neurosciences*, 943–954. Cambridge, MA: The MIT Press.

Mehler, J., & Dupoux, E. (1994). *What Infants Know: The New Cognitive Science of Early Development* (P. Southgate, Trans.). Cambridge, MA: Blackwell.

Moskowitz, A. K. (2004). 'Scared Stiff': Catatonia as an evolutionary-based fear response. *Psychological Review*, 111(4), 984–1002.

Nadel, L., & Jacobs, W. J. (1996). The role of the hippocampus in PTSD, panic, and phobia. In N. Kato (Ed.), *Hippocampus: Functions and Clinical Relevance*. Amsterdam: Elsevier Science.

Nijenhuis, E. R. S., & Van der Hart, O. (1999). Forgetting and re-experiencing trauma: From anesthesia to pain. In J. Goodwin & R. Attias (Eds.), *Splintered Reflections: Images of the Body in Trauma*, 39–66. New York: Basic Books.

Nijenhuis, E. R. S., van der Hart, O., & Steele, K. (2004). Trauma-related structural dissociation of the personality. Trauma Information Pages website, January 2004. Web URL: http://www.trauma-pages.com/nijenhuis-2004.htm .

Ogden, P., & Minton, K. (2000). Sensorimotor Psychotherapy: One method for processing traumatic memory. *Traumatology*, 6(3). Available online at http://www .fsu.edu/~trauma/v6i3/v6i3a3.html.

Otake, T., Hatano, G., Cutler, A., & Mehler, J. (1993). More or syllable? Speech segmentation in Japanese. *Journal of Memory and Language*, 32, 258–278.

Panneton, R. K. (1985). Prenatal Auditory Experience with Melodies: Effect on Post-Natal Auditory Preferences in Human Newborns. Dissertation, University of North Carolina, Greensboro.

Perry, B. D., Pollard, R. A., Baker, W. L., Sturges, C., Vigilante, D., & Blakely, T. L. (1995). Continuous heartrate monitoring in maltreated children [Abstract]. Annual Meeting of the American Academy of Child and Adolescent Psychiatry, New Research.

Perry, B. D., Pollard, R., Blakely, T., Baker, W., Vigilante, D. (1995b). Childhood trauma, the neurobiology of adaptation and 'use-dependent' development of the brain: How 'states' become 'traits'. *Infant Mental Health Journal*, 16(4), 271–291.

Pert, C. (1999). *Molecules of Emotion*. New York: Scribner.

Pert, C., Ruff, M., Weber, R. J., & Herkenham, M. (1985). Neuropeptides and their receptors: A psychosomatic network. *Journal of Immunology*, 135(2), Supplement, 820–826.

Piontelli, A. (1992). *From Fetus to Child*. London: Routledge.

Porges, S. W. (2011). *The Polyvagal Theory: Neurophysiological Foundations of Emotions, Attachment, Communication, and Self-regulation*. New York: W. W. Norton & Co.

Purpura, D. P. (1975). Normal and aberrant neuronal development in the cerebral cortex of human fetus and young infant. In M. A. G. Brazier, & N. A. Buchwald (Eds.), *Basic Mechanisms in Mental Retardation*, 141–169. New York: Academic Press.

Putnam, F. W. (Fall 2004). Stuck in the past. *Psychiatry: Interpersonal and Biological Processes*, 67(3), 235–238.

Righard, L., & Alade, M. (1990). Effect of delivery room routines on success of first breast feed. *Lancet*, 336, 1105–1107.

Righard, L., & Franz, K. (1995). *Delivery Self Attachment*. (Video). Sunland, CA: Geddes Productions.

Rosebush, P. I., & Mazurek, M. F. (1999). Catatonia: Re-awakening to a forgotten disorder. *Movement Disorders*, 14, 395–397.

Rothschild, B. (1996). *Applying the Brakes: Theory and Tools for Understanding, Slowing Down and Reducing Autonomic Nervous System Activation in Traumatized Clients*. Paper presented at the Tenth Scandinavian Conference for Psychotherapists working with Traumatized Refugees, May 24–26, 1996, Finland.

Rothschild, B. (1997). Slowing down and controlling traumatic hyperarousal. In L. Vanderberger (Ed.), *The Many Faces of Trauma, International Perspectives* (in press).

Rothschild, B. (Feb 1998). Post-Traumatic Stress Disorder: Identification and Diagnosis. *The Swiss Journal of Social Work*.

Roz, C. (2002). Lecture on affect regulation, in *Embodiment and Emotion*. London, Tavistock Clinic: Conference Seminar.

Satt, B. J. (1984). *An Investigation into the Acoustical Induction of Intrauterine Learning*. Dissertation, California School of Professional Psychology, Los Angeles.

Scaer, R. C. (2001). The neurophysiology of dissociation & chronic disease. *Applied Psychophysiology and Biofeedback*, 26(1), 73–91. Available online at http://www .trauma-pages.com/a/scaer-2001.php.

Scaer, R. C. (2005). *The Trauma Spectrum: Hidden Wounds and Human Resiliency*. New York: W. W. Norton.

Schore, A. (2003). *Affect Dysregulation and Disorders of the Self*. New York: WW Norton.

Seligman, M. (1975). *Helplessness: On Depression, Development and Death*. San Francisco: W.H. Freeman and Co.

Sella, Y. (March 2003). Soul without skin, bones with no flesh: bodily aspects of the self in the treatment of women patients with restrictive anorexic eating patterns. International Journal of Psychotherapy, 8(1), 37 – 51.

Siegel, D. (1999). *The Developing Mind: Toward a Neurobiology of Interpersonal Experience*. New York: Guilford.

Solomon, H. M. (2004). Self creation and the limitless void of dissociation: The 'as if' personality. *Journal of Analytical Psychology*, 49, 635–656.

Spitz, R. (1961). Some early proto-types of ego defense. *Journal of American Psychoanalytic Association*, 9, 626–651.

Squire. L .R. (1992). Memory and the hippocampus: A synthesis from findings with rats, monkeys, and humans. *Psychological Review*, 99(2), 195–231.

Stephens, B. D. (2003). The Sleep of Prisoners: Hypnogogic Resonance and the Vicissitudes of Analyst Sleep. *Journal of Jungian Theory and Practice*, 5(2), 1–22.

Taylor, M. A., & Fink, M. (2003). Catatonia in psychiatric classification: A home of its own. *American Journal of Psychiatry*, 160, 1233–1241.

Taylor, S. E. (2002). *The Tending Instinct: Women, Men, and the Biology of Our Relationships*. New York: Henry Holt and Company.

Trowell, J. (1982). Effects of obstetric management on the mother/child relationship. In C. M. Parkes & J. Stevenson-Hinde (Eds.), *The Place of Attachment in Human Behavior*, 79–94. New York: Basic Books.

Truby, H. M. (1975). Prenatal and neonatal speech, pre-speech, and an infantile speech lexicon. *Child Language 1975*, a special issue of WORD, 27, parts 1–3.

Van den Bergh, B. R. H., & Marcoen, A. (July 2004). High antenatal maternal anxiety is related to ADHD symptoms, externalizing problems, and anxiety in 8- and 9-year-olds. *Child Development, 75(4), 1085.*

van der Kolk, B. A. (1994). The body keeps the score: Memory and the evolving psychobiology of post-traumatic stress. *Harvard Psychiatric Review*, Vol. 1.

van der Kolk, B. A. (1996). The body keeps the score. In B. A. van der Kolk, A. C. McFarlane, & L. Weisaeth (Eds.), *Traumatic Stress: The Effects of Overwhelming Experience on Mind, Body and Society.* New York: The Guilford Press.

Vanderlinden, J. & Vandereycken, W. (1997). Trauma, dissociation and impulse dyscontrol. In *Eating Disorders.* New York: Brunner Mazel Publications.

Vaughn, H. G. (1975). Electrophysiological analysis of regional cortical maturation. *Biological Psychiatry*, 10, 313–326.

Winnicott, D. (1945). Primitive emotional development. In *Through Paediatrics to Psycho-Analysis.* New York: Basic Books (1975).

Winnicott, D. W. (1988). *Human Nature.* London: Free Association Books.

Winnicott, D. W. (1965). *The Maturational Processes and the Facilitating Environment.* New York: International Universities Press.

Wittine, B. (1993). Assumptions of transpersonal psychotherapy. In R. Walsh, & F. Vaughan, (Eds.), *Paths Beyond Ego: The Transpersonal Vision*, 165–171. New York: Jeremy P. Tarcher/Putnam.

Woodman, M. (Winter 1993). Stepping over the threshold: Into the black hole at the center of Self. *Noetic Sciences Review*, 28, 10–15.

Woodward, S. C. (1992). *The Transmission of Music into the Human Uterus and the Response to Music of the Human Fetus and Neonate.* Dissertation, University of Capetown, South Africa.

NOTES

INTRODUCTION
1. Halligan, S.L., Yehuda, R. (2000). "Risk Factors for PTSD." *PTSD Research Quarterly.* The National Center for Post-Traumatic Stress Disorder, VA Medical and Regional Office, White River Junction, VT.

CHAPTER 1
1. George Orwell. (1950). *Nineteen Eighty-Four.* London: Alfred A. Knopf Everyman's Library, pages 268–269.

CHAPTER 2
1. "Freud, in a famous metaphor, compared the psyche to an iceberg. Like an iceberg (Freud said) nine-tenths of the psyche is invisible to us, submerged in the unconscious." Quoted from "Psychology: An Introduction" by Russell A. Dewey, PhD, retrieved from http://www.intropsych.com/ch11_personality/super-ego.html [Sigmund Freud. (1990/1923). *The Ego and the Id* (The Standard Edition of the Complete Psychological Works of Sigmund Freud). New York: W. W. Norton & Company.]
2. Courtois, C. A. (2004). Complex trauma, complex reactions: Assessment and treatment. *Psychotherapy: Theory, Research, Practice, Training,* 41(4), 412–425.
3. Herman, J. L. (1992). Complex PTSD: A syndrome in survivors of prolonged and repeated trauma. *Journal of Traumatic Stress,* 5, 377–377.
4. Walsh, R., & Vaughan, F. (Eds.) (1993). *Paths Beyond Ego: The Transpersonal Vision.* New York: Jeremy P. Tarcher/Putnam, p. 47.
5. Maslow, A. (1968). *Toward a Psychology of Being,* second edition. Princeton, NJ: Van Nostrand, pp. 71–72.

6. Walsh, R., & Vaughan, F. (Eds.) (1993). *Paths Beyond Ego: The Transpersonal Vision*. New York: Jeremy P. Tarcher/Putnam, p. 110.

7. Metzner, R. (1998). *The Unfolding Self: Varieties of Transformational Experience*. Novato, CA: Origin Press, p. 258.

CHAPTER 5

1. Kalsched, D. (1996). *The Inner World of Trauma: Archetypal Defenses of the Personal Spirit*. London and New York: Routledge.

2. Kimbles, S. L., & Singer, T. (2004). *The Cultural Complex: Contemporary Jungian Perspectives on Psyche and Society*. Brunner-Routledge.

3. Ann Casement, *Post-Jungians Today: Key Papers in Contemporary Analytical Psychology*, Psychology Press, 1998

4. Kalsched, D. (1996). *The Inner World of Trauma: Archetypal Defenses of the Personal Spirit*. London and New York: Routledge.

CHAPTER 6

1. Siegel, D. (1999). *The Developing Mind: Toward a Neurobiology of Interpersonal Experience*. New York: Guilford.

2. Seligman, M. (1975). *Helplessness: On Depression, Development and Death*. San Francisco: W.H. Freeman and Co.

3. Squire. L .R. (1992). Memory and the hippocampus: A synthesis from findings with rats, monkeys, and humans. *Psychological Review*, 99(2), 195–231.

4. Porges, S. W. (2011). *The Polyvagal Theory: Neurophysiological Foundations of Emotions, Attachment, Communication, and Self-regulation*. New York: W. W. Norton & Co.

5. Scaer, R. C. (2005). *The Trauma Spectrum: Hidden Wounds and Human Resiliency*. New York: W. W. Norton, 195.

6. Alex Tresniowski, "There Goes the Bride," *People Magazine*, May 16, 2005, Vol. 63, No. 19.

7. Keleman, S. (1989). *Patterns of Distress: Emotional Insults and Human Form*. Berkeley, CA: Center Press.

8. Moskowitz, A. K. (2004). 'Scared Stiff': Catatonia as an evolutionary-based fear response. *Psychological Review*, 111(4), 984–1002.

9. Rosebush, P. I., & Mazurek, M. F. (1999). Catatonia: Re-awakening to a forgotten disorder. *Movement Disorders*, 14, 395–397.

10. Taylor, M. A., & Fink, M. (2003). Catatonia in psychiatric classification: A home of its own. *American Journal of Psychiatry*, 160, 1233–1241.

11. Dixon, A. K. (1998). Ethological strategies for defence in animals and humans: Their role in some psychiatric disorders. *British Journal of Medical Psychology*, 71, 417–445.

12. Gilbert, P., & Allan, S. (1998). The role of defeat and entrapment (arrested flight) in depression: An exploration of an evolutionary view. *Psychological Medicine*, 28, 585–598.

13. Moskowitz, A. K. (2004). 'Scared Stiff': Catatonia as an evolutionary-based fear response. *Psychological Review*, 111(4), 995.

14. American Psychiatric Association (1994). *Diagnostic and Statistical Manual of Mental Disorders Fourth Edition (DSM-IV)*. Washington DC: American Psychiatric Association, 765.

15. Moskowitz, A. K. (2004). 'Scared Stiff': Catatonia as an evolutionary-based fear response. *Psychological Review*, 111(4), 995.

16. Mann, S. C., Caroff, S. N., Keck, P. E., & Lazarus, A. (2003). *Neuroleptic Malignant Syndrome and Related Conditions* (2nd ed.). Arlington, VA: American Psychiatric Publishing.

17. Gurrera, R. J. (1999). Sympathoadrenal hyperactivity and the etiology of neuroleptic malignant syndrome. *American Journal of Psychiatry*, 156, 169–180.

18. Nijenhuis, E. R. S., van der Hart, O., & Steele, K. (2004). Trauma-related structural dissociation of the personality. Trauma Information Pages website, January 2004. Web URL: http://www.trauma-pages.com/nijenhuis-2004.htm .

19. Ibid.

20. Robert C. Scaer, M.D., *Applied Psychophysiology and Biofeedback*, (2001), 26(1), 73–91, based on a Keynote Address presented at the 31st annual meeting of the Association for Applied Psychophysiology and Biofeedback, March 29-April 2, 2000, Denver, CO.

21. Kosten, T. R., & Krystal, J. (1988). Biological mechanisms in posttraumatic stress disorder: Relevance for substance abuse. In M. Galanter (Ed.), *Recent Developments in Alcoholism*, 49–68. New York: Plenum.

22. Farkas, B. (2004). Etiology and pathogenesis of PTSD in children and adolescents. In R. R. Silva (Ed.), *Posttraumatic Stress Disorders in Children and Adolescents [Handbook]*, 126. New York: W. W. Norton.

23. Perry, B. D., Pollard, R. A., Baker, W. L., Sturges, C., Vigilante, D., & Blakely, T. L. (1995). Continuous heartrate monitoring in maltreated children [Abstract]. Annual Meeting of the American Academy of Child and Adolescent Psychiatry, New Research; Perry, B. D., Pollard, R., Blakely, T., Baker, W., Vigilante, D. (1995b). Childhood trauma, the neurobiology of adaptation and 'use-dependent' development of the brain: How 'states' become 'traits'. *Infant Mental Health Journal*, 16(4), 271–291.

24. Carmen, E. H., Reiker, P. P., & Mills, T. (1984). Victims of violence and psychiatric illness. *American Journal of Psychiatry*, 141, 378–379.; Jaffe, P., Wolfe, D., Wilson, S. K., et al. (1986). Family violence and child adjustment: A comparative analysis of girls' and boys' behavioral symptoms. *American Journal of Psychiatry*, 143, 74–77.
25. Woodman, M. (Winter 1993). Stepping over the threshold: Into the black hole at the center of Self. *Noetic Sciences Review*, 28, 12.
26. Taylor, S. E. (2002). *The Tending Instinct: Women, Men, and the Biology of Our Relationships*. New York: Henry Holt and Company.
27. Kosfeld, M., Heinrichs, M., Zak, P. J., Fischbacher, U., & Fehr, E. (June 2005). Oxytocin increases trust in humans. *Nature*, 435(7042), 673–676.
28. Freyd, J. J. (1994). Betrayal trauma: Traumatic amnesia as an adaptive response to childhood abuse. *Ethics & Behavior*, 4(4), 307–329.

CHAPTER 7

1. Winnicott, D. (1945). Primitive emotional development. In *Through Paediatrics to Psycho-Analysis*. New York: Basic Books (1975); Winnicott, D. W. (1965). *The Maturational Processes and the Facilitating Environment*. New York: International Universities Press.
2. H. J. Landy & L. G. Keith. *Human Reproduction Update*. European Society for Human Reproduction and Embryology, 1998, Vol. 4, No. 2, 177–183.
3. Huizink, A. C., Mulder, E. J. H., & Buitelaar, J. K. (2004). Prenatal stress and risk for psychopathology: Specific effects or induction of general susceptibility? *Psychological Bulletin*, 130(1), 115–142.
4. Giannakoulopoulos, X., Fisk, N., Glover, V., Kourtis, P., & Sepulveda, W. (1994). Fetal plasma cortisol and B-endorphins response to intrauterine needling. *Lancet*, 344, 77–81.
5. Spitz, R. (1961). Some early proto-types of ego defense. *Journal of American Psychoanalytic Association*, 9, 626–651; Fraiberg, S. (1982). Pathological defenses in infancy. *Psychoanalytic Quarterly*, 51, 612–634.
6. Bustan, M. N., & Coker, A. L. (Mar 1994). Maternal attitude toward pregnancy and the risk of neonatal death. *American Journal of Public Health*, 84(3), 411–414.
7. DiPietro, J. A., Novak, M. F. S. X., Costigan, K. A., Atella, L. D., & Reusing, S. P. (May 2006). Maternal psychological distress during pregnancy in relation to child development at age two. *Child Development*, 77(3), 573–587.
8. Ibid.

9. Van den Bergh, B. R. H., & Marcoen, A. (July 2004). High antenatal maternal anxiety is related to ADHD symptoms, externalizing problems, and anxiety in 8- and 9-year-olds. *Child Development*, 75(4), 1085.

10. Feldmar, A. (1979). The embryology of consciousness: What is a normal pregnancy?" In D. Mall & W. Watts (Eds.), *The Psychological Aspects of Abortion*, 15–24. University Publications of America.

11. Righard, L., & Alade, M. (1990). Effect of delivery room routines on success of first breast feed. *Lancet*, 336, 1105–1107; Righard, L., & Franz, K. (1995). *Delivery Self Attachment*. (Video). Sunland, CA: Geddes Productions.

12. Castellino, R. (1997). *The Caregiver's Role in Birth and Newborn Self-Attachment Needs*. Santa Barbara, CA: Birthing Evolution-Birthing Awareness, 19.

13. Emde, R. N., Swedburg, J., & Suzuki, B. (1975). Human wakefulness and biological rhythms after birth. *Archives of General Psychiatry*, 32, 780–783.

14. Klaus, M. H., Kennell, J. H., & Klaus, P. H. (1995). *Bonding: Building the Foundations of Secure Attachment and Independence*. Reading, MA: Addison-Wesley Publishing Company.

CHAPTER 8

1. Eigen, M. (1999). *Toxic Nourishment*. London: Karnac Books.

2. Ibid, 154.

3. Schore, A. (2003). *Affect Dysregulation and Disorders of the Self*. New York: WW Norton.

4. Deutsch, H. (1942). 'Some forms of emotional disturbance and their relationship to schizophrenia'. *Psychoanalytic Quarterly*, 11, 301.

5. Ibid, p. 302

6. Ibid.

7. Ibid, p. 303

8. Benz, D., & Weiss, H. (1989). *To the Core of Your Experience*. Charlottesville, VA: Luminas Press, 77; Kurtz, R. (1990). *Body-Centered Psychotherapy: The Hakomi Method*. Mendocino, CA: LifeRhythm Press.

9. Shari Roan, "Obesity Epidemic May Have Roots in 1950s," *Los Angeles Times*, December 19, 2011.

10. Porges, S. W. (2011). *The Polyvagal Theory: Neurophysiological Foundations of Emotions, Attachment, Communication, and Self-regulation*. New York: W. W. Norton & Co.

11. Truby, H. M. (1975). Prenatal and neonatal speech, pre-speech, and an infantile speech lexicon. *Child Language 1975*, a special issue of WORD, 27, parts 1–3.

12. Mehler, J., & Christophe, A. (1995). Maturation and learning of language in the first year of life. In M. S. Gazzaniga (Editor-in-Chief) & S. Pinker (Language Section Ed.), *The Cognitive Neurosciences*, 943–954. Cambridge, MA: The MIT Press.

13. Mehler, J., & Dupoux, E. (1994). *What Infants Know: The New Cognitive Science of Early Development* (P. Southgate, Trans.). Cambridge, MA: Blackwell.

14. Childs, M. R. (1998). Prenatal language learning. *Journal of Prenatal and Perinatal Psychology and Health*, 13(2), 99–121.

15. Otake, T., Hatano, G., Cutler, A., & Mehler, J. (1993). More or syllable? Speech segmentation in Japanese. *Journal of Memory and Language*, 32, 258–278.

16. Satt, B. J. (1984). *An Investigation into the Acoustical Induction of Intrauterine Learning*. Dissertation, California School of Professional Psychology, Los Angeles; Panneton, R. K. (1985). Prenatal Auditory Experience with Melodies: Effect on Post-Natal Auditory Preferences in Human Newborns. Dissertation, University of North Carolina, Greensboro.

17. DeCasper, A., & Spence, M. (1982). Prenatal maternal speech influences human newborn's auditory preferences. *Infant Behavior and Development*, 9, 133–150; Woodward, S. C. (1992). *The Transmission of Music into the Human Uterus and the Response to Music of the Human Fetus and Neonate*. Dissertation, University of Capetown, South Africa.

18. Hepper, P. G. (1988). Foetal 'soap' addiction. *Lancet*, ii, 1347–1348; Hepper, P. G. (1991). An examination of fetal learning before and after birth. *Irish Journal of Psychology*, 12, 95–107.

19. Pert, C. (1999). *Molecules of Emotion*. New York: Scribner; Pert, C., Ruff, M., Weber, R. J., & Herkenham, M. (1985). Neuropeptides and their receptors: A psychosomatic network. *Journal of Immunology*, 135(2), Supplement, 820–826.

20. van der Kolk, B. A. (1996). The body keeps the score. In B. A. van der Kolk, A. C. McFarlane, & L. Weisaeth (Eds.), *Traumatic Stress: The Effects of Overwhelming Experience on Mind, Body and Society*. New York: The Guilford Press.

21. Purpura, D. P. (1975). Normal and aberrant neuronal development in the cerebral cortex of human fetus and young infant. In M. A. G. Brazier, & N. A. Buchwald (Eds.), *Basic Mechanisms in Mental Retardation*, 141–169. New York: Academic Press; Vaughn, H. G. (1975). Electrophysiological analysis of regional cortical maturation. *Biological Psychiatry*, 10, 313–326.

22. Marquez, A. (2000). Healing through prenatal and perinatal memory recall: A phenomenological investigation. *Journal of Prenatal and Perinatal Psychology and Health*, 15(2), 146–172.

23. Hull, W. F. (1986). Psychological treatment of birth trauma with age regression and its relationship to chemical dependency. *Pre- and Peri-Natal Psychology Journal*, 1, 111–134; Lake, F. (1982). *With Respect: A Doctor's Response to a Healing Pope*. London: Darton, Longman & Todd, Ltd.

24. Porges, S. W. (2011). *The Polyvagal Theory: Neurophysiological Foundations of Emotions, Attachment, Communication, and Self-regulation*. New York: W. W. Norton & Co.

25. Givens, A. M. (1987). The Alice Givens approach to prenatal and birth therapy. *Journal of Prenatal and Perinatal Psychology and Health*, 1(3), 223–229.

26. Piontelli, A. (1992). *From Fetus to Child*. London: Routledge.

27. Lieberman, M. (1963). Early developmental stress and later behavior. *Science*, 141, 824.

28. "Births: Final Data for 2012," National Vital Statistics Reports, Volume 62, number 9, December 30, 2013. United States Centers for Disease Control and Prevention, http://www.cdc.gov/nchs/fastats/delivery.htm.

29. Porges, S. W. (2011). *The Polyvagal Theory: Neurophysiological Foundations of Emotions, Attachment, Communication, and Self-regulation*. New York: W. W. Norton & Co.

30. Vanderlinden, J. & Vandereycken, W. (1997). Trauma, dissociation and impulse dyscontrol. In *Eating Disorders*. New York: Brunner Mazel Publications.

31. Sella, Y. (March 2003). Soul without skin, bones with no flesh: bodily aspects of the self in the treatment of women patients with restrictive anorexic eating patterns. *International Journal of Psychotherapy*, 8(1), 37 – 51.

32. Roz, C. (2002). Lecture on affect regulation, in *Embodiment and Emotion*. London, Tavistock Clinic: Conference Seminar.

33. Sella, Y. (March 2003). Soul without skin, bones with no flesh: bodily aspects of the self in the treatment of women patients with restrictive anorexic eating patterns. *International Journal of Psychotherapy*, 8(1), 37 – 51.

CHAPTER 10

1. Tim Nudd, "Rihanna gives painful details of Chris Brown assault," *PEOPLE. com*, November 6, 2009, http://www.cnn.com/2009/SHOWBIZ/Music/11/06/rihanna.chris.brown/index.html?eref=ib_us.

2. "Chris Brown Diagnosed With Bipolar Disorder and PTSD, Ordered to Stay in Rehab for Two More Months," *US Magazine*, March 1, 2014, http://www.usmagazine.com/celebrity-news/news/chris-brown-diagnosed-with-bipolar-disorder-and-ptsd-ordered-to-stay-in-rehab-for-two-more-months-201413.

CHAPTER 11

1. The National Center for PTSD, U.S. Department of Veterans Affairs, retrieved from http://www.ptsd.va.gov/public/PTSD-overview/basics/how-common-is-ptsd.asp.

2. Donnelly, Elizabeth A., & Bennett, Michael. (Mar 2014). Development of a critical incident stress inventory for the emergency medical services. *Traumatology: An International Journal*, 20(1), 1–8.

3. Badly injured Colorado woman wrote messages on umbrella as she waited five days for rescue in wrecked car. *New York Daily News*, May 5, 2014. Retrieved from http://www.nydailynews.com/news/national/colorado-woman-missing-days-found-alive-wrecked-car-article-1.1779638#ixzz32VpKzsT8.

4. http://www.victimsofcrime.org/help-for-crime-victims/get-help-bulletins-for-crime-victims/how-crime-victims-react-to-trauma.

5. National Crime Victims Research and Treatment Center, Medical University of South Carolina, retrieved from www.dartmouth.edu/~eap/reactionstotrauma.pdf.

6. Burgess, Ann Wolbert and Lynda Lytle Holmström (1974). "Rape Trauma Syndrome". *American Journal of Psychiatry*, 131(9), 981–986.

7. Diane Zimberoff, *Breaking Free from the Victim Trap*, 1989

8. http://www.ptsd.va.gov/public/PTSD-overview/basics/how-common-is-ptsd.asp.

9. *War damaged vet kills girlfriend; Is PTSD to blame?* CBS News show Forty Eight Hours, July 11, 2012. Retrieved from http://www.cbsnews.com/news/war-damaged-vet-kills-girlfriend-is-ptsd-to-blame/.

10. Yarvis, Jeffrey (2008). Hypnotherapy under Fire: Efficacy of Heart-Centered Hypnotherapy in the Treatment of Iraq War Veterans with Posttraumatic Stress. *Journal of Heart-Centered Therapies*, 11(1), 3-18.

11. Shear, M. K., Simon, N., Wall, M., Zisook, S., Neimeyer, R., Duan, N., Reynolds, C., et al. (2011). Complicated grief and related bereavement issues for DSM-5. *Depression and Anxiety*, 28(2), 103–17.

12. Bonanno GA, Wortman CB, Lehman DR, et al. (2002). Resilience to loss and chronic grief: a prospective study from preloss to 18-months postloss. *Journal of Personality & Social Psychology*, 83, 1150–1164.

13. Susanne Babbel. The Trauma That Arises from Natural Disasters. *Psychology Today*, April 21, 2010. Retrieved from http://www.psychologytoday.com/blog/somatic-psychology/201004/the-trauma-arises-natural-disasters

14. Norris, F., Murphy, A., Baker, C., & Perilla, J. (2004). Post-disaster PTSD over four waves of a panel study of Mexico's 1999 flood. *Journal of Traumatic Stress*, 17, 283–292.

CHAPTER 12

1. Chögyam Trungpa, *Cutting Through Spiritual Materialism*, (Boston, MA: Shambhala New Edition, 2002), 3.
2. Leonard Shengold, *Soul Murder Revisited: Thoughts about Therapy, Hate, Love, and Memory*. (New Haven, CT: Yale University, 1999) Press, 2.
3. Ibid, 288.
4. Sigmund Freud. *The Ego and the Id (The Standard Edition of the Complete Psychological Works of Sigmund Freud)*. (New York: W. W. Norton & Company, 1990/1923).

CHAPTER 13

1. *Harvard Mental Health Letter*, May, 2009, http://www.health.harvard.edu/ newsletters/ Harvard_Mental_Health_Letter/2009/May/Take-a-deep-breath

CONCLUSION

1. http://nccam.nih.gov/news/2009/073009.htm
2. Eric Berne's, *Games People Play*, 1963.
3. Sigmund Freud, "Hypnosis", *The Standard Edition of the Complete Psychological Works of Sigmund Freud* Volume I, London: Hogarth Press, 1986, pp. 113–114
4. Carl Jung, *Memories, Dreams, Reflections*, 1961: New York: Vintage, pp. 117–119.
5. Emerson, William R. (Spring 1996). The Vulnerable Prenate. *Pre- & Perinatal Psychology Journal*, Vol 10(3), 125–142.
6. Bloch, G. (1985). *Body & Self. Elements of Human Biology, Behavior, and Health*. Los Altos, CA: William Kaufmann, Inc.
7. Magid, K., and McKelvey, C. (1988). *High Risk: Children Without a Conscience*. New York: Bantam Books.

APPENDIX 1

1. Jung, C.G. (1966). The Mana Personality. *The Collected Works of C. G. Jung: Two Essays on Analytical Psychology. Vol. 7, second edition*. Princeton: Bollingen.
2. Ibid.
3. Wittine, B. (1993). Assumptions of transpersonal psychotherapy. In R. Walsh, & F. Vaughan, (Eds.), *Paths Beyond Ego: The Transpersonal Vision*, 165–171. New York: Jeremy P. Tarcher/Putnam.
4. Bernstein, Jerome S. (2005). *Living in the Borderland: The Evolution of Consciousness and the Challenge of Healing Trauma*. London & New York: Routledge.
5. Porges, S. W. (2011). *The Polyvagal Theory: Neurophysiological Foundations of Emotions, Attachment, Communication, and Self-regulation*. New York: W. W. Norton & Co.

6. Felicia Mueller, "Complex Trauma," Counseling Washington, http://www
    .counselingwashington.com/ ardisplay.aspx?ID=33&SecID=131

7. Courtois, C. A. (2004). Complex trauma, complex reactions: Assessment and
    treatment. *Psychotherapy: Theory, Research, Practice, Training,* 41(4), 421.

8. Rothschild, B. (1996). *Applying the Brakes: Theory and Tools for Understanding,
    Slowing Down and Reducing Autonomic Nervous System Activation in Traumatized
    Clients.* Paper presented at the Tenth Scandinavian Conference for Psychotherapists
    working with Traumatized Refugees, May 24–26, 1996, Finland; Rothschild, B.
    (1997). Slowing down and controlling traumatic hyperarousal. In L. Vanderberger
    (Ed.), *The Many Faces of Trauma, International Perspectives* (in press); Rothschild,
    B. (Feb 1998). Post-Traumatic Stress Disorder: Identification and Diagnosis. *The
    Swiss Journal of Social Work.*

9. Ogden, P., & Minton, K. (2000). Sensorimotor Psychotherapy: One method for
    processing traumatic memory. *Traumatology,* 6(3). Available online at http://
    www.fsu.edu/~trauma/v6i3/v6i3a3.html.

10. Ibid, 110.

11. Nijenhuis, E. R. S., & Van der Hart, O. (1999). Forgetting and re-experiencing
    trauma: From anesthesia to pain. In J. Goodwin & R. Attias (Eds.), *Splintered
    Reflections: Images of the Body in Trauma,* 39–66. New York: Basic Books.

12. van der Kolk, B. A. (1994). The body keeps the score: Memory and the evolving psycho-
    biology of post-traumatic stress. *Harvard Psychiatric Review,* Vol. 1; Nadel, L., & Jacobs,
    W. J. (1996). The role of the hippocampus in PTSD, panic, and phobia. In N. Kato (Ed.),
    Hippocampus: Functions and Clinical Relevance. Amsterdam: Elsevier Science.

13. Putnam, F. W. (Fall 2004). Stuck in the past. *Psychiatry: Interpersonal and
    Biological Processes,* 67(3), 237.

14. Kalsched, D. (2013). *Trauma and the Soul.* London: Routledge, 179.

15. Schore, A. (2003). *Affect Regulation and the Repair of the Self.* New York: W.W.
    Norton, 263.

16. Winnicott, D. W. (1988). *Human Nature.* London: Free Association Books, 132.

17. Hollis, J. (2013). *Hauntings: Dispelling the Ghosts Who Run Our Lives.* Asheville,
    NC: Chiron Publications, 135.

18. Emerson, W. R. (2002). Somatotropic therapy. *Journal of Heart-Centered
    Therapies,* 5(2), 65–90.

APPENDIX 2

1. Jung, C. G. (1946). Psychology of the transference. *The Collected Works of C. G.
    Jung, Vol. 16, second edition.* Princeton: Bollingen, para. 364.

2. Stephens, B. D. (2003). The Sleep of Prisoners: Hypnogogic Resonance and the
    Vicissitudes of Analyst Sleep. *Journal of Jungian Theory and Practice,* 5(2), 3.